W9-ABC-676

E-COMMERCE BASICS,
SECOND EDITION

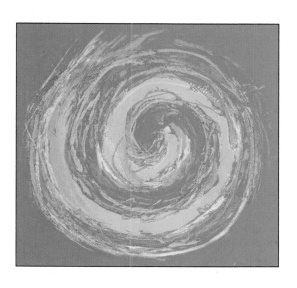

Dr. Bruce J. McLaren
Indiana State University
Dr. Constance H. McLaren
Indiana State University

THOMSON
★
COURSE TECHNOLOGY ™

Australia • Canada • Mexico • Singapore • Spain • United Kingdom • United States

THOMSON

COURSE TECHNOLOGY

E-Commerce BASICS, Second Edition

By Dr. Bruce J. McLaren and Dr. Constance H. McLaren

Senior Vice President
Chris Elkhill

Managing Editor
Chris Katsaropoulos

Senior Product Manager
Dave Lafferty

Product Manager
Robert Gaggin

Product Marketing Manager
Kim Ryttel

Associate Product Manager
Jodi Dreissig

Development Editor
Custom Editorial Productions Inc.

Production Editor
Anne Chimenti
Custom Editorial Productions Inc.

Compositor
GEX Publishing Services

Disclaimer
Course Technology reserves the right to revise this publication and make changes from time to time in its content without notice.

ISBN 0-619-05942-7

Get Back to the Basics...
With these *exciting new products!*

This new book from our *BASICS* series provides a step-by-step introduction to the fundamentals of business on the Internet.

Other books include:

NEW! Internet BASICS by Barksdale, Rutter, & Teeter
35+ hours of instruction for beginning through intermediate features

0-619-05905-2	Textbook, Soft Spiral Bound Cover
0-619-05906-0	Instructor Resource Kit

NEW! Microsoft OfficeXP BASICS by Morrison
35+ hours of instruction for beginning through intermediate features

0-619-05908-7	Textbook, Hard Spiral Bound Cover
0-619-05906-0	Instructor Resource Kit
0-619-05909-5	Activities Workbook
0-619-05851-X	Review Pack (Data CD)

NEW! Microsoft Office 2001 Macintosh BASICS by Melton & Walls
35+ hours of instruction for beginning through intermediate features

0-619-05912-5	Textbook, Hard Spiral Bound Cover
0-619-05914-1	Instructor Resource Kit
0-619-05913-3	Workbook
0-619-05915-X	Review Pack (Data CD)

Web Design BASICS by Stubbs & Barksdale
35+ hours of instruction for beginning through intermediate features

0-619-05964-8	Text, Soft Spiral Bound Cover
0-619-05966-4	Electronic Instructor's Manual Package
0-619-05977-X	Review Pack (Data CD)

Computer Concepts BASICS by Pusins & Ambrose
35+ hours of instruction for beginning through intermediate features

0-538-69501-3	Text, Hard Spiral Bound Cover
0-538-69502-1	Activities Workbook
0-538-69503-X	Electronic Instructor's Manual Package
0-538-69504-8	Testing CD Package

Join Us On the Internet **www.course.com**

How to Use This Book

What makes a good computer instructional text? Sound pedagogy and the most current, complete materials. Not only will you find an inviting layout, but also many features to enhance learning.

Objectives— Objectives are listed at the beginning of each lesson, along with a suggested time for completion of the lesson. This allows you to look ahead to what you will be learning and to pace your work.

Step-by-Step Exercises—Preceded by a short topic discussion, these exercises are the "hands-on practice" part of the lesson. Simply follow the steps, either using a data file or creating a file from scratch. Each lesson is a series of these step-by-step exercises.

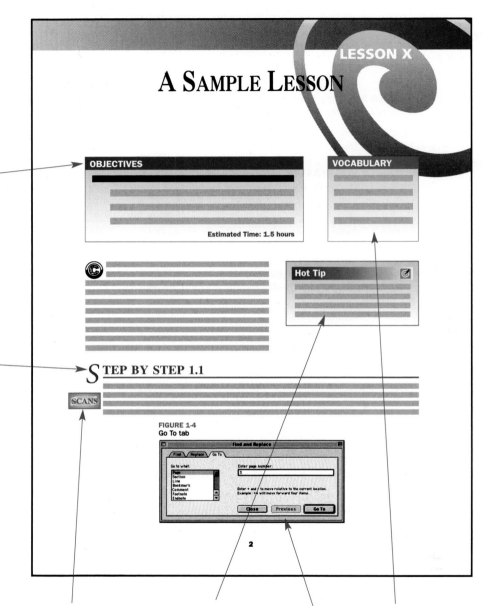

A SAMPLE LESSON

LESSON X

OBJECTIVES

Estimated Time: 1.5 hours

VOCABULARY

Hot Tip

STEP BY STEP 1.1

SCANS

FIGURE 1-4
Go To tab

SCANS—(Secretary's Commission on Achieving Necessary Skills)—The U.S. Department of Labor has identified the school-to-careers competencies.

Marginal Boxes— These boxes provide additional information, such as Hot Tips, fun facts (Did You Know?), Computer Concepts, Internet Web sites, Extra Challenge activities, and Teamwork ideas.

Vocabulary—Terms are identified in boldface throughout the lesson and summarized at the end.

Enhanced Screen Shots—Screen shots now come to life on each page with color and depth.

How to Use This Book

Summary—At the end of each lesson, you will find a summary to prepare you to complete the end-of-lesson activities.

Vocabulary/Review Questions—Review material at the end of each lesson and each unit enables you to prepare for assessment of the content presented.

Lesson Projects—End-of-lesson hands-on application of what has been learned in the lesson allows you to actually apply the techniques covered.

Critical Thinking Activities—Each lesson gives you an opportunity to apply creative analysis and use various resources to solve problems.

End-of-Unit Projects—End-of-unit hands-on application of concepts learned in the unit provides opportunity for a comprehensive review.

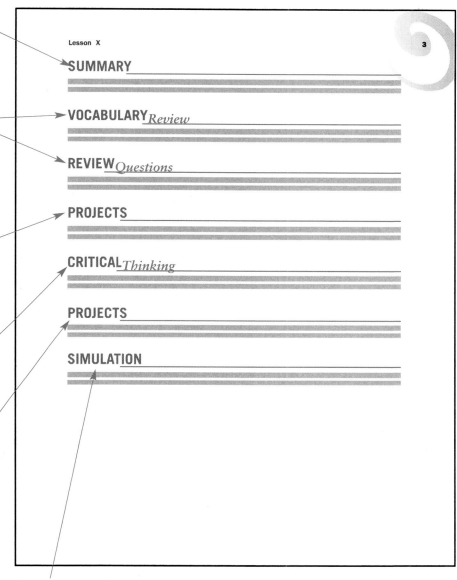

Lesson X

3

SUMMARY

VOCABULARY*Review*

REVIEW*Questions*

PROJECTS

CRITICAL*Thinking*

PROJECTS

SIMULATION

Simulation—Realistic simulation jobs are provided at the end of each unit, reinforcing the material covered in the unit.

PREFACE

Businesses and organizations of all kinds have learned that it makes good business sense to use the Internet to reach their audience. Almost every magazine ad or TV commercial makes sure that you know the address of the company's Web site. Other organizations, like universities and nonprofit groups, realize as well that they can give you much more information if you visit them online than they could ever afford to do by other means.

Why do businesses find it essential to have an online presence that will attract customers? How can customers make the most of what is available online? These are the two key questions that we answer in this book. Here you'll learn all about the sites developed for businesses of many different kinds. You'll see how to find them and learn what they have to offer. You'll also see how they are developed and learn what separates an adequate site from a great one.

Technical advances and the ever-increasing number of customers with Internet access are among the reasons for the massive development in online business. E-commerce has spurred the development of the technology that enables a company to post a product catalog, a buyer to select items to order, and payment information to be transferred securely and privately. E-commerce allows investors to find out how their portfolios have performed and to make stock trades in the privacy of their own homes. E-commerce makes it easy to use your computer to schedule a flight and buy a plane ticket, to apply for a job, or to read a company's annual report.

Some experts predict that Internet spending will reach at least $2.5 trillion within the next two years. Although consumer shopping might get the most publicity, transactions between businesses are expected to account for 80 to 90 percent of this activity. No matter whose projections you read, it is clear that e-commerce is an important part of our economy and our society.

By studying the activities and examples in this book, you'll learn to use e-commerce effectively. You'll have the confidence to enter this arena, knowing what you can find and how to use what you find. Using *E-Commerce BASICS* as your guide, you'll find that you can gather corporate information, make a purchase online, develop an effective company Web site, or find global trading partners. The more you look, the more you'll find.

E-Commerce BASICS is divided into units and lessons. You will learn a concept and then apply it through hands-on step-by-step activities and site visits. The book will take you through each step in a logical, easy-to-follow manner.

In *Unit 1: An Introduction to Electronic Commerce*, we'll introduce you to the impact of the Internet on our economy. We won't smother you with statistics, but you'll see enough trends to get the idea of the amazing success and growth potential of e-commerce. You'll also take a look at some typical business uses of the Net. Remember, it is not all about selling.

In *Unit 2: Personal and Business Services Online*, you'll see the effect of nonsales e-commerce. For example, a whole industry has sprung up to support online job searches. You'll see how one-stop career sites can help you discover what you want to do, how to prepare for it, and how to find the job you want. In another lesson, you'll learn how to manage your personal and business finances without ever going to the bank, the broker, or the insurance office. You'll also learn how to make travel plans, use the Internet to find a phone number, get up-to-the minute weather bulletins, and locate other information.

In *Unit 3: Buying Online*, you'll learn everything you need to know to be a savvy purchaser. You'll see examples of the goods and services you can shop for electronically—things like a paperback book, clothing for you to wear or to sell in your store, a shipment of light fixtures, or even a car. You'll see how to participate in an online auction or subscribe to an electronic magazine. You'll see how organizations conduct business with each other online and how the Internet enables businesses with similar needs to work together. Before you're finished, you'll know why it is important to deal with a reputable and secure online merchant.

In *Unit 4: Doing Business on the Web*, you'll take a look at e-commerce from the company's perspective. You'll learn how companies use the Internet for marketing, including e-mail targeted advertising, generating customer lists, and ways to deliver customer service over the Web. You will learn how banner ads can be linked to certain keywords in search engines. You will see how multinational corporations use the Web to reach customers in many countries. You'll also see how to use the Internet to research customs and economies of other countries before visiting those countries.

In *Unit 5: Developing an Electronic Commerce Web Site,* you'll learn about e-commerce Web sites, including Web servers and HTML files. You'll visit some award-winning Web sites to view good designs. You will use Microsoft FrontPage to build your own small personal Web site and even build a small e-commerce site as a project. You will learn about the details of processing credit card information securely and discover other ways to pay for goods and services purchased on the Internet.

Throughout the book you will find references to e-commerce Web sites and many figures that show the actual sites. Although you don't need to be connected to the Internet to learn about electronic commerce, you'll experience more by surfing the Web while you read this book. For those who have not had much experience with e-mail and Web browsers, the appendices contain brief tutorials on popular tools. An appendix about e-commerce security issues also is included.

Acknowledgments

We would like to express our appreciation to the many individuals who have contributed to the completion of this book. Putting this book together has been a pleasant experience due largely to the good work of the people whose names appear here.

- Robert Gaggin, Product Manager, Course Technology

- Dave Lafferty, Senior Product Manager, Course Technology

- Jodi Dreissig, Associate Product Manager, Course Technology

- Betsy Newberry and Anne Chimenti of Custom Editorial Productions Inc., with editing contributions by Priscilla Mullins and Jennifer Elworth

- Reviewer Becky Hodges

- GEX Publishing Services

We would also like to thank the administration of the School of Business at Indiana State University, especially Dean Ronald Green, for supporting our writing efforts. We also acknowledge the many contributions of our students. After all, that is why we write these books. And finally, we appreciate the understanding of our family who wait while we complete these writing tasks.

About the Authors

Bruce McLaren is a professor of Management Information Systems in the School of Business at Indiana State University. He serves as chairperson of the Organizational Department. He teaches courses in data communications, networking, and database management. He earned his Ph.D. from Purdue University. He is the author of more than a dozen textbooks in database management, word processing, spreadsheets, e-commerce, and the Internet.

Connie McLaren is a professor of Quality and Decision Systems in the School of Business at Indiana State University. She serves as QDS program coordinator and teaches courses in statistics, forecasting, management science, and decision analysis. She earned her Ph.D. from Purdue University. She is the author of several books in management science, spreadsheets, and e-commerce.

GUIDE FOR USING THIS BOOK

Please read this Guide before starting work. The time you spend now will save you much more time later and will make your learning faster, easier, and more pleasant.

Conventions

The different type styles used in this book have special meanings. They will save you time because you will soon automatically recognize from the type style the nature of the text you are reading and what you will do.

ITEM	TYPE STYLE	EXAMPLE
Text you will key	**Bold**	Key **Don't litter** rapidly.
Individual keys you will press	**Bold**	Press **Enter** to insert a blank line.
Web addresses that you might visit	*Italics*	More information about this book is available at *www.course.com*.
Web addresses that you should key	**Bold**	Start your browser and go to **www.course.com**.
Glossary terms in book	***Bold and italics***	The ***menu bar*** contains menu titles.
Words on screen	*Italics*	Click before the word *pencil*.
Menus and commands	**Bold**	Choose **Open** from the **File** menu.
Options/features with long names	*Italics*	Select **Normal** from the *Style for following paragraph* text box.

Instructor Resource Kit CD-ROM

The *Instructor Resource Kit* CD-ROM contains a wealth of instructional material you can use to prepare for teaching this course. The CD-ROM stores the following information:

■ ExamView® tests for each lesson. ExamView is a powerful testing software package that allows instructors to create and administer printed, computer (LAN-based), and Internet exams. ExamView includes hundreds of questions that correspond to the topics covered in this text, enabling learners to generate detailed study guides that include page references for further review. The computer-based and Internet testing components allow learners to take exams at their computers, and also save the instructor time by grading each exam automatically.

- Electronic *Instructor Manual* that includes lecture notes for each lesson, lesson plans, answers to the lesson and unit review questions, and suggested/sample solutions for Step-by-Step exercises, end-of-lesson activities, and Unit Review projects.

- Copies of the figures that appear in the student text, which can be used to prepare transparencies.

- Suggested schedules for teaching the lessons in this course.

- Additional instructional information about individual learning strategies, portfolios, and career planning, and a sample Internet contract.

- PowerPoint presentations that illustrate objectives for each lesson in the text.

SCANS

The Secretary's Commission on Achieving Necessary Skills (SCANS) from the U.S. Department of Labor was asked to examine the demands of the workplace and whether new learners are capable of meeting those demands. Specifically, the Commission was directed to advise the Secretary on the level of skills required to enter employment.

SCANS workplace competencies and foundation skills have been integrated into *E-Commerce BASICS*. The workplace competencies are identified as 1) ability to use resources, 2) interpersonal skills, 3) ability to work with information, 4) understanding of systems, and 5) knowledge and understanding of technology. The foundation skills are identified as 1) basic communication skills, 2) thinking skills, and 3) personal qualities.

Exercises in which learners must use a number of these SCANS competencies and foundation skills are marked in the text with the SCANS icon.

START-UP CHECKLIST

Hardware and Software Requirements

Concepts in this book are illustrated using screen captures from Microsoft Internet Explorer 6.0. You should have a compatible Web browser (such as Netscape Navigator 4.0 or higher or Internet Explorer 4.0 or higher).

Computer systems that support these browsers include PCs running Microsoft Windows and Macintosh systems. You should have an Internet connection with a modem or a direct connection to work the Step-by-Step activities and projects from this book. You need to have Microsoft FrontPage (2000 or later) installed on your computer to work the exercises and projects in Lesson 13.

Home Page

Access the home page for this textbook at *www.course.com*. Click "E-Commerce" in the product catalog and select "E-Commerce Concepts." Scroll until you find the home page for this textbook.

TABLE OF CONTENTS

UNIT 1 INTRODUCTION TO ELECTRONIC COMMERCE

UNIT 2 PERSONAL AND BUSINESS SERVICES ONLINE

UNIT 5   DEVELOPING AN ELECTRONIC COMMERCE WEB SITE

INTRODUCTION TO ELECTRONIC COMMERCE

Unit 1

Lesson 1   2 hrs.
The Internet in Our Economy

Lesson 2   3 hrs.
Business on the Internet

 Estimated Time for Unit: 5 hours

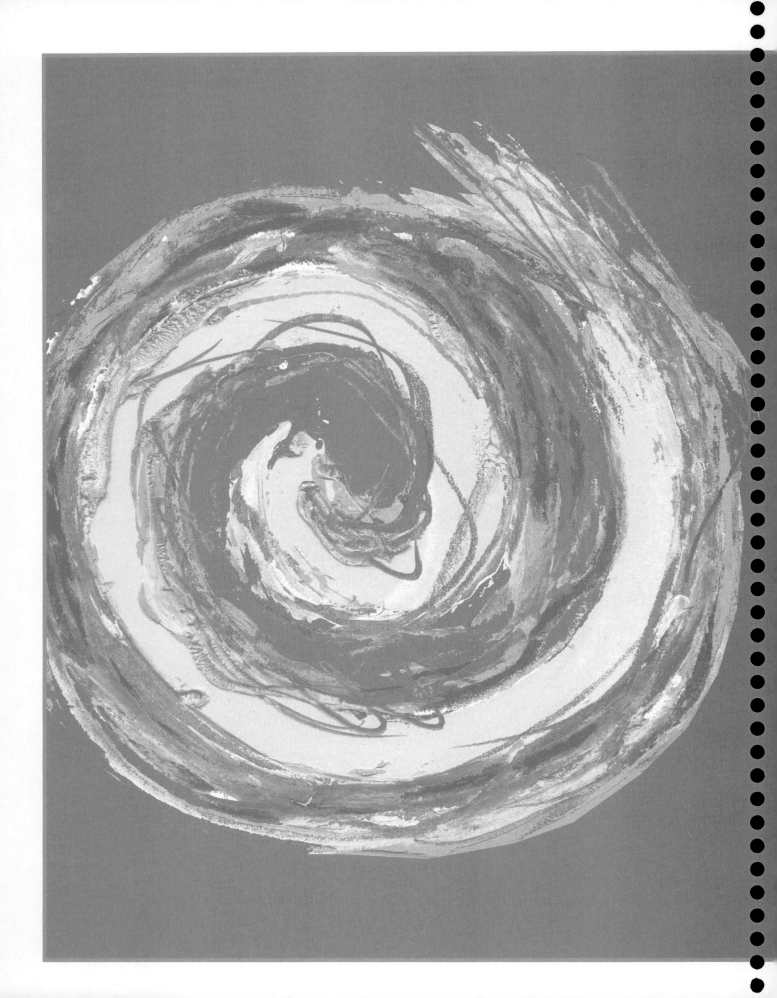

THE INTERNET IN OUR ECONOMY

OBJECTIVES

Upon completion of this lesson, you should be able to:

- Use the Internet to find information about electronic commerce.
- Use the Internet to find information about companies and products.
- Discuss companies that have achieved success with e-commerce and those that have had problems.
- Find information about the past, present, and future developments of e-commerce.

Estimated Time: 2 hours

VOCABULARY

Business-to-business (B2B) sales

E-commerce (electronic commerce)

URL (uniform resource locator)

An Introduction to Electronic Commerce

Electronic commerce is a tremendously popular phrase these days. *Time* and *Business Week* magazines devote cover articles to the idea. Newspaper and TV news stories weigh in on the future of traditional retailing, and everyone from The Gap to your local drug store wants to make sure you know their Internet address.

What do people mean by electronic commerce? How big is it, really? Will companies be left behind if they don't do business this way? Will you be left behind if you don't do business this way? And just what way are we talking about?

In this lesson, you'll learn what electronic commerce is to individuals in a variety of industries. You'll learn how the Internet affects our economy, both nationally and globally. You'll see, by the numbers, where it's been and where experts expect it to go. And you'll begin to see what part e-commerce will play in your future.

E-Commerce—It's More Than Buying and Selling

Have you ever stopped to think that not so very long ago, the letters "www" were meaningless to most people? Comedians didn't use funny Web addresses as punch lines, and a woman named "Dorothy Com," who uses the nickname "Dot," didn't attract much attention.

E-Commerce

Although the features that follow include all types of activities, they can be put into two categories: (1) The online sale of goods or services and (2) the online distribution of information. Some authorities use the term *electronic commerce* or *e-commerce* to mean buying and selling goods and services over the Internet. In this book, we'll use a broader definition: *e-commerce (electronic commerce)* is any electronic exchange of information to conduct business.

From Limited Beginnings

The Internet, as we know it, really isn't very old. The forerunner of the Internet was the Advanced Research Projects Network, or ARPANET. It was created in the 1960s for military and scientific use. Its main purpose was to maintain communications in case a nuclear war or natural disaster knocked out critical pieces of our communications systems. At that time, only researchers and other specialized users could access the network. Later, the National Science Foundation worked with universities to establish a network, and eventually improvements in modem speed, the development of the Internet Service Provider (ISP) industry, and domain name registration made the Internet accessible to businesses, educational institutions, and the average household.

As you might expect, the Internet provides a source of historical information about itself. Several sites offer timelines that can help you put the developments into perspective. Figures 1-1 and 1-2 show portions of a historic timeline created to accompany the PBS series, "Life on the Internet." Users can slide the pointer to the year they want to view. As you see, the Internet was not open to commercial use before 1991. Yet five years later, Internet shopping malls accounted for over $1 billion of activity.

FIGURE 1-1
PBS Internet timeline, 1991-1993

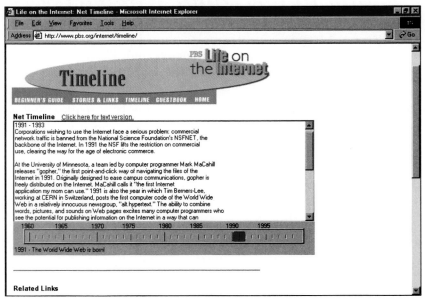

FIGURE 1-2
PBS Internet timeline, 1996

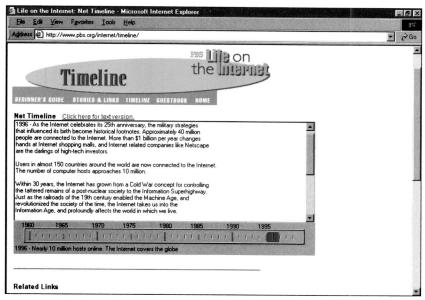

Businesses Establish a Presence

To get a feel for how widespread business use of the Internet has become, take your own informal survey. When you are driving down an interstate, check out the next semi-truck you pass. It probably displays the Web address, or *URL (uniform resource locator)* of the trucking company. Look on the title page or cover of your textbooks, and you'll probably find the Web address of the publisher. Go to your pantry or refrigerator, and see how many companies include their Web address on their product label. The January 28, 2002, issue of *Time* magazine contained URLs in at least 25 of the 27 ads that appeared. And *Time* puts *www.time.com* right on its front cover.

So why do all of these businesses want the world to know where to find them on the Internet? Some use the Internet for sales to consumers, and some use the Internet for sales to other businesses. All use their Internet presence to provide information about their company and products.

You can't order a new car from the Ford or Toyota or Honda Web sites, but you can read about models and options and configure the car you want to buy from your local dealer. If you visit the General Mills Web site, shown in Figure 1-3, you can't order a box of Cheerios, but you can learn that Cheerios were invented in 1941 and were originally called Cheeri Oats. You can also find out about career opportunities at General Mills and read the latest news about the company. For most companies, the goal of a Web site is to interest potential customers, employees, and investors in their company.

FIGURE 1-3
General Mills home page

Business-to-Business

For all the hype about consumers shopping online, forecasters predict that the overwhelming majority of sales—as much as 93% of the over $2.5 trillion predicted for 2004—will be business-to-business. *Business-to-business (B2B) sales* are sales made by one business to another, rather than directly to a consumer. If you need to buy a replacement hinge for a kitchen cabinet, it may be easier for you to make a trip to your local hardware store than to order it over the Internet. But if your company manufactures cabinets and you are searching for a supplier of hinges, examining online catalogs from hardware manufacturers can let you see at a glance which manufacturer has what you need.

The Internet also makes it easy for corporate buyers and sellers around the world to find each other and become trading partners. An Internet exchange formed by automakers connects the parts department at dealerships with body shops looking for repair parts. This joint venture ensures that by using Bell and Howell's electronic parts catalog, General Motors, Ford, DaimlerChrysler, and Saturn will get the correct shipments to the right places more quickly.

Non-Sales Benefits

A Web presence can have other benefits for companies besides sales. A company can enhance its image by providing corporate history, free advice for users about its products, and its financial information online.

It can post job openings and showcase new products. It can make its name familiar to customers in far-flung locations who would never hear of the company otherwise. And it can do all of this while gathering information on the number—and in some cases the individual characteristics—of the people who access its Web site.

Net Fun

You may not be able to order a box of Cheerios from the General Mills Web site, but there are such things as online grocery stores. Electronic shopping services, such as Netgrocer, will ship your order anywhere in the continental United States or to military personnel abroad.

The Partnership Between the Internet and Business

One of the easiest ways to understand the close alliance between the Internet and business is to search the Internet itself. Popular search engines, such as Yahoo and Google, show categories for business and related subjects. Some provide immediate links to business topics, such as stock price quotes or company names, on their opening screens. In the following Step-by-Step activity, you will visit several search engines to learn about e-commerce.

Did You Know?

CyberAtlas reported these sites as the top ten online properties for January, 2002, based on unique visitors: Microsoft Corp., Yahoo Inc., AOL Time Warner, Terra Lycos, U.S. Government, *Amazon.com*, eBay, Primedia, Google, and Walt Disney Internet.

Net Ethics

The Center for Business Ethics at the University of St. Thomas offers training and resources for ethical business practices. Although the Center's area of concern goes far beyond e-commerce, it has chosen the Internet as a vehicle for publishing the latest research in business ethics. You can read issues of the *Online Journal of Ethics* by visiting the Web site at *http://www.stthom.edu/cbes/oje.html*.

STEP-BY-STEP 1.1

SCANS

1. Start your Web browser and search for or go directly to the Yahoo home page. Yahoo is one of the Web's most popular sites, and it groups topics together to make it easier for you to find what you need. Which categories could you investigate to learn about e-commerce?

   _____

   _____

2. What link do you see under "Inside Yahoo" that relates to e-commerce? What other links on this page might provide useful information about e-commerce?

   _____

   _____

3. Click the **Business and Economy** category (you might have to scroll down the page to see the list of categories), and then click the link to **Business to Business**. Follow a link of your choice. What did you choose, why did you choose it, and what did you learn?

   _____

   _____

4. As you've learned, e-commerce includes just about any activity related to business. What Yahoo link would you follow to:
   a. learn about a company? _____
   b. find a stock price?_____
   c. look at job openings? _____
   d. find office furniture? _____
   e. learn current mortgage loan rates? _____
   f. order a birthday present? _____

STEP-BY-STEP 1.1 Continued

Figure 1-4 shows some of the Yahoo links to business sites. Tour the business section to see today's business news and other useful links.

FIGURE 1-4
Yahoo's Business and Economy links

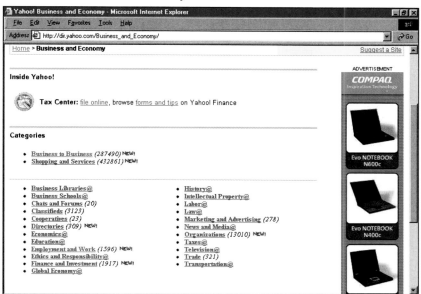

STEP-BY-STEP 1.1 Continued

5. One of the most useful things about the Internet is its ability to provide almost up-to-the-minute business information. For investors in the stock market, this is a very important feature. In the lists that go across the Web page, find the **Personal** category and click **My Yahoo**. Your screen should look similar to the one shown in Figure 1-5. What changes can you make in Yahoo's front page?

FIGURE 1-5
My Yahoo choices

6. There are several features of a page that would be useful for a business owner. If you were starting a business to manufacture toys, you might want to keep track of your competition. Name three companies you would list in the stocks section.

7. Scroll through the **My Yahoo** page. If you were preparing to go to a toy maker's convention, what features might you use, and why would they be useful?

Extra Challenge

How do you use the Internet? How do your friends use it? Is the Internet a way to communicate with people, a tool for doing schoolwork, a source of fun, a business tool, or all of these?

Finding Company Information on the Web

As you have seen, companies use the Web to sell products and services and to make information available. E-commerce can help them control costs by not having to print and mail catalogs and brochures. They can advertise and communicate on the Web, reaching a worldwide audience that they might never be able to reach otherwise. They can make themselves available to customers 24 hours a day, 7 days a week.

Why would you want to find a specific company on the Internet? There are many reasons. You might want to:

- learn more about the products and services a company offers.

- make a purchase.

- download information, such as a parts manual.

- apply for a job with the company.

- read the company's financial reports before you buy its stock.

- write an e-mail letter to the company's customer service representatives.

> **Hot Tip**
>
> An AOL survey showed Web users were cautious about purchasing insurance online. Even if you have concerns about privacy or service, you can comparison-shop online and then contact an insurance company by phone or by mail.

In some instances, you might have a product or service in mind, but not know the name of a company that sells it. You might need to buy a new copier for your business, and want to investigate copier models from a number of manufacturers and retailers. Or you might want to see which banks offer online banking services.

In the following Step-by-Step activity, you will learn how to search the Web for specific companies. You'll also learn how to locate companies by their products.

S TEP-BY-STEP 1.2

1. There are many ways that you can search for information about a company. If you want to get to the company's Web site, you can take a chance and guess at the URL you think it would have. You can also conduct a general search with a search engine for the company's name. Go to Yahoo, Google, and Lycos, and search for the phrase "Pizza Hut." How many hits appear?

SEARCH ENGINE	NUMBER OF HITS
Yahoo	
Google	
Lycos	

STEP-BY-STEP 1.2 Continued

The list of matches picks up all kinds of references to Pizza Hut, as you can see by the titles that appear. The variety makes it a bit difficult to see exactly which one will lead you to the company. Luckily, each of these search engines makes it easier for you to go to a company site directly.

2. When you search with Google, the **I'm Feeling Lucky** button will take you to the site that best matches your search string. Do this for Pizza Hut. Click **More Pizza Hut®** and then click **PR**. Click **The Pizza Hut Story®** to find out more about the company.

   a. Where was the first Pizza Hut located? _____

   b. In what state is the company headquarters? _____

   c. What is the company URL? _____

   d. What company once owned Pizza Hut? _____

   e. What company owns it now? _____

3. Information about specific companies can be found at Hoover's Online. You can search by company name or by other identifiers, or you can check **Companies and Industries** and go to a **Company Directory**. Go to **Hoover's Online** and search for Pizza Hut by Company Name, as shown in Figure 1-6.

   a. What is the New York Stock Exchange ticker symbol for the parent company? _____

   b. Who is the president of Pizza Hut? _____

   c. In what sector and industry is Pizza Hut classified? _____

FIGURE 1-6
Hoover's Online search for Pizza Hut

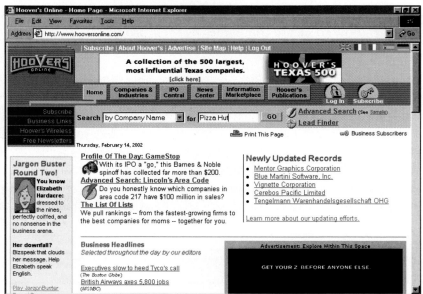

STEP-BY-STEP 1.2 Continued

4. How would you search for information about specific products? Although you can narrow your search with most search engines by using successively more specific categories, you will eventually need to type in the product and do a search. Using the search engine of your choice, search for information about digital cameras by going through representative categories. You need to find Web sites of three manufacturers. What hierarchy of categories did you follow to find the companies?

a. Search engine _____

b. First category _____

c. Second category _____

d. Third category _____

e. Additional categories _____

f. Company 1 URL _____

g. Company 2 URL _____

h. Company 3 URL _____

E-Commerce Success Stories (and Dot-Bombs)

> **Did You Know?**
>
> U.S. online retail revenue (excluding travel, prescription drugs, and autos) is forecast to reach $130.3 billion in 2006. This is nearly four times the amount ($34.1 billion) for 2001.

There have been some marvelous successes in e-commerce. Established companies have found new customers and a new way of doing business by going online. Other companies have been created just to take advantage of this new technology. They may not have a physical presence anywhere. Still other companies have sprung up to provide a product or service for this new technology. Without the technology, there would be no e-services companies.

In 1993 and 1994, the Internet world was full of promise and many companies jumped aboard. In 1995, things slowed a bit, and some companies found that they had moved too quickly, or that the early promise of e-commerce did not live up to their expectations. Some small companies withdrew, and some large companies lost quite a bit of money. But many companies, particularly those with a niche targeting a narrow market with a specific product or service, found great success. The stock market soared for companies such as Cisco Systems, a firm that provides networking equipment to handle the ever-growing volume of Internet traffic.

Some companies that do business in malls and shopping centers decided to add an e-commerce division. These bricks-and-clicks companies complement their regular retail presence with electronic catalogs. For example, at *Staples.com* you can shop online and then pick up your purchase at the local store, saving the shipping charges and having the product almost immediately.

However, some companies were not particularly successful at the e-commerce business model. *Pets.com* became very well known by its TV advertising campaign featuring a sock puppet. *Pets.com* went out of business in 2000; if you visit *Pets.com* now you are forwarded to another company, *petsmart.com*. The bubble seemed to burst in 2000, with dot-bomb failures being blamed by some analysts for the decline in the stock market. The NASDAQ, the stock exchange comprised primarily of new technology companies including e-commerce firms, was hit particularly hard.

Another example, eToys, was the darling of Wall Street. The per-share value of its stock rose as high as $90. The company's market value (total number of shares multiplied by share price) was more than $8 billion. When the stock price fell to 12 cents a share, eToys declared bankruptcy in 2001. Its Web identity was purchased by K-B Holdings and combined with the *KBKids.com* Web site.

> **Did You Know?**
>
> Over 500 Internet companies went out of business in 2001, almost twice as many as in 2000. Analysts expect the numbers to improve in 2002 because today's new e-companies are increasingly based on sound business principles.

STEP-BY-STEP 1.3

1. Number one on almost everyone's list of successful e-commerce sites is *Amazon.com*. This book-seller has done everything right. In 1997, net sales were $148 million. In 2001, the figure was over $3 billion. In the 4th quarter of 2001, *Amazon.com* showed an operating profit for the first time in its history. Customers can search for books by title, by author, and by subject. They can browse and read book reviews. Amazon also sells other products, such as electronics, toys, games, and music CDs. Purchasing is easy and secure. Shipping is not cheap, but items are discounted. Figure 1-7 shows the results when you search for books by a popular mystery author.

FIGURE 1-7
Book search results from *Amazon.com*

Go to **Amazon.com**. Search for books by your favorite author. (Need an idea? Try Tom Clancy, John Grisham, or Bruce McLaren.) Is it easy to perform this search? What do you like or dislike about it?

_____

_____

STEP-BY-STEP 1.3 Continued

2. For one of the books you found, do a bit of comparison-shopping. With shipping, what is the book's final price at *Amazon.com*?

_____

3. What is the book's price at your local bookstore? Don't forget to include sales tax and your cost of traveling to the store.

_____

4. Which way would you purchase the book? Would it make a difference if you needed it by the end of this week?

_____

_____

5. In late 2001 the CNET *News.com* Web site featured a story about dot-com failures. Go to the **News.com** site and search for dot-com failures (December 27, 2001). Read the "Dot-Com Failures Up from Last Year" article to learn about the failures of these companies. From their stories, develop four reasons for e-commerce failure.

    a. _____

    b. _____

    c. _____

    d. _____

6. One of the hottest services on the Internet is travel. In 1997, online travel sales accounted for $654 million in sales. In 2000, online travel sales accounted for $18 billion in sales. In January 2001, online sales for travel accounted for nearly one-third of the sales in e-commerce transactions. By 2006, travel sales are expected to reach $63 billion. Visit your search engine's travel category. What kinds of things can you do? What links appear? Would you feel confident making your own travel plans this way?

_____

_____

Net Fun

Tenagra Corporation, a public relations and Web design firm, presents awards to e-commerce sites it finds particularly effective. You can see the list of winners and visit their sites to judge for yourself. Go to **www.tenagra.com**, and click the link to **Internet Marketing Excellence Awards**.

Who Is Keeping Track?

One industry that has flourished in the past few years is the industry dedicated to keeping track of the Internet and all of its associated activities. Old and new research companies have found a market for reports about the Internet. Consultants, economists, market researchers, and statisticians provide information to the public and sell research reports to subscribers.

Why is it important to know the numbers? The most obvious reason is to spot trends and understand how your company fits into the grand scheme of things. Research companies can supply anything from demographic information (age, gender, and other personal information) of Internet users to forecasts for market segments of the Internet economy. In this Step-by-Step activity, you will visit some of these companies. Throughout this book you will see references to the information they can provide.

S TEP-BY-STEP 1.4

SCANS

1. Figure 1-8 shows the home page for Forrester Research, one of the sites that reports measurements of the Internet economy. One of its features is an e-mail newsletter with links to research reports. Other companies concentrate on reporting e-commerce usage. Find the URL for each company listed in the following table.

COMPANY	URL
CyberAtlas	
Jupiter Media Metrix	
NUA	
Nielsen//NetRatings	

FIGURE 1-8
Home page for Forrester Research

STEP-BY-STEP 1.4 Continued

2. Visit each of these companies. Each offers some information to the visiting public. Look at the information, and record at least one statistic that is interesting to you from each site.

a. CyberAtlas _____

b. Jupiter Media Metrix _____

c. NUA _____

d. Nielsen//NetRatings _____

3. What kinds of information do these sites sell, and what does it cost?

_____

_____

Extra Challenge

The Nielsen Company also tracks the number of people who watch television programs. Why might a business want to know how many Internet users visit its site? What similarities do you see between the reasons for measuring site visitors and the reasons for measuring TV viewers?

Did You Know?

Are you wondering how the research companies count Internet users? If you'd like to find out, read the sampling information from your sites. Do they follow different procedures? Would you expect their statistical results to be very different?

Technology Careers

The research companies you've learned about in this lesson hire market researchers, statisticians, Web designers, and other software specialists. They also need a sales force. Account executives sell research to new clients and work with clients to understand their information needs. With experience, this position can lead to other marketing positions. Being a computer genius is not a requirement for this kind of a job, but excellent communication skills are necessary.

SUMMARY

In this lesson, you learned:

- You can find information about electronic commerce on the Internet.

- You can use the Internet to find information about companies and products.

- Some companies have been very successful with e-commerce, but others have struggled.

- There are Web sites that gather and report information about who uses the Internet for e-commerce.

VOCABULARY *Review*

Define the following terms:

Business-to-business (B2B) sales	E-commerce (electronic commerce)	URL (uniform resource locator)

REVIEW *Questions*

TRUE / FALSE

Circle T if the statement is true or F if the statement is false.

T   F   1. Most e-commerce involves retail consumers rather than business-to-business exchanges.

T   F   2. Travel sales account for a large portion of e-commerce sales.

T   F   3. You do not have to pay for most of the company information that you find on the Web.

T   F   4. *Amazon.com* has made a profit in nearly every year of its existence as the number one e-commerce firm.

T   F   5. Many e-services companies were developed to provide technology products for e-commerce firms.

WRITTEN QUESTIONS

Write a brief answer to the following questions.

1. What is e-commerce?

2. What are three reasons that businesses would want to use the Internet? Describe a company or a product for each reason.

3. What kinds of products sell well to consumers over the Internet? Why do you suppose these products work so well?

4. How could a business use the Internet to interact with another business?

5. What kinds of information do companies that research Internet usage provide? Why is this information valuable to businesses that use the Internet?

PROJECTS

 PROJECT 1-1

1. Find the Web site for VELCRO®, the hook and loop fastener.

2. Who invented VELCRO®? What gave him the inspiration?

_____

_____

3.　Click the link for **Automotive**. List three ways the product is used by the automotive industry.

_____

_____

_____

4.　Click the link for **Industrial**. Click the link for **Products**, and then the link for **ONE WRAP®** ties. How can these ties be used around a computer workstation?

_____

_____

_____

5.　Click the link for **Consumer**. How do gardeners use VELCRO®?

_____

_____

_____

6.　Read about VELCRO DIRECT ONLINE(SM). What are the five services it provides to VELCRO's business customers?

_____

_____

_____

_____

_____

SCANS **PROJECT 1-2**

1.　Find the Web site for Epson, a maker of ink jet printers.

2.　Click the appropriate place on the world map for your location.

3.　What is the print speed (ppm, or pages per minute) and the cost for the least expensive ink jet printer?

_____

_____

4.　Return to the Epson home page for your region. Click the link for **Contact Us** at the bottom of the page.

5.　Click the link for **Dealer Locator**.

6. Select the link for **Ink Cartridge—Color—Stylus Color 777/777i** (or another Epson printer if this is not listed). Select your country and your zip code. What is the name and address of the closest dealer located in your region that carries the ink cartridge for this printer?

_____

_____

  TEAMWORK PROJECT

Choose a consumer product that is interesting to the members of your group. Each member of the group should go shopping online for that product. Compare what you found. What range of prices did you find? Would you be able to buy that product online? What consumer information did you find about the product? Did the product come in a variety of brands or models? As a group, decide whether you would buy online, and if so, from which seller.

CRITICAL *Thinking*

ACTIVITY 1-1

For one 24-hour period, write down every URL you see or hear. Exclude those that you find when you are surfing the Internet, but include the ones you see in ads or on products and delivery trucks when you are not at the computer. Group them according to the purpose you think they serve. Using about 100 words, describe the types of references you saw and heard.

BUSINESS ON THE INTERNET

Upon completion of this lesson, you should be able to:

■ Describe how the unique capabilities of the Internet allow business to connect with other groups.

■ Discuss the advantages for businesses to work with each other online.

■ Explain how businesses and consumers can benefit from the Internet.

■ Discuss how government can use the Internet to provide services.

■ Explain how other organizations use the Internet.

Estimated Time: 3 hours

VOCABULARY

Bricks and clicks

Business-to-consumer (B2C) sales

Consumer

Entrepreneurs

Portable document format (pdf)

Private trading networks (PTN)

Request for quotation (RFQ)

Retailing

Supply chain

A Net for All Reasons

As you learned in Lesson 1, many different kinds of businesses have a home on the Internet. Some use the Internet for *retailing*—selling goods and services to the *consumer*, the ultimate owner or user of the product. With or without a physical store, these businesses can reach new consumers, take orders, and complete transactions electronically. Some companies use the Internet to sell things to other businesses rather than to consumers. Some businesses feature their product information online, but require a phone contact or a personal visit in order to finalize the sale.

Some businesses use the Internet for transactions with other businesses, exclusively. The Internet has made it much easier for businesses to manage the *supply chain*—how businesses get what they need at the right place and at the right time.

Not all of e-commerce involves a sales transaction. Businesses and organizations have discovered the value of the Internet for showcasing their operations and placing their information in front of a target audience. Web sites are also useful for an organization whose main purposes are information and public relations. It can put its best foot forward, share its story, and be available whenever anyone wants to look. By providing online access to corporate information, businesses can avoid mass mailings, improve communications with their customers and investors, and reach new audiences.

In this lesson, you'll look at several businesses that use the Internet for e-commerce. In later lessons, you'll learn more specifically how to shop for goods and services, and how to set up your own e-commerce site.

E-Commerce Models

Although you may think that e-commerce means online stores selling products to consumers on the Web, business-to-business e-commerce dwarfs the consumer side. In this section you will learn how the Web has affected all kinds of online commerce, from business to consumers to government to universities and colleges. First we will explore some e-commerce acronyms in Table 2-1.

TABLE 2-1
E-commerce models

SYMBOL	EXPLANATION	EXAMPLE
B2C	Business-to-consumer	Buy tax preparation software and download from the Internet
B2B	Business-to-business	Post RFQ (request for quotation) in eMarketplace
C2C	Consumer-to-consumer	Sell old 35mm camera through online auction
G2C	Government-to-consumer	Download a tax form from the IRS site
U2S	University-to-student	Register for classes and pay fees online

 Net Ethics

In several references in this lesson, you'll see the ™ symbol for a company's registered trademark. This mark clearly indicates that no one else may use this name. Copyrighted material is a bit different. For example, at the Merriam-Webster Dictionary Web site (*http://www.m-w.com*), the term *copyright* is defined as "the exclusive legal right to reproduce, publish, and sell the matter and form." Because the definition is copyrighted, this book has to show it in quotation marks and attribute its source. It is so simple to copy and paste text or graphic images from a Web document that companies must protect themselves legally by placing copyright, or terms of use, statements with their material. This doesn't prevent a user from lifting something from a site, but it does establish legal protection for the owner of the site. The only real protection is the sense of ethical responsibility shown by those who visit the site. Hundreds of Web pages are devoted to Internet copyright issues. These also address fair use policies and issues of intellectual property rights. For a sample, see the information from the Stanford University Libraries at *http://fairuse.stanford.edu*.

B2C: Business-to-Consumer

Business-to-consumer (B2C) sales represent the traditional type of e-commerce marketplace in which an online company provides a product to an end consumer. The product might be delivered over the Internet (such as an electronic greeting card, your SAT scores, or downloaded software and music) or shipped from a distribution center to the customer. Package delivery companies such as UPS and FedEx have played an important role in this kind of e-commerce by completing the transaction in an efficient manner. Products may be goods or services, including information.

B2B: Business-to-Business

In the B2B e-commerce model, businesses work with other businesses through the Internet. B2B e-commerce marketplaces provide ways to bring buyers and sellers together. For example, the Just For Plastics Web site, shown in Figure 2-1 allows sellers with excess inventory to meet industrial plastics buyers to bid for these items. Another example is at the *ContractorHub.com* Web site, which claims to "shave off approximately 10 percent of the time traditionally required to compare and organize bids."

FIGURE 2-1
Just for Plastics Web site

C2C: Consumer-to-Consumer

Online auction sites have enabled end users to sell items they no longer need on the Web. Auction sites such as eBay and Yahoo make it easy to list products for sale. To pay for goods, customers can send a money order or personal check to the seller, but these must travel through the mail, delaying the completion of the transaction. New payment services like PayPal and BidPay are intermediary sites that permit sellers to receive payment from auction winners directly through the Internet without the seller having to establish a merchant account for credit card processing.

G2C: Government-to-Consumer

Government sites provide all sorts of helpful information to consumers and businesses. For example, when you are preparing your income tax returns, you can download printable forms from the IRS Web site, or search through the documentation library for information about a tax question. You can even file certain important forms over the Web. The FAFSA (Free Application for Federal Student Aid) form can be filed electronically by answering questions on the Web.

U2S: University-to-Student

This category represents the e-commerce activities performed in specialty industries. Many colleges and universities list class schedules online. You can register for classes over the Web and then pay for them with a credit card. Students can order transcripts and check financial aid status online. Library resources are available online. Many schools now offer a broad range of distance education classes on the Web, eliminating the bricks and mortar classroom and face-to-face contact with an instructor. Figure 2-2 shows how students can study online at Rio Salado College, part of Maricopa Community College in Arizona.

FIGURE 2-2
Online learning opportunities at Rio Salado College

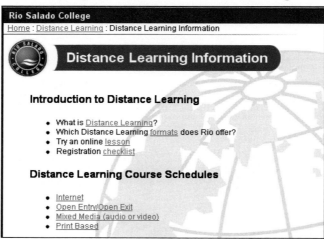

STEP-BY-STEP 2.1

1. The first site you will visit is the Kelley Blue Book site at **http:www.kbb.com**. This company provides information on car prices. Go there and scroll to examine the entire page. As you look through the page, note the services that are available for car buyers and sellers.

   a. What type of e-commerce model does this site represent?

   _____

   b. What used car services are available from this site?

   _____

   _____

STEP-BY-STEP 2.1 Continued

    c. What information about new cars is available on this site?

    _____

    _____

    d. Because this site does not charge for its services, revenue must be generated in other ways. Can you tell from the site why advertising here would be a good idea for automotive industry companies?

    _____

    _____

2. The Rock & Dirt Web site at **www.rockanddirt.com** is designed for the heavy equipment industry. Find this site and examine the choices found on the home page.

    a. What e-commerce model represents the activities done at Rock & Dirt?

    _____

    b. After examining the buttons in the banner at the top of the page, list four activities that can be accomplished at this site.

    _____

    _____

3. The Internal Revenue Service Web site at **www.irs.gov** offers numerous services for business and individual taxpayers. Visit this site and click the **Contents** section for Individuals.

    a. Click the **e-file** link. Click the **e-file Using Your Computer** link under Individual Taxpayers. What are the benefits of using e-file in this manner?

    _____

    _____

    _____

    b. Most of the site provides information in English. In what other language(s) does the IRS provide information?

    _____

    c. Click the link called **Where to File** in the menu at the left under Resources. Click your state on the map and look up the address for returns _with payment_. If you are not in the United States, select Indiana (IN) on the map.

Extra Challenge

It would be unusual for a computer-related business—a computer store, an Internet service provider, or a Web design firm—not to have an Internet presence. What other businesses would consider a Web site critically important? Are there any businesses whose customers would not look for them on the Internet? Why might these businesses want to have a site anyway?

B2B: Business-to-Business E-Commerce

The B2B sector of e-commerce is booming, and a large reason for this success has to do with savings in time and money. A university might have a relationship with Office Depot so that departments can place orders for office supplies and equipment, bypassing the purchasing department and saving time and money. The pricing is pre-arranged based on a negotiated agreement between the two parties. Orders are placed online and delivered the next day to campus locations. It is estimated that a manual purchase order that goes through a purchasing agent could cost 10 to 20 times

Did You Know?

According to International Data Corporation, the total worldwide value of goods and services purchased by businesses through e-commerce will increase from $282 billion in 2000 to $4.3 trillion by 2005, an annual growth rate of 73 percent.

more than the same order placed online. Think about the simplicity of sending an e-mail message versus writing a letter, typing the envelope, and mailing it to your party. Office Depot also offers business services to small businesses as you will see in the next Step-by-Step.

The supply chain network refers to the integrated relationship between raw material providers, component part suppliers, manufacturers, and the distribution system that moves finished products to the final customer. The use of *private trading networks* (PTNs) brings business buyers and sellers together through the Internet. PTNs provide an online trading post where buyers can post *requests for quotations* (RFQs) for products they wish to purchase. Sellers can list excess equipment and merchandise or advertise their company's products to potential buyers. For example, the Rock and Dirt Web site allows heavy equipment operators to list used equipment they wish to sell. *FastParts.com* is a B2B net marketplace where electronic parts and equipment can be bought and sold. There is no fee to offer a lot for sale or to request a lot to buy, but a small transaction fee is charged to the seller when the transaction is completed.

B2B PTNs are moving beyond purchasing toward improving collaboration between business sellers and buyers. The *PowerWay.com* Web site focuses on improving quality in the automotive industry supply chain by organizing the relationships between suppliers and buyers. For example, PowerWay's private Web site consolidates documentation between supply chain partners. Automotive engineering changes can be quickly communicated with partners, smoothing the process of developing new products and making both parties more effective.

S TEP-BY-STEP 2.2

1. Open the Office Depot site shown in Figure 2-3 and click the **Business Center** link in the top banner menu. You will reach the **Partner Services** link where third-party providers offer business services to Office Depot customers.

FIGURE 2-3
Office Depot site

Small Business Center

Business Tools	Business News	Business Partners
Office Depot is your source for Small Business and Home-based Business Solutions.	Office Depot has partnered with bizjournals.com to bring you:	Money Matters
		Sales & Marketing
		Office Administration
FREE Downloadable Forms OSHA forms, Job reference forms, Workers Comp info.	• Breaking news	Internet Postage
	• Small Business Tools	Website Services
	• Industry Journals	HR & Staffing
Small Business Handbook Everything you need to know to run your business.	• Award-winning Local Coverage	**Microsoft**
Working the Web	Local News	Build a Website
A complete online directory of Web resources that inform, educate and help.	Select a City ▾ Go	Improve Sales & Marketing
		Respond to Customers
		Create a Network

a. What HR & Staffing services are available to small businesses through this Web site?

_____

_____

b. What Sales & Marketing services are available to small businesses?

_____

_____

c. List at least three reasons why a business would want to purchase its office supplies through an e-commerce provider like *OfficeDepot.com*.

_____

_____

_____

STEP-BY-STEP 2.2 Continued

2. Open the **www.WoodworkingSite.com** Web site shown in Figure 2-4. This is a PTN for the wood products industry.

FIGURE 2-4
WoodworkingSite.com private trading network site

a. List the types of services offered for *Sourcing* (buying) products.

_____

_____

b. List the types of services offered for *Selling* products.

_____

_____

c. Look at the remaining services offered at this site. Pick one and explain why it would benefit a business user.

_____

_____

3. Open the **www.PowerWay.com** site and take the tour. Answer the following questions based on the tour.

a. What is the industry's goal for the design time for a new car?

_____

_____

b. What are quality gates?

_____

_____

STEP-BY-STEP 2.2 Continued

c. List some of the items associated with a project that might be found on the *Powerway.com* home page.

_____

_____

d. *PowerWay.com* uses the **portable document format** (**PDF**) to display documents in its Web site. PDF files are documents that have been converted from their original format so that they can be transferred over the Internet to your Web browser without changing their look. What software is used to view PDF documents?

_____

Extra Challenge

What products are well suited for an online catalog? Why would these products work well for online catalog sales? Name three that are well suited to online ordering and three that are not. Why are some products better candidates for online catalog sales than others?

B2C: Business-to-Consumer E-Commerce

Online shopping is what many people think of when they hear the phrase B2C. They think of the ease and comfort of sitting at home and not fighting traffic to go to the mall, being able to shop 24/7—24 hours a day, 7 days a week—and finding access to goods that don't appear in local stores. All of these benefits are very real, and online sales of consumer goods have exceeded early expectations. Even in the fourth quarter of 2001, U.S. sales from online retailers totaled over $10 billion. In December alone, 18.7 million American households spent $5.7 billion online.

What do consumers spend their money on? Software, music, books, clothes, computers, food, and furniture are just some of the things consumers buy online. These are items, with the exception of clothing, that consumers feel comfortable buying without touching. They can comparison-shop more effectively than they can in stores, and there is little uncertainty about what they are getting. Clothing is slightly different, but most clothing retailers make it relatively simple for consumers to return what doesn't fit.

Bricks and clicks is a phrase that describes retailers, such as Target, Gap, and Toys "R" Us, that have regular stores and also offer online shopping. Other online retailers do not have a storefront, but exist only on the Internet. *Amazon.com*, the online bookseller, falls into this category. Borders Book Stores, a company with over 360 stores nationwide, teams with Amazon for its online sales. Consumers can also buy airline tickets, make hotel and car reservations, and have flowers delivered by working through an Internet site.

Buying and selling are not the only activities that take place in B2C e-commerce. Some companies use their Web sites to influence consumer buying and selling, even though consumers don't buy online. Car companies are a good example of this. You can learn all about models, colors, and options from the corporate Web site, but customers still contact dealers to buy a car.

Corporate Web sites provide a good source of information. Consumers who have misplaced the instruction manual for their DVD player can go to the manufacturer's Web site and download another one. Gardeners can go to the seed company's Web site to read everything from planting tips to pest advice to recipes for their produce. Some software companies offer an e-mail link to their Help Desk on their company site. Restaurants can show their menus, and sports teams can show their schedules. Connecting with their customers in this way helps companies build loyalty and attract new customers. And it helps consumers get more for their purchasing dollar.

STEP-BY-STEP 2.3

1. How does a giant retailer use the Internet? To see, begin by finding Wal-Mart's Web site.

2. Examine the folder tabs at the top of the page, shown in Figure 2-5. Click the tab for **Movies**. What is the price for a DVD of *Monsters, Inc.*? Does this price include shipping?

_____

FIGURE 2-5
Wal-Mart home page

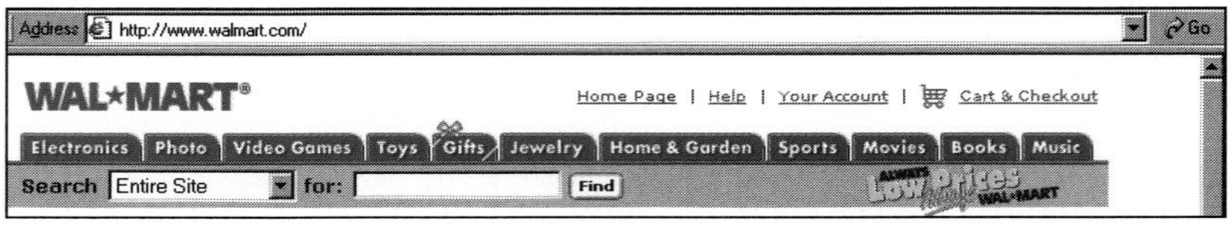

3. Make a list of five items you normally buy at a store like Wal-Mart. Are these items that you would buy online? Why or why not? Do you think every item for sale at the local Wal-Mart is available at the Web site? Why or why not?

_____

_____

4. Next, examine the Web site of a specialty retailer by going to **www.sephora.com**. You can find a Wal-Mart almost anywhere in the country, but the same isn't true for Sephora. Go to **Sephora Stores and Events** at the top of the page and find the closest store to your location. Why is it important for this kind of retailer to have the ability to reach consumers through a Web site?

_____

_____

5. Businesses need to reach consumers in other ways. Go to the Web site of the Whitehall Inn in Maine at **www.whitehall-inn.com**. Look at the history of the inn, the accommodation choices, and information about the restaurant. What does this business do at its Web site to attract guests?

_____

_____

STEP-BY-STEP 2.3 Continued

6. Some businesses use their Web site to build loyalty among their customers rather than specifically selling them anything. For example, search for the Purina site using the keyword *Purina*. List five ways you could use this site for help if you had a new puppy or kitten. Do you think that going to this site for information would make you more likely to buy Purina brand food for your pet? Why?

_____

_____

_____

_____

E-Government and B2G

Federal, state, and local governments use their Web sites to provide information to citizens and to conduct business. The U.S. government encourages companies to use the Internet to bid on government contracts, and federal agencies post information, recruit employees, and encourage contact through their Web sites.

The federal government uses the Internet to both buy and sell items. During 2000, the Treasury Department sold over $3.3 billion in bonds and notes online. But there are other kinds of government sales, too. The government sells oil drilling leases, surplus military goods, documents, and real estate. Fed Biz Opps, found under Federal Business Opportunities, is the government's single point of entry for its procurement of goods in amounts totaling over $25,000. A wide variety of possibilities are listed—the government buys everything

Hot Tip

If you have studied French, you may recognize that both *entrepreneur* and *enterprise* come from French roots and are related to *undertake*. ***Entrepreneurs*** undertake nearly everything associated with the businesses they start. Visit the St. Louis University Web site at *www.slu.edu* to learn more about its academic programs and support for entrepreneurship through the Jefferson Smurfit Center for Entrepreneurial Studies.

from nuclear weapons to tractors, lighting fixtures, and toiletries. The Fed Biz Opps site is one of the many links at *www.firstgov.gov*, an official U.S. Government site that guides the user through its Web presence. Figure 2-6 shows some of the categories of links available at the FirstGov site. State and local governments also take advantage of the Internet to work with their citizens.

FIGURE 2-6
First Gov

S TEP-BY-STEP 2.4

1. Begin with a visit to the FirstGov Web site to see how online access to the Federal Government is organized. Click the link for **Passport Applications** under Online Services for Citizens.

   a. What size must the picture on your passport application be?

   _____

   b. Return to the FirstGov Web site. Click the **and much more** link under Online Services for Citizens, then click **Government Shopping Mall** to find information about purchasing a flag that has flown over the U.S. Capitol. From whom must you order a flag?

   _____

   c. Return to **Online Services for Citizens** and click **Social Security Online**. What would you have to do to replace a lost Social Security card? What were the most common names for babies born in 1885?

   _____
   _____

STEP-BY-STEP 2.4 Continued

2. Official Web sites for each state are found at **www.state.xx.us**. Use the two-letter abbreviation of the state's name in place of "xx" in the URL. The site for Indiana is shown in Figure 2-7. Choose three states you have visited or would like to visit, and write their URLs here.

_____

_____

_____

FIGURE 2-7
State of Indiana Web site

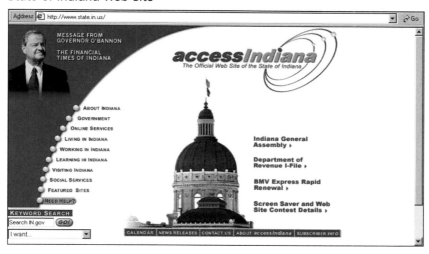

Visit the three state sites and see whether or not there are links on the main page to these services.

A welcome from the Governor	Yes ___	No ___
Visiting the state	Yes ___	No ___
Paying state taxes electronically	Yes ___	No ___
Renewing license plates electronically	Yes ___	No ___
Doing business in the state	Yes ___	No ___

Why does it make sense for all official state government sites to have a similar Internet address?

_____

_____

STEP-BY-STEP 2.4 Continued

3. Does your town or city have a government Web site? Use a search engine to see. If it does not, choose another town or city you know.

Which of the following kinds of information were you able to find on the city's Web site?

Welcome from city government	Yes _____	No _____
City map	Yes _____	No _____
Community events calendar	Yes _____	No _____
Schools	Yes _____	No _____
Parks and recreation facilities	Yes _____	No _____
Local weather	Yes _____	No _____

Extra Challenge

Do other countries have official government Web sites? If you click **I'm Feeling Lucky** in Google when you search for Canada, you will arrive at the official government site shown in Figure 2-8. For other countries, you may have to specify the country name in the language of the country. Search for a corresponding government site for Mexico and see what you find.

FIGURE 2-8
Web site of the Canadian government

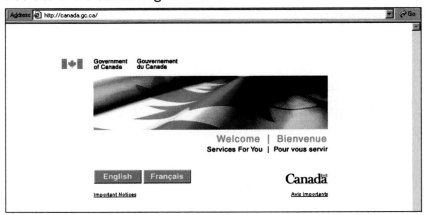

Organizations on the Web

A wide variety of organizations that are not companies use the Web to do business electronically. Because the Internet provides such a wonderful way to disseminate information to anyone at any time and at any place, organizations use their Web sites to tell visitors about their work, to provide links to services, and to enable donors to make contributions. For example, in the first two weeks after 9/11, the Red Cross collected $61 million in *online* donations. Prior to this, the largest online total was $2.7 million in 1999.

Charities are not the only organizations that have a strong Web presence. Trade associations, professional organizations, schools, religious organizations, and cultural organizations all benefit from telling their story online. Figure 2-9 shows the Web site for the T. rex exhibit at the Field Museum in Chicago.

FIGURE 2-9
"Sue" museum site

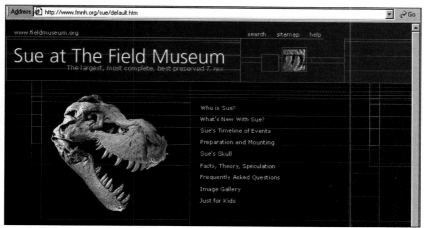

STEP-BY-STEP 2.5

1. Find the Web sites for these organizations and record the URL for each.
   Habitat for Humanity _____
   American Cancer Society _____
   Society for the Prevention of Cruelty to Animals _____
   United Way _____
   Charity of your choice_____
   a. Does every site provide information about the history of the organization?

   _____
   _____

   b. Can you find a mission statement for each organization?

   _____
   _____

STEP-BY-STEP 2.5 Continued

    c. Is there a way to locate a local branch of the organization?

_____

_____

    d. Can you make a donation online?

_____

_____

    e. Can you find out what portion of donations reaches those in need?

_____

_____

2. Trade associations are associated with particular industries. These associations also act as information sources for members and consumers alike. Many of them provide educational material and Web links to their members' sites and to related sites. If you have a business, it would be valuable to be able to learn from others who face the same issues you do. The Internet can make it easy to find and communicate with your peers. A portion of the Web site for the American Sportfishing Association is shown in Figure 2-10. Not only can individuals visit this site to learn more about fishing, but professionals involved in the industry—such as fishing equipment retailers and manufacturers, environmentalists, and camp owners—can also find each other in the database, learn about legislation, and benefit from the association's research.

FIGURE 2-10
American Sportfishing Association

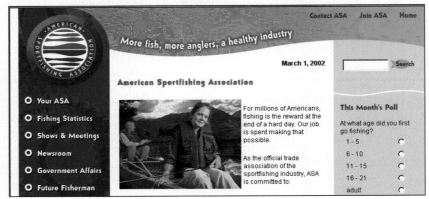

STEP-BY-STEP 2.5 Continued

Search for trade associations for these industries, and then use what you find to complete the table.

INDUSTRY	URL	NAME OF ASSOCIATION
Textiles		
Lighting		
Desktop publishing		
Soap		
Consumer electronics		

3. Cultural organizations use the Web for promotion and information. Go to the Web sites for the Metropolitan Museum of Art, the Boston Pops, the Indianapolis Children's Museum, and the San Diego Zoo. Confirm that you can find schedules and cost information at each site. How do these sites entice online visitors to make a real visit to the attraction?

_____

_____

Did You Know?

Where would you go if you wanted to volunteer but didn't know where to begin? *Volunteermatch.org* and *helping.org* both lead interested people to agencies and organizations that need them. Figure 2-11 shows you how the Web can match volunteers with organizations that need them.

FIGURE 2-11
VolunteerMatch site

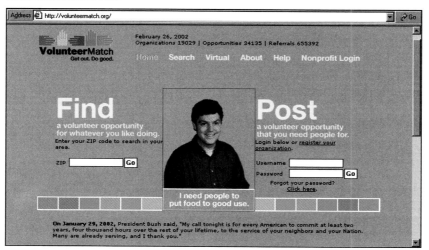

SUMMARY

In this lesson, you learned:

- The unique capabilities of the Internet allow businesses to connect with other groups.

- There are advantages for businesses to work with each other online.

- Businesses and consumers can benefit from the Internet.

- Government can use the Internet to provide services.

- Organizations use the Internet to reach people.

VOCABULARY *Review*

Define the following terms:

Bricks and clicks	Portable document format	Request for quotation (RFQ)
Business-to-consumer	(pdf)	Retailing
(B2C) sales	Private trading networks	Supply chain
Consumer	(PTN)	
Entrepreneurs		

REVIEW *Questions*

TRUE / FALSE

Circle T if the statement is true or F if the statement is false.

T   F   1. Between 8 and 10 million American households shopped online in December of 2001.

T   F   2. *Bricks and clicks* describes a business that has both a physical store and an online store.

T   F   3. For electronic commerce to be classified as B2C, the consumer must buy something online.

T   F   4. The site that provides access to all the agencies of the U.S. government is *Fedgov.com*.

T   F   5. Based on the standard pattern, the official state government Web site for Texas would be *www.state.tx.us*.

WRITTEN QUESTIONS

Write a brief answer to the following questions.

1. How can a business use the Internet to its advantage without making a sales transaction?

2. What kinds of information can a business put on its Web page to support sales? Use a music store as an example.

3. Why would a business that knows it will not be making online sales still want to have an online catalog? Use a business that sells antique cars as an example.

4. How can a business benefit by linking its Web page to a trade association Web page?

5. Where would a business begin to look for online instructions on how to obtain government contracts?

6. How can a very large company use a Web site to educate its customers?

7. List three reasons a consumer might want to buy a gift online rather than from a traditional store.

8. Why does it make sense for a charity to accept donations online?

9. Explain why a business would want to join a private trading network.

10. What advantages would come to a company with existing stores by creating an online store?

PROJECTS

 PROJECT 2-1

There are many online resources for developers and owners of small businesses. In addition to the Small Business Administration, the financial site Quicken has a section for small businesses. Also, *www.smallbizhelp.net* offers advice.

Visit the sites for the resources listed below. Compile a list of the three best suggestions from each site for a small business that wants to do e-commerce.

The Small Business Administration suggestions:

1. _____

2. _____

3. _____

Quicken suggestions:

1. _____

2. _____

3. _____

Smallbizhelp suggestions:

1. _____

2. _____

3. _____

SCANS PROJECT 2-2

1. Visit the Kodak Web site to see what features are available. Can you buy products directly from Kodak, or is this site only for information?

2. What features of this site would be attractive to someone who feels they have taken good photographs and would like to share them?

3. What features of this site would be attractive to someone who wants to learn more about digital photography?

4. How should you protect your film during airport security checks?

5. Click **Email postcards**. Follow the instructions to select a sample picture, a border, a greeting, and a message. If you wish, send your postcard to someone.

6. Click the folder tabs for **Manage, Edit, Play, Share,** and **Learn**. Which do you think Kodak is emphasizing at this site—selling to consumers or helping to attract new consumers to Kodak?

SCANS PROJECT 2-3

1. Visit the Kelley Blue Book Web site. Find out the **Trade-In Value** for your family vehicle. If you are not sure about your car, choose a 1999 Dodge Grand Caravan SE with a V6 3.8 liter engine in excellent condition. Assume this car has 55,000 miles.

2. Repeat the previous step and find the **Private Party Value** for the same vehicle. Why is there a difference between these prices?

3. Return to the Kelley Blue Book home page. Click the **recalls** link under **Tools, Tips, Advice** and search the NHTSA to determine if your family vehicle has been recalled. If you are not sure about your car, choose a 1999 Grand Caravan from the Dodge Truck group.

CRITICAL *Thinking*

ACTIVITY 2-1

Imagine that you have been asked to give a speech to the clients of a local Small Business Development Center. Your topic is "How the Internet Can Improve Your Business." In about 100 words, write a sentence outline of your speech.

INTRODUCTION TO ELECTRONIC COMMERCE

REVIEW *Questions*

TRUE/FALSE

Circle T if the statement is true or F if the statement is false.

T   F   1.   To be considered e-commerce, a transaction must include buying and selling.

T   F   2.   The forerunner of today's Internet was developed for military and scientific purposes.

T   F   3.   You can order a new car from the Toyota corporate Web site.

T   F   4.   B2B is the largest segment of e-commerce.

T   F   5.   Selling directly to buyers is the primary function of most corporate Web sites.

T   F   6.   It is possible to configure Yahoo to show automatically business items of interest.

T   F   7.   There are companies whose business is collecting and selling statistical information about the use of the Internet.

T   F   8.   B2C, C2C, and G2C each connect a segment of e-commerce to a company.

T   F   9.   The supply chain establishes relationships that integrate a manufacturer's raw material and provides subcontractors and distribution centers.

T   F   10.   Government Web sites provide information but are prohibited from sales transactions.

MATCHING

Match the description in Column 2 to its correct term in Column 1.

Column 1

__ 1. Hoover's Online

__ 2. Google

__ 3. FirstGov

__ 4. I'm Feeling Lucky

__ 5. Dot bomb

__ 6. *Amazon.com*

__ 7. E-file

__ 8. B2B

__ 9. B2C

__10. Plane ticket

Column 2

A. A choice that leads to the most logical search match

B. Online transactions between businesses

C. Online transactions between a business and consumers

D. Popular search engine

E. Successful online company that sells books and other consumer items

F. Enables citizens to pay taxes online

G. Web site for corporate information

H. An item that sells well online

I. An online business that failed

J. Web site for U.S. government information

PROJECTS

SCANS **PROJECT 1-1**

1. Find the Web site for Paramount's King's Island, an attraction near Cincinnati, Ohio.

2. Under **Rides and Attractions** on the main menu, click **Thrill Rides** and read about **The Beast**.
   A. From what material is this roller coaster constructed? _____
   B. How long is the track? _____
   C. What is the top speed of this roller coaster? _____

3. Click **Special Events** on the main menu and then choose **Math and Science Days**. List three activities that students do on these days.

_____

_____

4. Click **Plan a Visit** on the main menu and look at the map, tips, and other features provided there. Why does it make good business sense for the park to provide this information on a Web site?

_____

_____

5. Scroll down to the bottom of the page and click the link for **Jobs.** How old do you have to be to get a job at King's Island? How many seasonal workers are employed at the park?

_____

_____

6. Can you buy tickets online? Why would a customer want to do this? What benefit does this have for the park?

_____

_____

SCANS PROJECT 1-2

1. Search for and go to the Web site for the Pew Internet and American Life Project.

2. Click **About Us,** click the **Our Mission** link, and read the Mission Statement. Although e-commerce is not listed as a facet of this study, how does it impact the groups, such as families and communities, that are listed in the Mission Statement?

_____

_____

3. Click **Internet Data Dump** under **Net Resources** at the left of your screen. Click **Market Research.** Select **comScore Networks.** Click **About comScore** and read about **Who We Are.** ComScore provides information on Internet users' surfing and buying behavior. How do they do this?

_____

_____

4. Return to the Pew Internet and American Life Project page and click the link for **Our Reports.** Find the report from November 12, 2001, titled "The Dot-Com Meltdown and the Web." Click **Read the Report.**

5. Instead of downloading the entire report, click **Major Findings.** Click **2** under **Table of Contents.** What two changes have affected Internet users, and how widespread are these changes?

_____

_____

6. Why does the Pew Project publish its results on its Web site? Do you think it publishes these results in other places? Why?

_____

_____

PROJECT 1-3

1. Visit the Web site for Innovative Metal Designs at **www.innovativemetals.com**. What kinds of products does this company make?

   _____

   _____

2. Click **Links,** and you should see a list of motorcycle manufacturers. Does Innovative Metal Designs manufacture motorcycles?

   _____

   _____

3. What does this company show on its Web site to demonstrate that it makes high quality products?

   _____

   _____

4. Click **Quotes** to see how the company interacts with its customers. Do not fill out or submit the order form! Who are the customers of this company?

   _____

   _____

SIMULATION

 JOB 1-1

Evan Peters has enjoyed selling things ever since he first went around the neighborhood selling candy bars for an elementary school fundraiser. Lately, Evan has been helping his friends buy, sell, and trade computer hardware, cell phones, and other electronic equipment. As more people learn about his services, Evan's popularity has grown until he now has a room full of equipment to sell and a list of 165 people he's helped.

Evan thinks he is ready to take the next step and launch Evan's Trading Mart. Before he does so, though, he knows he will need to learn more about running a business. Use the Web resources you learned about in Unit 1 to investigate Small Business Development Centers in your state and the services they offer to someone like Evan.

 JOB 1-2

Gloria Fernandez is the senior real estate agent at Castillo Bay Realty in Florida. She wonders how the Internet could help her company. One of her friends works for a marketing company that creates advertising plans, including new media projects for the Internet. She asked her friend to think of ways that the Internet could benefit Castillo Bay Realty. Suppose you are an intern at the advertising company. What would you advise Gloria?

PERSONAL AND BUSINESS SERVICES ONLINE

Unit 2

 Estimated Time for Unit: 7 hours

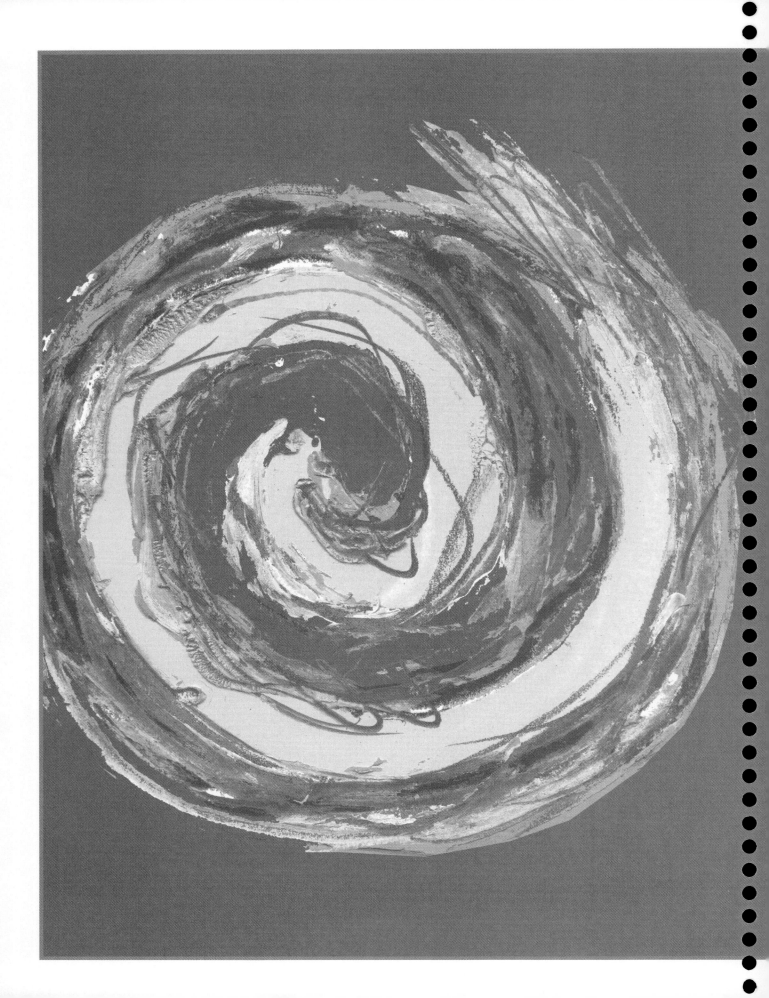

SEARCHING FOR A CAREER

LESSON 3

OBJECTIVES

Upon completion of this lesson, you should be able to:

- Locate career-planning information online.
- Prepare an electronic resume and post it.
- Search for job listings.
- Find relocation information.
- Match educational institutions with your needs.

Estimated Time: 3 hours

VOCABULARY

Acronym

Assessment tools

Career

Clearinghouses

Job

Meta-sites

Resume

Personal and Business Services Online

As you're learning, e-commerce means more than buying and selling goods online. It describes business conducted electronically that takes advantage of the speed, access, and data handling capabilities of the Internet.

Companies that provide services instead of products can take advantage of these capabilities in the same way that companies that sell goods can. Even though they may not have an object to sell, service companies still have customers (or clients), and they need to reach them. With the Internet, they can bring their services to anyone with a connection.

In this lesson, you'll learn how to access information about careers and see how the Internet can help you decide what you want to do with your life. You'll be able to find information about a particular career and explore how to prepare for it. You'll learn how to find job listings in online job banks and at company Web sites. You'll also see how to prepare an electronic resume.

Your Career Awaits You . . . on the Internet

You probably already know that computers are necessary to do almost any job today, whether you are in the medical profession or manufacturing, law enforcement or sales. What you might not realize is that you can use the computer and the Internet to help determine the career that might be best for you and to find your dream job. Sites available on the Web will teach you how to present information about your qualifications and experience in an attractive resume. A *resume* is a list of your personal information, educational background, and professional experience. Through the Internet, you can post your resume, view position announcements, make contacts, and even calculate the cost of living and look for an apartment in your new location.

And there's more. If you are an employer wanting to hire capable employees, what better place to look for them than on the Internet? You have instant access to a huge number of resumes, and you can reach applicants all over the world. By listing open positions on your company's Web site or through a job bank, you get immediate and extensive exposure for your openings. With available software, you can automatically scan the resumes you receive to filter out the ones that aren't appropriate for the position.

The Internet has a huge amount of employment information. Individuals post resumes on their personal home pages, and company Web sites post openings. Government and academic placement centers list openings, and many commercial sites have links to thousands of jobs. There is also a large and growing amount of career-planning advice online. Career related super- or *meta-sites* (the prefix *meta* means going beyond or higher) can be gigantic. These sites offer not just their own information, but also indexes of related information.

Some sites appear on everyone's list of the top Web employment sites. Most of these are multipurpose, allowing you to access career-planning advice, work on and post your resume, post and search for jobs, and learn about industry trends. You can find helpful information at Career Journal, JobWeb, Monster, America's Job Bank, and other meta-sites.

In this lesson, you'll learn how job applicants can use the Internet to help with career planning and resume writing. You will also learn how applicants and prospective employers can find each other.

Career Planning

You may already have a clear idea of the career you'd like to pursue. But whether you do or not, you'll benefit from some career planning. Experts recommend that you always have both short- and long-term career goals, and that you examine them frequently. And circumstances, or your interests, might lead you in directions you have yet to consider.

Most people change jobs several times during their lifetimes. What some don't realize is that there are differences between jobs and careers. A *job* is simply a specific position you have with a specific employer. A *career*, on the other hand, is a profession, including the training you receive and the goals you set. A person with a career in pharmaceutical sales may have jobs with several different companies over the years. You need to devote time and energy to career planning, and the Internet can help you.

STEP-BY-STEP 3.1

1. Most search engines have a category for jobs or careers. Open a search engine, go to this category, and search for career-planning sites. Eliminate sites that seem to be selling materials for career counseling or are for particular geographic areas, and go to five sites that seem to offer useful online guidance. (*Hint*: university career planning sites provide helpful—and free—information.) You may want to choose sites that end in *.edu,* such as the career planning sites at the University of Waterloo, Emory University, and Bowling Green State University. Write the addresses of your five sites below, along with helpful advice you found at each one.

CAREER-PLANNING URLS	HELPFUL INFORMATION AT EACH SITE
a.	
b.	
c.	
d.	
e.	

2. Some career-planning sites offer free online **assessment tools**. These are questionnaires that help you discover characteristics about yourself, such as your interests, aptitudes, or skills. One of the best career-planning sites is the Job Hunter's Bible. This site, shown in Figure 3-1, is related to the best selling book *What Color Is Your Parachute?* by Dick Bolles. Go to this site and click **Tests and Advice**.

a. Click **Career Tests** and read about online tests. Choose one of the assessments that appear and read about it. What is this test supposed to reveal to the test taker? Does it cost anything to get the test results?

_____

_____

FIGURE 3-1
The Job Hunter's Bible

STEP-BY-STEP 3.1 Continued

b. Figure 3-2 shows some questions from a sample test. Read the *Seven Rules About Taking Career Tests*. Which rule seems to be most applicable to you, and why?

_____

_____

FIGURE 3-2
Sample career test questions

Address	http://www.review.com/career/careerQuiz1.cfm?careers=6&menuID=0

Instructions

In order for us to estimate your personal Interests and Usual Style, you will first need to answer a series of questions. Read each pair of phrases below and decide which one of the two most describes you, then select the radio button next to that phrase.

As you make your choices, **assume that all jobs are of equal pay and prestige**. When you have answered all of the questions, click "Continue" to go on.

There are 24 total questions.

(1)
- ○ I would rather be a wildlife expert.
- ○ I would rather be a public relations professional.

(2)
- ○ I would rather be a company controller.
- ○ I would rather be a TV news anchor.

(3)
- ○ I would rather be a tax lawyer.
- ○ I would rather be a newspaper editor.

(4)
- ○ I would rather be an auditor.
- ○ I would rather be a musician.

(5)
- ○ I would rather be a production manager.
- ○ I would rather be an advertising manager.

3. Have you ever been interviewed for a job? Some applicants are very apprehensive when they sit down to talk with a prospective employer. Knowing what to expect, and practicing what you have to say, can help you make a better impression. Read through the interviewing advice at the Job Hunter's Bible, at **CollegeGrad.com,** and at **RileyGuide.com**. Record five interviewing hints that would be helpful to you.

a. _____

b. _____

c. _____

d. _____

e. _____

Extra Challenge

After reading the career planning advice you've found, what do you think you need to do before you can begin searching for a job? What careers are you considering now? How can you use the Internet to gather information about your options?

Your Resume

Ｈow do you present yourself to a prospective employer? When you answer a newspaper ad or visit a placement center, you will need to submit a copy of your resume. Electronic job searches are no different. Your resume needs to present you in the best possible light, and it needs to reach the right people. The Internet can help you with both. Figure 3-3 shows advice for resume writing on the JobWeb Web site.

Did You Know?

Many individual resumes are available for viewing when you search for resume links. You can see what you like and what you don't like in a resume by looking at examples.

FIGURE 3-3
Resume-writing tips

Build the Resume Employers Want

Matt Longino has read student resumes on college and university campuses throughout the nation. He has pored over pages of bond, vellum, and plain printer paper in hotel rooms, airports, and airplanes. He has seen faxed resumes, e-mailed resumes, and resumes posted on the Internet. Very little surprises him.

It's much the same for Stephanie Calhoun and Seth Feit. Like Longino, they're familiar with the ways students describe their skills and themselves. They know how to quickly scan paper and electronic documents, to pull out the ones they'd like to examine more closely, and to toss the others aside.

Longino, a college recruiter for GTE Corp. in Irving, Texas, says he looks at the education portion of a resume first.

"I look for the degree, the major, and the graduation date," he says. "And, of course, the GPA. It's kind of a lump sum of things that I look for."

Calhoun, college relations manager at JC Penney Co. Inc. in Dallas, Texas, says she looks at the experience section first.

"I look to see if the student has retail experience," she says, adding that she then checks out the graduation date and the GPA.

Feit, corporate staffing manager at America Online in Fairfax, Virginia, says he looks first for skills and experience.

All three recruiters agree that aside from containing the education, skills, and experience they seek, a resume needs to communicate those elements clearly and be free of glaring grammatical and spelling errors.

*Ｓ*TEP-BY-STEP 3.2

1. Return to the Job Hunter's Bible and follow the link for **Resumes**. Click the link for **Build Your Resume**. Write down the addresses (URLs) of five sites you find that you think will help you develop a good resume. List five tips you discovered for writing an effective resume.

RESUME ADVICE URLS	RESUME-WRITING TIPS	
a.	a.	
b.	b.	
c.	c.	
d.	d.	
e.	e.	

STEP-BY-STEP 3.2 Continued

2. If you are the author of books and articles about electronic resumes, it makes sense for you to use the Internet not only to describe your service but also to post samples. One well-regarded site included in the Job Hunter's Bible Resumes links is that of Rebecca Smith. This author, consultant, and Web designer offers reprints of her articles, tutorials for site design, and links to other career-related sites. In addition to providing an extensive amount of free advice, this site will also prepare your resume for a fee. Go to Rebecca Smith's site. Click **eResumes101** and then **What It Costs**. How much does this service cost, and what can you expect to receive?

_____

_____

3. You can submit your resume by pasting parts of it into a company's application form. Go to the Microsoft Web site and click the link for **Jobs** in the list of resources at the left. Click **Submit Resume** and examine how you could submit resume information. Unless you are interested in proceeding, don't complete the submission. You can see instructions in Figure 3-4.

FIGURE 3-4
Microsoft's resume submission form

STEP-BY-STEP 3.2 Continued

4. Applicants can also submit their resumes to online job *clearinghouses*. These are large databases that store information about jobs and job seekers, and match jobs with people. Go to **Monster.com** and find the resume-posting instructions shown in Figure 3-5. Now go to **Yahoo! Careers** and examine the process at that site. Which one appeals to you more, and why?

_____

_____

FIGURE 3-5
Resume posting at Monster.com

Extra Challenge

Artificial intelligence software searches for keywords in a resume that match the employer's needs. It determines which candidates should be dropped and which should stay in the list of potential employees. Some authorities believe that applicants can improve their chances if they load their resumes with buzzwords that they think the software will recognize. However, an applicant should use up-to-date terminology when describing experiences. Avoid fancy fonts and formatting that can confuse the scanning software.

The Job Search

Employers and applicants gain huge advantages by using the Internet. Employers can post job openings with no geographical limitations or response delays. Using search tools, employers can narrow applicant lists to just those most suitable for the position. As an applicant, you can use search tools to narrow the list of positions to the most promising ones. If you find a job posting that interests you, you can use the Internet to learn more about the company and its location. If you decide to apply, you can get your resume to the employer immediately.

STEP-BY-STEP 3.3

1. If you are looking for a job, you can look at one of the large clearinghouses, or you can go directly to a company's listings. Let's begin by looking at some of the general sites. Many of these ask you to specify a geographical location and a job title or category. For this Step-by-Step, select a location and job title or category that interest you. If you need an idea, search for healthcare positions in the Midwest. In the space below, write the choices you want to investigate.

   a. Position or job category _____

   b. Location _____

   c. Other keywords _____

2. Go to **America's Job Bank**, **Monster**, and **CareerWeb**. Record the URL of each service in the spaces below. Search for openings that fit your criteria, and list the three that interest you most from each service. Next to each opening, list the company offering it. As you see, you can find out more about the job and the company, and in some cases, submit your application through these services. Figures 3-6 and 3-7 show steps in a search at Monster.com.

America's Job Bank   URL: _____

Position: **Company:**

a. _____   a. _____

b. _____   b. _____

c. _____   c. _____

Monster   URL: _____

Position: **Company:**

a. _____   a. _____

b. _____   b. _____

c. _____   c. _____

CareerWeb   URL:_____

Position: **Company:**

a. _____   a. _____

b. _____   b. _____

c. _____   c. _____

STEP-BY-STEP 3.3 Continued

FIGURE 3-6
Monster.com search form

FIGURE 3-7
Monster.com search results

STEP-BY-STEP 3.3 Continued

3. a. What if you are an employer? How do employers post openings in these three job banks?

_____

_____

_____

_____

Extra Challenge

If you were an entrepreneur with a small business, which of these job services would you want to use? Which contact methods would you want to publicize in your listing: your e-mail address, your phone number, your street address, or your URL? Why?

b. Go to **America's Job Bank**, **Monster**, and **CareerWeb**. Read the instructions for posting a job. Be sure to read the Code of Conduct for employers at America's Job Bank. What does it cost to post a job with each of these services?

America's Job Bank _____

Monster _____

CareerWeb _____

SCANS

Relocating

Congratulations! You've successfully used the Internet to post your resume, search for open positions, and get past the first interview. Now you're ready to talk about salary and your new community. How expensive is it to live there? What recreational activities does the area offer? What are the schools and healthcare like? The Internet can help you gather all of this information.

STEP-BY-STEP 3.4

1. Using a location you've always liked, or one you found in Step-by-Step 3.3, decide on a city to use for this activity.

2. Go to **DataMasters.com**. Click the **Cost of Living** calculator. Use the calculator to see what a salary of $50,000 in Chicago would equal in New York, Los Angeles, and your new location.

a. New York _____

b. Los Angeles _____

c. Your new location _____

3. Search for your new location, and see what information you can find about schools and healthcare. How do the schools and healthcare services in the new location compare to the place you live now? How do the recreational activities in your current and new locations compare?

a. School information

_____

_____

STEP-BY-STEP 3.4 Continued

b. Healthcare information

_____

_____

c. Recreation

_____

_____

4. How would you find a place to live? You may find real estate links when you look up the new location, and most major real estate firms have Web sites. You also can search for nationwide apartment information, as shown in Figure 3-8. See what rental property is available in your new location, and determine what it would cost.

_____

_____

_____

FIGURE 3-8
Apartment hunting at Homestore.com

Net Fun

Yahoo.com lets you draw a map based on an address. You can even get driving directions, which would be a big help if your job interview were in an unfamiliar city. Try out one of these by asking for a map and directions to a place you know well.

Back to School

SCANS An important part of career planning is an understanding of the education and training required to enter and stay current in a field. What do you do if the career you want requires certification or continuing education? Most educational institutions have a Web presence. By searching for a particular school, you can find its home page. But you can also use the Internet to search for institutions that offer a particular program that interests you. The curriculum you want might even be offered online.

S TEP-BY-STEP 3.5

1. Assume you want to enter the medical field and become a nurse practitioner. Look for information about the requirements for this degree. At what Web site did you find the information?

   _____

2. *Acronyms*, which are abbreviations made up of the first letters of words, can become confusing, particularly in the computing field. Search for the meanings of these computer career acronyms: CNA, CNE, MCP, and MCSE. How can you achieve certifications for these computer careers?

ACRONYM	MEANING	HOW TO ACHIEVE CERTIFICATIONS
a. CNA		
b. CNE		
c. MCP		
d. MCSE		

 Net Ethics

When a job applicant or an employer looks for information in an online database, each would like to be assured that the listings are correct and accurate. However, postings tend to work on an honor system. If you are an employer, you trust that the information provided in a resume is factual. If you are a job seeker, you trust the position is as advertised. Undoubtedly, though, this kind of system can be abused. Participants are open to scrutiny by anyone who comes across their listing, and they should give careful thought to the amount of information they wish to publicize. For an interesting discussion of the legal and ethical concerns involved, read the copyright notices and acceptable site-use rules of some of the big job search companies you've found.

STEP-BY-STEP 3.5 Continued

3. You may decide you need to investigate colleges and universities to see what programs they offer. Go to **CollegeNET.com**. Click the **Custom Search** choice under **College Search** to locate schools that offer a program of interest to you. Figure 3-9 shows how CollegeNET lets you search for schools that meet your criteria. Were you able to find useful information? Explain.

_____

_____

_____

FIGURE 3-9
CollegeNET search

Net Fun

Take a virtual tour of a college campus. You can search for a school by name, or search on College AND Virtual AND Tour to find some very realistic replacements for actually being there.

SUMMARY

In this lesson, you learned:

■ You can locate career-planning information online.

■ You can use the Internet to prepare an electronic resume and you can post it online.

■ You can search individual company sites and job search sites to find job openings.

■ You can use the Internet to find information about a new community, including housing choices.

■ Educational institutions have Web sites that make it easy to match your needs.

VOCABULARY *Review*

Define the following terms:

Acronym	Clearinghouses	Meta-sites
Assessment tools	Job	Resume
Career		

REVIEW *Questions*

TRUE / FALSE

Circle T if the statement is true or F if the statement is false.

T   F   1. It is important to secure a job before you start planning your career.

T   F   2. You should expect to pay a fee in order to post your resume at a major job search site.

T   F   3. Employers should expect to pay a fee in order to list their openings at a major job search site.

T   F   4. The best way to submit an online application is to save your resume electronically and attach the file to an e-mail message to the company.

T   F   5. The salary that lets you live comfortably in one location may not provide enough funds for you to live at the same level in a different location. You should examine the cost of living in each place.

WRITTEN QUESTIONS

Write a brief answer to the following questions.

1. Why is career planning important?

2. Using the experience of someone you know, illustrate the difference between a job and a career.

3. Describe five types of information that you, as a prospective employer, would expect to see on a resume.

4. Your nervous friend has a job interview tomorrow. Give three pieces of useful advice for the interview.

5. How can the Internet help you with decisions about continuing education?

PROJECTS

SCANS PROJECT 3-1

Yahoo has links on its home page to both Careers and Jobs. Visit these sites and study the similarities and differences between them. Write a paragraph explaining what you find.

_____

_____

_____

_____

_____

SCANS PROJECT 3-2

Catelynn is looking for a summer job as an intern or a technician in a pharmacy so that she can see firsthand what the work would be like.

1. Use America's Job Bank, JobWeb, and Monster to search for these kinds of positions. Do you see the same position listed on more than one service? What does this tell you?

_____

_____

2. Now search for openings at Walgreens, CVS, and a pharmacy of your choosing. Do these corporate Web sites list temporary positions online, or do they list only openings for registered pharmacists?

_____

_____

3. Use the resources at CollegeNET to list at least five universities that offer the degree of Doctor of Pharmacy.

A. _____

B. _____

C. _____

D. _____

E. _____

SCANS PROJECT 3-3

Simone Landes has always been interested in moving to Houston. She likes the idea of living in Texas. Also, she has followed America's space program since she was very young, and Houston is the nerve center for space exploration. Although Simone grew up in Minnesota, she doesn't think that she'll have any trouble adapting to Houston's warmer weather.

What Simone doesn't have, though, is a job waiting for her in Houston. She is currently working as the assistant director of a corporate childcare center, although her college degree is in creative writing. Simone would prefer to find a position that makes use of her education. However, she would be willing to consider other positions as long as

- she can work for an established company and receive health and retirement benefits,

- she can start at a salary of at least $30,000 annually, and

- she is, or can become, qualified for the position.

1. Visit one of the career planning sites. Put yourself in Simone's situation. What careers might be possible for someone with an interest in creative writing? For someone with experience working with young children? For someone with interest, but little formal training, in physics and astronomy?

_____

_____

2. Draft a rough copy of Simone's resume, using the information you know about her. You will have to be creative with the missing pieces, but make them consistent with the facts you do have.

3. Use one of the large job search sites to find at least five open positions in the Houston area that fit Simone's criteria. For each, record the position, company, salary, and application procedure.

_____

_____

_____

_____

_____

4. Visit the Web site of at least one of the five companies. What can you learn about the company? What kinds of products or services does it offer? Does the Web site make the company appealing to you?

_____

_____

_____

5. Visit NASA's Web site at **Nasa.gov**. Write a paragraph telling Simone about space-related tours she can take in Houston.

_____

_____

_____

_____

_____

_____

SCANS **TEAMWORK PROJECT**

Share the careers you found for Simone with your teammates. Then, as a team, vote on one career to investigate further from among those everyone discovered. On the Internet use links to government data to investigate the potential for growth in that career. You may want to visit the Department of Commerce, the Department of Labor, and the Census Bureau. Divide tasks among team members. After everyone has gathered their information, write a memo from your team to Simone, describing the projections for this career. Act as career counselors and conclude with your recommendations to her.

CRITICAL*Thinking*

SCANS ACTIVITY 3-1

Interview a friend or family member who has had the same job for at least eight years. Ask how the person found out about the job and how he or she applied for it. On a separate piece of paper, write a 100-word report that compares and contrasts that job search with an Internet job search. Will you use the Internet to help find your next job? Why or why not?

PERSONAL FINANCE ON THE INTERNET

OBJECTIVES:

Upon completion of this lesson, you should be able to:

- Discover which banks and other financial institutions offer online banking and learn how to access the services they offer.

- Find up-to-date information about stock and bond prices, track a portfolio of investments, and use online brokerage services.

- Search for loan information and see how a borrower can apply online for a mortgage or other loan.

- Investigate online sources of insurance information and learn to use the Internet to comparison-shop for insurance.

- Find tax preparation help from both the government and private agencies, and learn how to file your taxes electronically.

Estimated Time: 2 hours

VOCABULARY

Automatic withdrawal

Direct deposit

Discount broker

Interest (loan)

Interest rate (loan)

Mortgage

Portfolio

Pull technology

Push technology

Socially responsible investing

Term

Ticker symbol

Managing Your Money Without Leaving Home

Although you might enjoy holding your actual paycheck in your hand, going to the bank to deposit it can be a nuisance. Considerations of time and security have led many people who receive regular checks, such as employees and Social Security recipients, to sign up for *direct deposit* of their checks. With this system, your employer electronically deposits your paycheck to the account you have specified.

You might also instruct your bank to make *automatic withdrawals* to pay bills due at regular intervals and for the same amount of money each time, such as a car payment. With this system, you authorize the bank to remove the amount you specify from your account and actually make the payment for you. You could also set up an automatic withdrawal to transfer money regularly to a savings account or other investment. In many communities, you can arrange to have the utility company collect their payment from your bank account. The monthly statement you receive in the mail is stamped DO NOT PAY. It looks just like a regular bill, showing you the amounts used and the payment owed, and it tells you how much will be withdrawn from your bank account on what date.

Electronic transfers save time, help you make your payments and deposits on time, and reduce your need to write checks. If it is this easy to do some of your banking electronically, why not consider doing the rest of it that way?

With the Internet, you can write checks and skip addressing envelopes, buying stamps, and mailing them. You can research the financial performance of your favorite companies and buy and sell stocks. Do you need a loan or want to buy insurance? Some banks and insurance companies allow their customers to apply online. You can get help with your taxes and even submit payments online. And this is just a small sample of the many ways you can manage your finances online.

A few words of caution are in order, though. As you will see in the next unit, it is important to use care whenever you conduct any kind of financial transaction online. Do not provide any personal financial information to a Web site unless you have confirmed that you are working with a reputable business and that your privacy is guaranteed. Do not let the ease of online purchasing cause you to overextend your credit cards. Avoid any site that makes an offer that is too good to be true.

The Yahoo site pictured in Figure 4-1, CNBC, CBS MarketWatch, and SmartMoney are examples of companies that have established financial meta-sites. These sites give you financial news and tools to use for personal and business finance. They also provide wonderful learning opportunities to help you get started with financial planning. These sites can help you do just about anything you want with your money!

FIGURE 4-1
Yahoo Finance meta-site

Banking Online

How does online banking really work? Most banks offer two ways for you to pay your bills electronically. You may work with a specialized financial software package on your computer and then connect to the bank to complete the transaction, or you may link to the bank through the Web and use the bank's software. Most experts expect the second, called Internet banking, to become the system of choice in the next few years.

When you pay your bills electronically, the bank immediately withdraws the money from your account. If your payee—say, the phone company—has established an electronic system with your bank, then the amount will go immediately into the phone company's account. But sometimes the payee has no electronic relationship with your bank. In this case, the bank holds the payment. Later, after collecting more customers' payments to that company, the bank sends the total owed to the company, either by check or wire transfer.

Why would this kind of system be attractive to a bank? There are several reasons, but they all have to do with the bank's profitability. First, by moving money electronically, a bank can keep deposits for the maximum amount of time to earn as much interest as possible. But probably more enticing to a bank are the cost savings. With less paper, less processing, and fewer employees, banks can achieve tremendous cost savings. Figure 4-2 lists some of the Internet banking features available at one bank.

FIGURE 4-2
Internet banking services

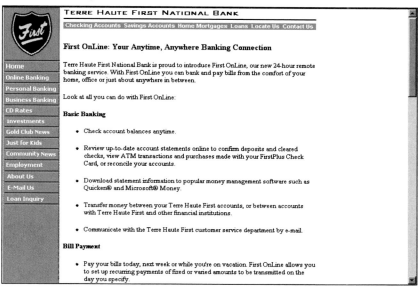

CyberAtlas—a Web marketer's guide to online facts—reports that 87% of community banks are expected to offer some form of Internet banking by 2003. The number of households who use it is expected to grow from 12.2 million at the end of 2001 to 18.3 million by 2004. Yet the numbers are not as large as was expected a few years ago. Both online banking and online bill paying have advantages for consumers, but banking experts warn that banks will have to offer customers a wide variety of online services to persuade them to participate.

Bankrate.com is an award-winning site that provides a wealth of information about online banking and other Internet financial tools. In a discussion of electronic bill payment, you can read that businesses spend over $10 billion each year to print bills and process their customers' payments. Customers spend over $4 billion just to mail their payments. It certainly seems reasonable to expect customers to begin to pay their bills electronically if enough of their accounts can be paid that way and if the fees charged by the bank are judged to be reasonable.

STEP-BY-STEP 4.1

SCANS

1. In 2001, Citibank's Web site, shown in Figure 4-3, was nominated for a Webby Award. These awards are given by the International Academy of Digital Arts and Sciences and recognize achievement in technology and creativity. Visit the bank site at **MyCiti.com** and click **Learn More** to see what this site can provide. Name three banking activities that you can do from this site.

   a. Activity 1 _____

   b. Activity 2 _____

   c. Activity 3 _____

FIGURE 4-3
MyCiti home page

2. Under **Take the Tour,** click the link for **FAQs.** Use the information to answer these questions.

   a. Customers who enroll with **My Accounts** can view financial statements online. What does this service cost?

   _____

   b. What measures protect the privacy of your information?

   _____

   c. What statements can you view in addition to your bank statements?

   _____

3. Return to the MyCiti home page and click **Life Events**. Select **I'm a College Student.** In the Credit Cards section, click **Student Credit Matters**. Choose **How Credit Cards Work**. What is the difference between the account balance and the minimum payment? Which one do you need to pay in order to avoid additional charges?

   _____

   _____

STEP-BY-STEP 4.1 Continued

4. Next, read about business banking online. Go to **Bankrate.com** and use the site's search feature to go to its **Small Biz** home page. You should see information about interest rates, taxes, credit, and articles that are tied to current financial events. Why would it be helpful for a small business owner to subscribe to Bankrate's e-mail newsletter?

_____

_____

5. Banks offer many other services online. Investigate online banking at your bank or another one in your community.
   a. Write the URL of the bank here. _____
   b. List three online services the bank provides. _____
   Service 1 _____
   Service 2 _____
   Service 3 _____
   c. List at least one bank service that is not provided online but that must be completed in person.

_____

Online Investing

Many financial sites on the Internet enable you to create a group of investments to watch. You don't have to own the stocks to keep track of their movements, and you can learn about companies' financial performance this way. In fact, you should thoroughly study a stock's history, along with the company's financial statements, before you consider purchasing any shares.

What is a Discount Broker?

Discount brokers are agents who buy and sell stocks for you, but don't provide all of the market analysis and customer service that a full-service broker provides. Why do people trade online? For the same reasons they bank online: it is fast, cheap, and easy. You can order your trade at any time of day, not just when the broker's office is open.

Net Fun

Do you want to know what banks are like in other countries? Go to **aaadir.com**. By choosing a country, you'll find a directory of local banks. Information is listed for each one, including the availability of Internet banking. For example, five banks are listed for Finland, and two of them offer Internet banking.

Several Internet sites allow users to rate online brokerage firms. One site that provides information on discount brokers and other financial services is The Motley Fool at *fool.com*. Figure 4-4 shows the kind of table the site provides to help investors compare discount brokers. The site also provides information on full-service brokers.

FIGURE 4-4
The Motley Fool discount broker comparison

Address http://www.fool.com/dbc/tables/compare.htm?ref=60broker ▾ Go

Discount Broker Comparison Table

	Ameritrade Open Account More Info	**Datek** Open Account More Info	**CSFBdirect** Sign up now! More Info	**TD Waterhouse** Open Account More Info
Account Minimum Information				
Cash Account	$2,000	$500	No minimum	$1,000
Margin Account	$2,000	$2,000	$2,000	$2,000
Retirement Account (IRA)	$1,000	$500	No minimum	No minimum
Commission Schedule -- Online Trades				
Market Order	$8.00	$9.99	$20.00	$14.95
Limit Order	$13.00	$9.99	$20.00	$17.95
Commission Schedule -- Touchtone Phone Trades				
Market Order	$12.00	$15.01	$20.00	$35.00
Limit Order	$17.00	$15.01	$20.00	$38.00
Commission Schedule -- Broker Assisted Trades				
Market Order	$18.00	$25.00	$30.00	$45.00
Limit Order	$23.00	$25.00	$30.00	$48.00
Fee Schedule				
Account Maintenance Fees	$15/quarter [waived if > $2,000 in assets OR 4 trades/6 months]	$15/quarter [waived if > $5,000 in assets OR 4 trades/rolling 6 months]	$15/quarter [waived if > $10,000 in total assets OR 4 trades/year]	$20/quarter [waived if > $10,000 in assets OR 4 trades/year]
Account Transfer Fees	$25.00	None	$25.00 (outgoing)	$50.00, IRA account excluded
IRA Custodian Fees	None	None	$35.00 per account per year ***	None

In Lesson 2, you saw how to find a company's information on its Web site. In this Step-by-Step, you'll learn how to follow the financial markets on the Web. You'll learn how to create a collection of stocks and other investments, called a ***portfolio***, to watch. You'll also investigate ways to buy and sell stocks online.

S TEP-BY-STEP 4.2

1. Many Internet sites allow you to follow a stock. Even the opening screens of some browsers, such as Yahoo, offer users the opportunity to request a current stock price. In this Step-by-Step, you will be visiting several sites for stock information. Find the URL for each of the following companies and check the services they offer.

BROKERAGE	URL	FREE QUOTES?	FREE PORTFOLIO WATCH?	TRADING?
a. American Express Financial Services				
b. ETRADE				
c. SmartMoney				

STEP-BY-STEP 4.2 Continued

2. All stocks have a *ticker symbol*, which is a company abbreviation made up of several letters. Ticker symbols are used for easy reference in stock quotes. For example, the ticker symbol for the Mauna Loa Macadamia Partners, a Hawaiian grower of macadamia nuts, is NUT. Go to **CBS.marketwatch.com**. Use the **Find symbol** link to find the New York Stock Exchange ticker symbol for the following companies in the North American markets. By clicking **Quote**, you will be able to see stock price information, such as that shown for Disney in Figure 4-5. For each company in the table below, record the symbol, today's high, the 52-week high, and the 52-week low.

FIGURE 4-5
Stock price information for Disney

TICKER SYMBOL	TODAY'S DATE	TODAY'S HIGH	52-WEEK HIGH	52-WEEK LOW
a. Disney				
b. Procter & Gamble				
c. Chrysler				
d. Maytag				
e. Merck				

3. Go to the ETRADE home page and read about the site. Visit **Portfolios** under the **Investing** section of the tour and look at the information provided. What is the difference between a portfolio and a watch list?

_____

_____

STEP-BY-STEP 4.2 Continued

4. ETRADE and other online brokers are evaluated by Jupiter Media Metrix with a CORE (Composite Rating of Online Effectiveness) Index, based on visitors' behavior at the site. Figures 4-6 and 4-7 show the CORE ratings for banks and brokers in the first publication of this index. Go to **Jupiter Media Metrix**. Under **JMM Vital Stats** find **CORE Report** and click **Learn more**. Which of the factors included in the index do you think are the best indicators of a bank's or broker's effectiveness?

FIGURE 4-6
Jupiter CORE rating for online banks

Table A: Top 20 Online Banks Ranked According to the Jupiter Banking CORE*		
Rank	Bank	Overall Index
1	BankofAmerica.com	100
2	WellsFargo.com	99
3	KeyBank.com	88
4	BankOne.com	81
5	Chase.com	73
6	HSBC.com	70
7	Washington Mutual	66
8	Citigroup Banking Sites	65
9	Fleet.com	65
10	SunTrust.com	64
11	PNCBank.com	62
12	AmSouth.com	62
13	NavyFCU.org	61
14	UBOC.com	59
15	Fifth Third Bank	59
16	Wachovia.com	55
17	BbandT.com	51
18	Huntington.com	51
19	Peoples.com	44
20	USBank.com	43

STEP-BY-STEP 4.2 Continued

FIGURE 4-7
Jupiter CORE rating for online brokers

Table B: Top 19 Online Brokerages Ranked According to the Jupiter Brokerage CORE*		
Rank	**Brokerage**	**Overall Index**
1	E*Trade Financial Network	100
2	TDWaterhouse.com	100
3	ShareBuilder.com	82
4	Fidelity.com	80
5	Ameritrade.com	72
6	Schwab.com	72
7	Datek.com	61
8	ML.com	61
9	CSFBDirect.com	57
10	Vanguard.com	48
11	AmericanFunds.com	45
12	BuyandHold.com	42
13	EdwardJones.com	40
14	AmericanCentury.com	40
15	PutnamInvestments.com	34
16	PRUFN.com	29
17	TrowePrice.com	27
18	Janus.com	26
19	Scottrade.com	0.0

Did You Know?

When you search the Internet and retrieve information from a location, you are using *pull technology*. However, you can also have information sent to you. Using *push technology*, you can specify the kinds of information you want, and the system finds and downloads it automatically to your computer. For example, you can subscribe to have financial information sent to you, such as stock market reports or news stories.

STEP-BY-STEP 4.2 Continued

5. If your ISP permits, create a portfolio to watch. Go to **SmartMoney.com**. Click **My Portfolio**, and then **Watchlist**. A default list of stocks will appear. You can delete stocks from this list and add others of your choosing.

a. What is the symbol of the first stock that appears?

_____

b. What company has this symbol? Right click the symbol and select **News** to find the information.

_____

c. Go back to the Watchlist window, right click the first symbol again, and choose **Remove symbol**. You can do this for any company you don't want to track.

d. At the bottom of the Watchlist, click **Add** to add another ticker symbol. Enter the symbol of one of the companies you investigated in Step 2 and press **Enter**. What is the difference in the red and green color coding of the chart information?

_____

_____

6. To see how online trading actually works, go to **Ameritrade.com**. You won't actually make a trade, but you will view the Trading Demo. Click **Open an Account** and then click **Trading Demo**. Click **Start the Demo**. As you view, answer these questions.

a. How is the privacy of your trade guaranteed?

_____

_____

b. What does your Home Page show you?

_____

c. Proceed through the Demo. What is SnapTicket?

_____

_____

d. Go to **Rates & Fees** under **Services**. What is the minimum cost for a trade at Ameritrade?

_____

Financing Your Home or Car

When you get ready to buy a house or other property, you will most likely need a *mortgage*, a loan for a major part of the purchase price. Mortgages are usually for quite large amounts of money, typically about 80 percent of the purchase price of a home. Borrowers usually repay their mortgages over 20 or 30 years.

A mortgage, like most loans, requires the borrower to pay *interest*, which is a fee for the use of the money. This fee is usually figured as a percentage of the loan amount, and this percentage is called an *interest rate*. Over the 20- or 30-year life of a mortgage, a difference of just a half of a percentage point in the interest rate can mean thousands of extra dollars you must pay. The *term* of the mortgage—the number of years you have to repay—also dramatically affects the overall cost of the loan. So when you shop for a mortgage, it's worth the time to look around for a low rate and a term that suits your repayment abilities.

Banks, credit unions, savings and loans, and other financial institutions offer mortgages. Some of these institutions encourage their customers to apply for a mortgage online. The Internet can also provide expert advice to help you understand mortgages and compare features. Yahoo Finance has an Education section in the Mortgage Center that helps homebuyers understand mortgages. Some of its links are shown in Figure 4-8.

 Net Ethics

If you feel strongly that companies should consider the best interests of society and the environment in their operations, then you may want to use your investment dollars to promote such corporate behavior. *Socially responsible investing* (SRI) is a policy of promoting environmentally and socially responsible operating practices by investing in corporations with good records in these areas.

Several Internet sites provide guidance and information about SRI. One of these is Goodmoney. Unlike some watchdog organizations that criticize companies thought to have poor social or environmental histories, the Goodmoney site presents an objective view of the companies that it examines. This enables you to decide if a company's practices are in line with your values before you invest.

Being a socially responsible investor does not mean that you have to make financial sacrifices. Socially responsible companies can be just as profitable as any other. You can find out more information about SRI by following your browser's links to the S-R-Invest resource guide.

FIGURE 4-8
Mortgage education at Yahoo Finance

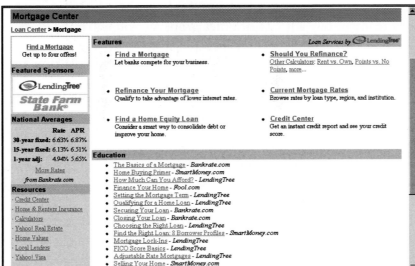

Automobile loans are for smaller amounts than mortgages and are repaid more quickly. Unlike home financing, vehicle financing is heavily advertised by car manufacturers and is used as a marketing tool. Banks and other lenders also make car loans, and Web sites such as Carsdirect, E-loan, and Moneycentral help you apply for loans online.

STEP-BY STEP 4.3

1. Go to **Yahoo! Finance**. Scroll down the left side to **Personal Finance** and click **Mortgage** in the **Loans** section. Click the article **The Basics of a Mortgage** from **Bankrate.com**. Go to the section on **Fixed Rate Mortgages**.

   a. What are the most common term lengths in numbers of years for fixed-rate mortgages?

   _____

   b. Compare the benefits and drawbacks of short-term mortgages and long-term mortgages.

   _____

   _____

   c. Click the link for **Survey of Interest Rates**. Choose a state and city to investigate. What is the best rate that you can find for each of these mortgages?

   30-Year Fixed-Rate Mortgage _____

   15-Year Fixed-Rate Mortgage _____

STEP-BY STEP 4.3 Continued

2. Return to the **Education** section under **Mortgage** at Yahoo! Finance. Examine the **Home Buying Primer** from **SmartMoney.com**.

   a. What are points?

   _____

   b. What do banks look at before granting a homebuyer a mortgage?

   _____

   _____

3. **LendingTree.com** is a clearinghouse for loans. An applicant who visits this site can submit information about an automobile purchase, home purchase, or other need for financing and receive information from potential lenders. Go to the Lending Tree Web site. In the **Find It Now** section, click **Auto & Motorcycle**. Unless you are ready to apply for a car loan and abide by the regulations of the site (see the question at the end of the form) do not submit the form. Why does the lender need all of this information from an applicant?

   _____

   _____

4. You can find out how much debt can you afford. **Bankrate.com** offers calculators to help you understand what your payments would be. Go to the Bankrate Web site and click **Calculators** in the main menu bar. Find the monthly payment for these two loans.

   a. A 15-year mortgage for $90,000 starting on January 1, 2003 with a 7.5% interest rate. _____

   b. A 5-year auto loan for $20,000 starting on January 1, 2003 with a 5.9% interest rate. _____

Searching for Insurance Online

Enabling customers to comparison-shop without actually having to contact assorted retailers is one of the features that make Internet marketing so attractive to buyers. Experts state, and common sense agrees, that comparison-shopping works best for products that the customer doesn't need to examine in person, such as books and computers. Although insurance is not considered to be a retail product, it has the same potential for Internet marketing. Customers need to comparison-shop, but they don't need to see or touch the product to make a buying decision.

Customers have told insurance companies that they are interested in being able to use the Internet for customer service. Being able to check the progress of a claim online at any time (and without being placed on hold!) is a very attractive service for insurance companies to offer their customers.

Net Fun ☼

If you like to dream about living in your own "castle," visit one of the more upscale real estate sites. You can look at property in some of the world's most spectacular locations by going to the DuPont Registry. Of course, you can always bring yourself back to earth by calculating the monthly mortgage payment for one of these homes!

S TEP-BY-STEP 4.4

SCANS

1. The financial sites that you have visited in this lesson have links to insurance information, but for the most direct information, go to **Insweb.com**. Click the tab for **Learning Center**. Under Learn More About, click **Other**. In the list of articles, click Tips for **Online Insurance Shopping**. Write a short summary of the three tips that make the most sense to you.

_____

_____

_____

2. Click **Other** under the **Insurance Information** tab. Choose the **Glossary**, and use it to learn the meaning of insurance terminology. Write definitions in your own words for the following terms:

   a. deductible

_____

_____

   b. rate

_____

_____

   c. term

_____

_____

   d. premium

_____

_____

3. **Quicken.com** is a financial site that uses Insweb for its insurance quotes. Go to Quicken, and click **Insurance Quotes**. Click **Term Life Needs Analyzer**. Answer the questions based on reasonable assumptions about a person you know. How much more insurance does your example need?

_____

STEP-BY-STEP 4.4 Continued

4. Figure 4-9 shows the home page for Moneycentral, Microsoft's financial site. It can also be reached at **CNBC.com**. Go to the site and search MSN Money for insurance. Click the link for **Auto Quotes**. Choose your state, and click the link for one of the insurance providers that appear.

FIGURE 4-9
Moneycentral home page

a. Which insurance companies provide online quotes in your state through this system?

_____

_____

b. Continue answering the questions in the form, using your personal information. This should take about 10 minutes for most companies. Do not submit any information to an agent unless you are serious about buying insurance. How did you like this experience? Can you actually buy the insurance coverage this way, or is this just a preliminary step before meeting with an agent? Figure 4-10 shows a sample quote.

STEP-BY-STEP 4.4 Continued

FIGURE 4-10
Sample auto insurance quote through MSN Money

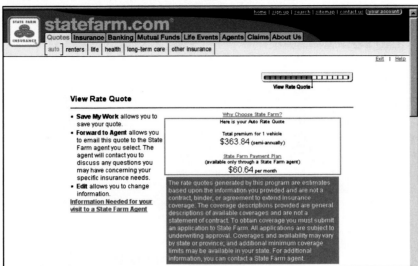

Extra Challenge

What costs would an insurance provider have to consider when processing applications? List three pieces of customer information that the insurance company would want to verify before selling a policy. Does your insurance company have a Web site and offer quotes online?

Internet Tax Tips

If you earn a paycheck, paying taxes is probably one of your least favorite activities. The Internet can make it simpler for you. The Internal Revenue Service Web site has links to forms, publications, instructions, and revenue departments in all 50 states. You can also file your taxes electronically. Although the number of taxpayers who file their returns electronically is growing every year, the IRS encourages more taxpayers to take advantage of this method. In this Step-by-Step, you'll see how it works. Let's take a tour.

S TEP-BY-STEP 4.5

1. The IRS home page is **www.irs.gov**. Go there and click the **e-file** logo. Scroll through the *e-file* page, shown in Figure 4-11, to see what's available.

FIGURE 4-11
The IRS *e-file* page

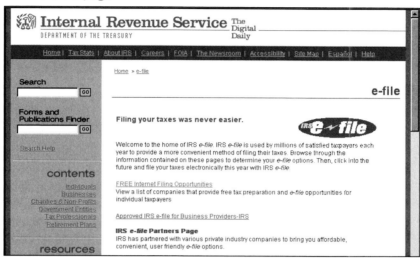

2. Scroll down to Individual Taxpayers and click **e-file Using Your Computer**. Answer the following questions.

   a. Do you have to work with a professional tax preparer?

   _____

   b. What equipment do you need to file electronically?

   _____

   c. How much does it cost to file online?

   _____

   d. Is your state one that allows you to also file the state tax return electronically?

   _____

3. Return to the *e-file* page and click the link for **EFTPS** under **Businesses**. What advantages does this system offer to businesses and employees?

   _____

   _____

SUMMARY

In this lesson, you learned:

■ You can access banks and other financial institutions online.

■ You can find up-to-date information about stock and bond prices, track a portfolio of investments, and use online brokerage services.

■ You can search for loan information and see how to apply online for a mortgage or other loan.

■ You can investigate online sources of insurance information and use the Internet to comparison-shop for insurance.

■ You can find tax preparation help from both the government and private agencies, and file your taxes electronically.

VOCABULARY *Review*

Define the following terms:

Automatic withdrawal	Interest rate (loan)	Push technology
Direct deposit	Mortgage	Socially responsible investing
Discount broker	Portfolio	Term
Interest (loan)	Pull technology	Ticker symbol

REVIEW *Questions*

TRUE / FALSE

Circle T if the statement is true or F if the statement is false.

T   F   1. In order for you to pay a bill online, the organization sending you the bill must have established a relationship with your bank.

T   F   2. Financial Web sites allow you to get stock price information without actually owning shares.

T   F   3. To apply for a loan online, you will need to fill out a form with information about your financial status.

T   F   4. Not all states allow you to buy insurance online, but you can get personalized insurance quotes online.

T   F   5. Filing your federal taxes online usually means that if you are owed a refund, you will receive it sooner than if you had mailed your tax return to the IRS.

WRITTEN QUESTIONS

Write a brief answer to the following questions.

1. Name three services commonly offered by online banking.

2. What information can you find from an online portfolio watch? Do you have to own the stock to take advantage of this feature?

3. Explain why you should comparison-shop for a mortgage.

4. What kinds of insurance can you purchase over the Internet? Why would an insurance company that does not provide online quotes want to be included in an online insurance quote search?

5. What are the benefits of filing taxes electronically?

PROJECTS

SCANS **PROJECT 4-1**

Find the URL for your bank or for a bank in your community and visit the site. Why do you think the bank has an Internet presence? Does it offer online services? Make a list of them. How does a current customer access these services? If the bank doesn't offer online services, why do you suppose it has a Web site?

_____

_____

_____

_____

SCANS **PROJECT 4-2**

Visit the home pages of Yahoo! Finance, Quicken, CNBC, CBS MarketWatch, and The Motley Fool. At each site, search for the current price of a share of common stock in Thomson Learning, the publisher of this textbook. Which financial site is easiest to use, and why? Try to consider each site as if it were the first one you visited. _Hint_: Thomson stock is traded on the Toronto and London stock exchanges.

_____

_____

SCANS **PROJECT 4-3**

In addition to home and automobile loans, you can investigate student loans online. Go to **lendingtree.com** and click **Student Loan.**

1. Investigate government loans by clicking **Stafford** under **Federal Loans.** Click **Finding and Applying** under **Financial Aid.**

2. Read the information about completing the FAFSA form under **Applying.** What is FAFSA and how is it used?

   _____

   _____

3. Click the link to **FAFSA on the Web.** What are this year's deadlines for completing the form?

   _____

4. What documents should you have available before you begin working on the FAFSA? Why do you think this list is provided? Why does the site give you the opportunity to save the form while you are working on it?

_____

_____

5. How do you sign your form electronically?

_____

  ## TEAMWORK PROJECT

With your team, select a bank in your area to investigate. Different teams should select different banks. Make an appointment with someone at the bank who is familiar with the bank's online services. Each team should create a list of questions about online banking to ask the bank employee. Be sure to include questions about kinds of services offered, costs, and future online plans. Then meet with the bank employee, and present the results to the class.

CRITICAL *Thinking*

 ## ACTIVITY 4-1

Jeremy Clark is pleased with himself. He has one semester left in college, has a part-time job that pays reasonably well, and has just bought a new car. After watching a TV show, he's become convinced that it is not too early to start an investment program. He doesn't know much about the stock market, but he'd like to buy a few shares of a good stock. Jeremy's downfall, though, is that he is not very good at keeping track of things. He pays his tuition monthly, but sometimes he forgets to send the check on time. His part-time job pays him every two weeks, and he is too embarrassed to tell the payroll department that he lost one of his January paychecks. Besides, he keeps hoping it will turn up somewhere in his room.

In about 100 words, write a letter to Jeremy, explaining how he could use his computer and the Internet to help organize his personal finances.

INTERNET INFORMATION SERVICES

Information as an Internet Service

The Internet is a rich source of information that can support businesses in their daily operations. As you've seen, a large amount of e-commerce consists of one business selling a product to another business or to a consumer. Sometimes, this product is a service, and there is no direct charge. Companies, agencies, organizations, and individuals publish a huge amount of information on the Web, and wise business and consumer users have learned how to find the information they need.

Internet search engines can be particularly useful if you are trying to find information and you are not exactly sure what is out there or where to look for it. Spend some time looking at several search engines to see what they feature and how their links are organized. Figure 5-1 shows part of the opening screen from Yahoo. The links give easy access to some of the services Yahoo provides. How might a small company use these links?

For example, suppose you are the owner of a small company that manufactures tennis rackets. If you wish to approach retailers in a new location, you could use the Internet Yellow Pages listing to search for sporting goods stores for sales contacts. The Maps and Travel feature can help you arrange trips to tennis tournament sites. And knowledge from News, Sports, and Weather could help you react quickly to changes on the tournament circuit. The other search categories are also useful. You could read about fitness in the Health section or find community recreation programs in the Regional section.

In this lesson, you'll explore several of the services the Internet offers. Although you'll concentrate on business uses for these services, many of them are valuable to consumers, too.

FIGURE 5-1
Yahoo home page services

Travel Planning

Professional travel agents have used computerized databases for years to keep track of flight schedules and airfares. A *database* is a large collection of information arranged in linked tables for easy search and retrieval. A travel agent's database contains flights, fares, passenger reservations, and schedules. Authorized users can easily search the system electronically for the information they want.

The huge amount of detailed information used in the travel industry lends itself perfectly to electronic storage and retrieval. Although the Internet certainly hasn't replaced travel agents, consumers now have the ability to search for deals and make arrangements on their own. You can buy tickets online if you wish. You can also examine available flights while you talk with a travel agent on the phone. This can help you find a special deal. In this Step-by-Step activity you'll look at several online travel services and plan a trip.

STEP-BY-STEP 5.1

SCANS

1. Go to the search engine of your choice, such as **Lycos** or **Google**, and look for a travel category. Click to see what links appear. Figure 5-2 shows part of the screen that appears when you click Netscape's travel link. This is an all-purpose travel site whose developers have tried to anticipate any need you might have and provide a link for it.

FIGURE 5-2
Netscape's Travel link

Figure 5-3 shows the result of clicking the Yahoo! Travel link under Recreation & Sports. As you can see, the information is presented in a much different format. The presence of all of these categories may help you focus your search in a very specific way.

FIGURE 5-3
Yahoo's Travel link

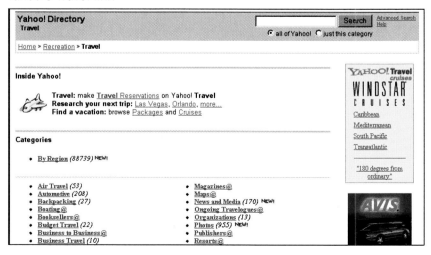

STEP-BY-STEP 5.1 Continued

a. How is your chosen search engine's site different from these?

_____

_____

b. Which kind of site would you rather use if you were planning business travel?

_____

_____

c. Would your choice be different if you were planning a family vacation? Why or why not?

_____

_____

2. Travelocity and Orbitz are two Internet travel sites that are widely used. For this Step-by-Step activity, you will use **Travelocity.com**. Travelocity is powered by a system called Sabre. Here, the phrase **_powered by_** means that a large search engine or database provides the background resources for the site. As you can see in Figure 5-4, the opening screen provides a simple way to search for a round trip airfare.

FIGURE 5-4
Travelocity's home page with flight information

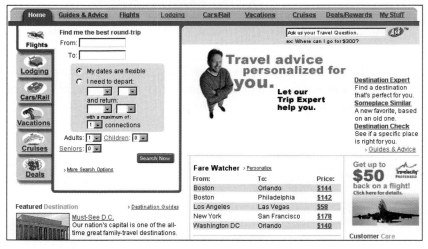

STEP-BY-STEP 5.1 Continued

Plan a round trip using the **Lowest Price** search. You will be departing from Columbus, Ohio, and traveling to Atlanta, Georgia. Leave a week from today and stay for five days. Use whatever times you wish. Plan for one adult traveler. Fly coach class without restrictions. Search all airlines. The search results will show you information about the flights that meet your requirements. Figure 5-5 shows some of the flights that appeared in April 2002. The first of these was a special promotion, requiring online booking within 30 minutes.

FIGURE 5-5
Results from airfare search

Complete the table below with your three lowest fares. The first line of the table is completed as an example.

AIRLINE	FLIGHT	DEPART AT	ARRIVE AT	NONSTOP?	PLANE	COST
Delta	636	9:10 a.m.	10:37 a.m.	yes	Boeing 757	$272

STEP-BY-STEP 5.1 Continued

3. Return to the Travelocity opening page and click **Lodging**. Note how the screen has changed to emphasize hotels instead of flights. The dialog box (shown in Figure 5-6), allows you to submit very general information. To refine your search, click the link for **More Search Options**. Specify Atlanta, Georgia as your destination. Use the dates you used in Step 2. Show only available properties and leave the distance and rate information as they appear. Specify Hampton Inns as your special preference. Click **Search Now**. If a map appears, be sure to specify Atlanta, GA. When the hotel list appears, select a hotel. Click on the hotel name again to get a Hotel Summary.

FIGURE 5-6
Travelocity's Lodging dialog box

a. How many rooms does your hotel have?

_____

b. Is breakfast included?

_____

c. Does it have a pool?

_____

d. Do the rooms have refrigerators and microwaves?

_____

e. A *data port* is a jack in the side of a telephone. By plugging into the jack, you are assured of an analog line, which is essential for making an Internet connection. Many hotels wire their telephones into the wall to prevent theft, so don't plan to unplug the phone and plug in your computer. How would you find out if your room has a data port, so you could connect your laptop to the Internet through the hotel telephone?

_____

_____

f. To reserve a room, click **Book Now**. Examine the room choices available. What is the least expensive non-smoking room rate available?

_____

STEP-BY-STEP 5.1 Continued

4. What will you want to do in Atlanta when you are not working? For this step, go to **Netscape** and click **Travel**. Under **Travel Departments**, click **Destination Guides**. Enter Atlanta, GA under **Destinations Search** and click **Go**. Choose the **Netscape Visitor's Guide to Atlanta, GA**. Choose **What's Going On?** in the **Entertainment Guide** to learn about upcoming events. What three events would you enjoy? Write the information here.

a. _____

b. _____

c. _____

5. If you're not familiar with a new location, it is helpful to have a map to find your way around. There are many commercially available types of map software, and you can get free maps from many Internet sources. After you land at the Atlanta airport, you need to go to the Georgia World Congress Center (GWCC) at 285 International Blvd. NW. You can get directions from the car rental company when you get there, but why not print out your own map before you leave home? Go to **Yahoo** and click **Maps**. Enter **ATL** as the airport code in the Address dialog box. Click **Get Map**. Under **Driving Directions,** click **To this location.** Enter **ATL** under section number 1. Enter the address you are trying to find under section number 2. Click **Get Directions**. Figure 5-7 shows the map you should find. Scroll down to follow the driving directions. How far is it from the airport to the GWCC?

Extra Challenge

How can the Internet make traveling easier? You've seen how to plan trips, find maps, and learn about local destinations. If you were writing a guidebook for travel to a vacation spot such as Hawaii, would you worry that all the information available on the Internet would harm the sales of your book? Would you consider having a Web site for your book? How could you use that site to encourage people to buy the book?

FIGURE 5-7
Map of driving directions from Hartsfield International Airport to International Blvd.

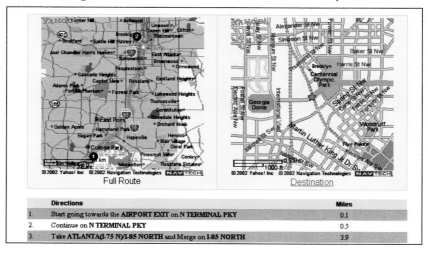

Online News and Weather

All of the major television news networks have an Internet presence, and so do many local stations. Newspapers also have established significant Web sites. Through these media sites, you can find television schedules, follow breaking news, read feature articles, and find links to community information. As businesses, these media have seen how providing an Internet site for their users can increase the number of viewers or readers they have.

Why would businesses want to monitor a media site? It may be easier to answer this question if you try to think of a business that is not affected by local, regional, or world events. Can you think of many that operate in a vacuum? If not, then you know why a business needs the media. Immediate access to the news of the day can help any business make timely and well-informed decisions.

S TEP-BY-STEP 5.2

1. Which of the following search engines provide links to current news headlines? Check the home pages of each to find out.

SEARCH ENGINE	LINKS TO CURRENT NEWS?
Altavista	
Excite	
Infoseek	
Netscape	
Yahoo	

Technology Careers

Who makes sure that a Web site does what it is designed to do? Who tests the systems and tools, and makes sure that the databases work properly? When companies develop online services, quality assurance engineers (QAEs) participate from the beginning of the design stage. They help create and execute test plans, work with software engineers, track problems, and work with outside vendors and customers. QAEs work in a team environment with other software professionals. They are trained in testing and programming, and they should have excellent written and oral communication skills.

STEP-BY-STEP 5.2 Continued

2. Find the URL for each of these major television networks. Do they allow you to search for local news? Do they show current news headlines?

NETWORK	URL	LINK TO LOCAL NEWS?	HEADLINES?
ABC			
CBS			
CNN			
Fox			
NBC			

3. Weather reports are important to all kinds of businesses. If you use an agricultural commodity, you would certainly be affected by price increases following droughts, floods, or freezes. If your company sells snow removal equipment, you'd base your order quantities on the long-range weather forecast. If you are involved in transportation, you would certainly want to know weather and road conditions. You can find links to weather information through each of the search engines and networks listed in Step 2. However, there are other dedicated weather sites, and we'll visit several of these to see what they provide.

When you search at Google for the National Weather Service, almost two million hits appear. You may find many weather links that are especially interesting to you. Some of them are designed for users with knowledge of meteorology, but others can be understood by any visitor. Begin by visiting the National Weather Service at **www.nws.noaa.gov**. Its home page is shown in Figure 5-8.

FIGURE 5-8
National Weather Service home page

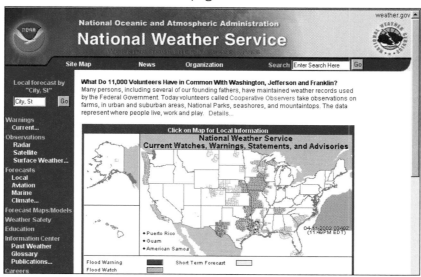

STEP-BY-STEP 5.2 Continued

4. The U.S. map shows current weather activity with color-coded weather warnings. Click your state and then click your location. What kinds of information do you find? Name at least five kinds.

a. _____

b. _____

c. _____

d. _____

e. _____

Read the Zone Forecast to see the weather forecast for your location. Are there any current warnings and advisories for your area?

_____

5. The National Hurricane Center provides a Web site at **www.nhc.noaa.gov**. During the hurricane season, this site receives a huge amount of traffic. In fact, the service has at times been overloaded when a hurricane is bearing down on the U.S. Why is it important that this site has information in English, in French, and in Spanish?

_____

Use the links on the NHC home page to answer these questions.

a. What was the most expensive Atlantic hurricane in history?

_____

b. When did it occur, and what was the cost?

_____

c. How often are North Atlantic hurricane names reused?

_____

Extra Challenge

At least one major U.S. insurance company keeps televisions (and likely the Internet) at its corporate headquarters tuned to breaking news and weather stories. What effects would this instantaneous knowledge have on the way an insurance company operates?

Internet Information Providers

You are no doubt coming to the conclusion that you can find the answer to almost any question you might have by searching the Internet. You've seen how to find a map and driving directions for a specific location, as well as how to find out what is going on in the world. You can also use the Internet to find reference information. Publicly accessible databases, such as phone books, are also accessible online. And if you need to know something—whether it is how to spell a word, the population of Richmond, Virginia, or a quotation to support a speech you are giving—you can find it in a Web reference section.

> **Net Fun**
>
> Have you ever wondered what the difference is between a Webmaster and a Web guru? How about between Cold Fusion and Hotmail? NetLingo, the Internet Dictionary, defines these terms and hundreds more. You can even learn what all the smiley faces mean by checking out *www.netlingo.com.*

Most public libraries have a collection of telephone books from major cities around the world. If you need to look for Jane Doe in Los Angeles, you can make a trip to your library and look for her in the LA phone book. If you want to find a dry cleaner in Milwaukee, you can look through the Milwaukee Yellow Pages. You can also do both of these searches on the Internet. Search engines offer data searches for phone numbers, street addresses, and e-mail addresses for individuals and businesses.

To find general information about a person, you can enter the name in Google or another search engine. But to find contact information, the simplest way is to look on a search engine's home page for a link to People Finder or People Search. For business information, look for Yellow Pages. All search engines support such searches. The results you find will vary slightly, depending on who powers the search. Some search engines even have a link to send a gift to the person you look up, and some help you get a map to the person's house. You can find Zip code lookup information from the post office at *www.usps.gov*. In this Step-by-Step activity, you'll see how to locate this kind of information.

S TEP-BY-STEP 5.3

1. Sites such as Yahoo provide ways to search for people. Some companies that wouldn't normally be thought of as Internet businesses also provide ways for users to conduct searches. One of these is AT&T, which offers **Anywho.com.** The home page is shown in Figure 5-9. Go to this site and search for people in your state who have your last name.

    a. Do you recognize any of the listings? Are they correct for the people you know?

    _____

    _____

    b. Now use Anywho's Yellow Pages to search for printers in Seattle, Washington. How many do you find?

    _____

STEP-BY-STEP 5.3 Continued

c. The Anywho site also allows you to do a reverse lookup by entering a phone number and finding the person's name and address. What do you see as the benefits and drawbacks of this feature?

_____

_____

FIGURE 5-9
Anywho home page

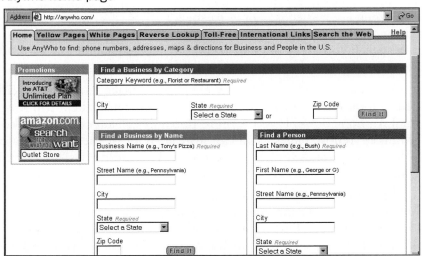

2. You can find many kinds of reference materials by looking at the links from any search engine. For example, go to **Google.com**. Select **Directory** and click **Reference**, then **Libraries**, then the **Virtual Reference Desk** category. Here, you find links to dictionaries, fact books, encyclopedias, grammar, bibliographies, thesauri, and quotes. Other search engines provide similar links. Using the search engine of your choice, locate an example of each of these reference tools. Record its URL, and describe how a landscape design company could use the information in its business. The first one in the table is done for you.

REFERENCE TOOL	URL	EXAMPLE
Dictionary	http://www.m-w.com/home.htm	Check the spelling of a word in an advertising brochure
Fact book		
Encyclopedia		
Grammar		
Bibliography		
Thesaurus		
Quote		

STEP-BY-STEP 5.3 Continued

3. Writing tools aren't the only academic references available online. Use your favorite search engine to locate four sources that help with math and science. Start by searching for "Ask Dr. Math."

REFERENCE TOOL	URL	KIND OF HELP
a. Ask Dr. Math		
b.		
c.		
d.		

4. The Internet also supplies medical and legal information. However, be advised that just because information appears online does not mean that it is accurate. In Lesson 8, you will learn more about how to determine which sites are trustworthy. For now, search for the Web site of a hospital or university medical school in your area.

a. Does it have a link to a medical information service?

_____

b. Figure 5-10 shows the opening page of the Laurus Health link from a local hospital. Why is this sort of link valuable to someone who needs general medical information?

_____

FIGURE 5-10
Laurus Health link

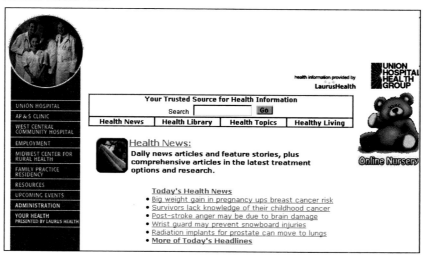

Internet Links to Government Information

Federal, local, and state governments maintain massive amounts of information, and much of it is open to the public. By creating Internet access to the information, the government saves printing and storage costs, and users can retrieve exactly the information they need at any time. Information that is arranged logically and organized according to search patterns makes it relatively easy for users to locate the facts they need. This can be especially useful to businesses. You learned in earlier lessons how to conduct business with the federal government and how to pay your taxes electronically. In this lesson, you'll see how to access even more information.

A good place to start looking for federal information is the Federal Web Locator, sponsored by the Center for Information Law and Policy. This site is organized according to the three branches of government, with additional links to organizations closely related to the federal government. At this site you can find information on your elected representatives or read about cases coming before the Supreme Court. You can visit the Web site for the State Department, the Department of Commerce, or any of the other cabinet level departments. Each section has link after link to the agencies under its jurisdiction. In this Step-by-Step activity, you'll look at just a few of them.

STEP-BY-STEP 5.4

1. Go to the Federal Web Locator, shown in Figure 5-11, and click the link to the **Department of Commerce** and then to the **Bureau of the Census.** Select your state in the **State and County Quick Facts** area. By selecting your county, you can see how its counts compare with the figures from your state. Use the table to answer the following questions.

   a. What is the total population of your county?

   _____

   b. Has your county population increased or decreased since 1990?

   _____

   c. Are retail sales per capita higher or lower for your county than they are for the state?

   _____

STEP-BY-STEP 5.4 Continued

FIGURE 5-11
The Federal Web Locator page

2. Select **Browse more data sets** for your county, and click the **County Business Patterns Economic Profile** for the most recent year. Find out how many people are employed in these areas:

a. retail computers and software

_____

b. restaurants

_____

c. real estate agents

_____

d. business consulting

_____

STEP-BY-STEP 5.4 Continued

3. Return to the **Federal Web Locator** and visit the **Women's Bureau of the Department of Labor**, shown in Figure 5-12. Search the site for information about GEM-SET and WANTO. What are these programs, and how can they help improve technological skills?

_____

_____

FIGURE 5-12
Department of Labor Women's Bureau home page

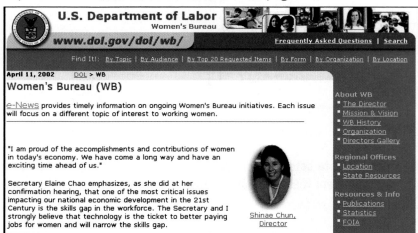

4. Laws passed by the U.S. Congress affect businesses. Senators and representatives are keenly interested in electronic commerce and the potential for taxation and regulation. If you are running a business, you will want to keep up with congressional hearings and know how to contact your elected representatives. One way you can find them is to go to **www.Congress.org**. This is not an official government site, but, nevertheless, is very useful and accurate. Go there now, and key your Zip code in the **Write Elected Officials** box.

a. Who is your representative in the House?

_____

b. Who are your senators?

_____

c. Click the photo of one of your elected representatives. Does this person have a Web page?

_____

STEP-BY-STEP 5.4 Continued

d. When you click to send e-mail through this site, a preset topic will appear as will the opportunity to compose your own letter. Investigate how this works. Would this make you more likely to contact one of your representatives in Congress? Explain.

_____

_____

> ### Extra Challenge
>
> The Internet makes it possible for government offices and elected officials to offer detailed information to citizens. What benefits do you see when you compare this capability to earlier times? What responsibility remains with the government to be sure that all citizens, whether they are online or not, can receive the information they need?

SUMMARY

In this lesson, you learned:

- You can plan a trip and make your reservations online.
- You can use the Internet to find up-to-date news and weather reports.
- You can locate phone numbers, draw maps, and search for services online.
- You can use the Internet to find government information useful to a business.

VOCABULARY _Review_

Define the following terms:

Data port	Database	Powered by

REVIEW *Questions*

TRUE / FALSE

Circle T if the statement is true or F if the statement is false.

T   F   1. Travel sites are good if you know where you want to go, but they don't help you plan a trip.

T   F   2. You can make airline reservations online, but you will have to contact the airline directly or work through a travel agent to pay for your tickets.

T   F   3. Most search engines show news headlines on their opening pages.

T   F   4. Many reference books that are found in libraries, such as dictionaries and encyclopedias, are available electronically over the Internet.

T   F   5. By investigating information from the Bureau of the Census Web site, a building contractor could see how many local housing permits had been issued.

WRITTEN QUESTIONS

Write a brief answer to the following questions.

1. Give examples of three organizations that use the Internet to provide information, but are not involved in sales transactions.

2. How could you use the Internet to find your way to a job interview?

3. How could you use the Internet to find information about a winter storm warning in South Dakota if you live in Ohio?

4. How could you use the Internet to learn the correct pronunciation of a word?

5. How could you use the Internet to learn if a bill was scheduled for a vote in the House of Representatives?

PROJECTS

 PROJECT 5-1

Plan a business trip from Pittsburgh, PA, to Denver, CO, one week from today. Stay for four days. Find the three cheapest flights. Check for room availability in two moderately priced hotel chains, one near the airport and one downtown. Use an information service to find the address for a company called Decisioneering. Locate INVESCO Field at Mile High Stadium. Use the Department of the Treasury site to find information about the U.S. Mint in Denver. Find driving directions from the airport to each of these locations. To help decide what to pack, get a weather forecast for Denver.

 PROJECT 5-2

You are a summer intern at a Web development company. Part of your job involves meeting with prospective clients to discuss the links that they would like to feature on their home pages. In the next month, you are scheduled to meet with the editor of the local newspaper, the program director of the television station, the director of the city's convention and visitors' bureau, and the superintendent of schools. In preparation for your meeting, locate a comparable Web site for each of these clients. Using what you see there, develop two lists. In one, include at least two common information links that you think these four sites should feature. In the other, list at least two unique information links for each of them.

  TEAMWORK PROJECT

You and your teammates work for a company in Kansas City, Missouri, that makes souvenir baseball apparel. To launch a new product, you are planning to travel from Kansas City to attend games at five different major league parks in five days. The parks are located in San Diego, New York, Chicago, Atlanta, and St. Louis. Each park has a home game in the afternoon of each day.

There are many different orders in which you can visit the parks. Each person on the team should take one order and put together an itinerary of flights that will let you visit all five parks. Assume that you would need to arrive in each city no later than noon, and you wouldn't be able to leave until 6:00 p.m. Compare your flight schedules and the total cost. Which of these would you choose, or would you keep looking? What criteria are the most important in this scheduling?

CRITICAL *Thinking*

SCANS **ACTIVITY 5-1**

During severe weather, the Internet weather sites are sometimes jammed with traffic. Write about 100 words describing how the availability of constantly updated weather information has changed the ability of business owners to make plans. As a business owner, if you knew a blizzard was coming to your area, what decisions would you have to make about your hours of operation, protecting your building from damage, and cleaning up afterward? How would the up-to-the-moment information you could find online help you plan?

PERSONAL AND BUSINESS SERVICES ONLINE

REVIEW *Questions*

TRUE/FALSE

Circle T if the statement is true or F if the statement is false.

T   F   1. An employee might have a variety of careers while pursuing a single job.

T   F   2. Career related Web sites often have career planning information as well as listings of particular job openings.

T   F   3. For an employer, listing a job opening online provides the same exposure as listing a job in the newspaper.

T   F   4. Online banking allows you to check your balance but prohibits transactions such as transferring funds between accounts.

T   F   5. The major benefit of online billing for both the billing company and the bill payer is convenience, not cost savings.

T   F   6. In order to track a portfolio of stocks on a financial site, you must be the registered owner of those stocks.

T   F   7. The Internal Revenue Service and state tax agencies would like more people to file their tax returns electronically.

T   F   8. Travel sites let you see the flights or hotel rooms that are available, but you cannot book reservations online.

T   F   9. Online maps illustrate locations and can even provide detailed driving directions from one location to another.

T   F   10. In order to find a person's telephone number online, you must also know the address.

MATCHING

Match the term in Column 1 to its correct description in Column 2.

Column 1	Column 2

___ 1. Portfolio   A. Company abbreviation used for stock quotes

___ 2. Resume   B. A tool to determine what you would owe from a loan

___ 3. Payment calculator   C. Cost of borrowing money, expressed as a percentage

___ 4. Acronym   D. Popular search site to find people

___ 5. Ticker symbol   E. Popular job search site

___ 6. Cost of living   F. Popular travel and lodging site

___ 7. Interest rate   G. A word created from the first letter or letters of other words

___ 8. Anywho   H. Group of stocks or other investments

___ 9. Travelocity   I. Allows comparison of basic expenses in different locations

___ 10. Monster   J. A list of personal information, education, and experience

PROJECTS

SCANS PROJECT 2-1

What kinds of skills does the FBI look for in applicants who want to become agents? In the past, many applicants had a background in law or accounting, but in recent years the FBI has tried to increase the diversity of its agents, in both background and personal characteristics. Use the Internet career and government information search tools you learned about in this unit to answer the following questions.

1. Describe the stages in the application process to become an FBI agent.

   _____

   _____

2. What percentage of FBI agents are women? What percentage are minorities? Describe any initiatives to increase these percentages.

   _____

   _____

3. Are there educational requirements? Are there physical requirements? What are they?

_____

_____

SCANS PROJECT 2-2

1. Using a financial site of your choice, create a portfolio watch list that includes these company stocks: Apple Computer, Microsoft, Nokia, and Schlumberger.

2. Using your watch list, track your portfolio's performance for five trading days. Assume you buy one share of each stock at the opening price on the first day and that you sell all of your stock at the closing price on the fifth day. At the end of five days of trading, determine how much money your portfolio would have gained or lost and the percentage gain or loss.

_____

_____

_____

SCANS PROJECT 2-3

1. Your neighbors have asked you to use your Internet skills to help them plan a trip to celebrate their 25th wedding anniversary. They are considering trips to San Francisco, New York City, Miami, and Toronto. Their budget for round-trip airfare from Minneapolis and four nights' lodging is $2500. Assume they will be leaving a month from today and locate a flight for each trip. Find an upscale hotel in each city that has a room available for those four nights.

_____

_____

2. In each city, find a sporting event and a cultural attraction. Create a map of each location pinpointing the airport, the hotel, and the locations of the sporting event and cultural attraction.

_____

_____

SIMULATION

 JOB 2-1

Evan Peters has learned a great deal about running a small business. Evan is more certain than ever that he will make his fortune with Evan's Trading Mart. He has begun to gather inventory (cell phones, digital cameras, and scanners) but has begun to worry that while he may know how to sell these items, he doesn't really know much about how they work. What would he do if a customer asks him the difference between an analog and digital cell phone, or to explain the specifications for a digital camera?

Evan needs information about his products and remembers seeing ads for **about.com** and **askjeeves.com**. Investigate these sites to see how they can help Evan learn what he needs to know.

 JOB 2-2

Gloria Fernandez, a Florida real estate agent, is ready to implement some of the suggestions she received for using the Internet to help her clients. One client, who is currently living in another state, likes to do business electronically and has asked Gloria to send information about banking, mortgages, and the demographic characteristics of the people in the Ft. Myers (Lee county) area. What sites do you think Gloria should recommend to help this client learn more about the area from a distance?

BUYING ONLINE

Unit 3

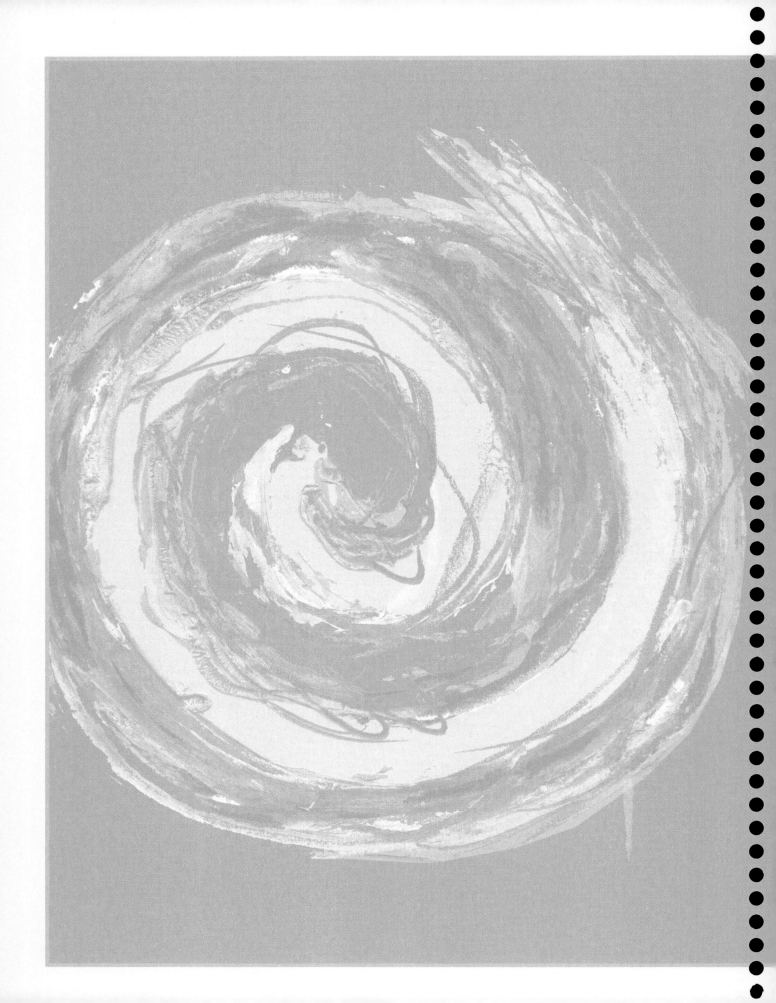

B2C: BUSINESS-TO-CONSUMER

OBJECTIVES

Upon completion of this lesson, you should be able to:

- Locate goods and services for purchase.
- Comparison-shop and configure big-ticket purchases.
- Place a secure order for a consumer product and track its delivery status.
- Participate in an online auction.

Estimated Time: 2 hours

VOCABULARY

Auction service

Cookie

Drill down

Shopping cart

Buying Online

The Internet can teach you to use your computer, help you find a job, download an e-mail program, or book a flight to Cancun. It can also let you buy, without visiting a store, just about anything you want. It doesn't matter if you are buying a best-selling book for yourself or sending flowers to a friend. Buying online is quick, easy, and safe if you know what to do.

All kinds of products and services are offered for sale online. In Lesson 6, you will see how to shop online. You'll learn how to locate the retail product you want and how to place your order safely. You'll learn how to use the Internet to price expensive products like computers and cars. Online auctions provide another way for buyers and sellers to exchange goods, and you'll learn in this lesson how they work.

The Internet—A Buyer's Dream

A television commercial for a major credit card company shows a harried mom chasing her three young children in the backyard. The announcer tells us that she shopped online for the Cozy Coupe™ and other things the children are using. Her comment: "Go shopping with these three? No way. I shop online!"

Online shopping is one of the more attractive features of the Internet. Parents can peruse their favorite shopping sites after the kids are down for a nap as easily as an investor can track a stock portfolio when away from the office. At any time and any place, consumers can access information via the Internet. At the beginning of the 20th century, rural homeowners relied upon mail-order catalogs, which were often viewed as wish books, for purchasing consumer goods. Today, anyone with an Internet connection can buy gourmet food from New York, tulips from

Holland, tickets to a concert in San Francisco, or clothing from stores in far corners of the world—all from a single location in a matter of minutes. It doesn't matter where you live or when you shop, as long as you have an Internet connection and a way to pay for the item.

All of the major search engines have shopping sections. Yahoo's shopping link shows ads from retailers as well as links to a number of major categories, as you can see in Figure 6-1. Clicking a category link such as DVD and Videos leads to more specific links for that area. You can also conduct a direct search for a product. If shopping for a digital camera, you can either follow links or enter the phrase in the search box.

FIGURE 6-1
Portion of Yahoo Shopping home page

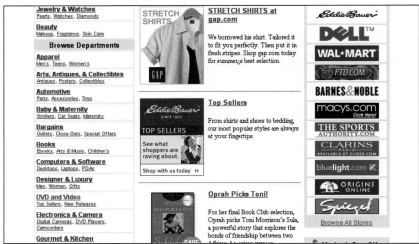

The Google Web Directory also has many shopping topics within its shopping category. You'll see links for everything from Antiques and Collectibles to Wholesale. One of these shopping links is for Weddings. Clicking Weddings brings up more categories and allows you to *drill down*, refining your search to more and more specific topics. Figure 6-2 shows the sites that appear when the Cakes link is clicked. Notice that this list of hits is different from one you would receive if you searched Google using cakes as a keyword. Here, the search engine restricts the hits to shopping for wedding cakes, saving you from wading through hundreds of references for bakeries.

FIGURE 6-2
Google's Shopping links for wedding cakes

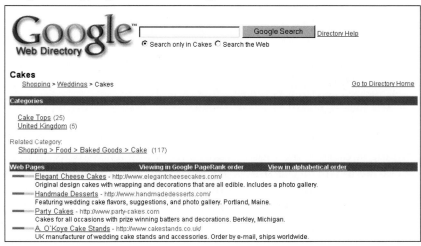

What portion of Internet traffic is online shopping activity? How does shopping online fare as compared to all retailing? What do experts predict will happen in the future? Are traditional stores going to be left behind as consumers switch to online shopping? As you learned in Lesson 1, millions of Internet users have made an online purchase. Jupiter Media estimates that half of the 150 million online users in the U.S. will make an online purchase in 2002. Researchers at eMarketer estimate B2C e-commerce revenues in the U.S. will be $75 billion in 2002. This is a huge increase from 1997's actual amount of $2 billion, but will have to continue to grow to reach the $3.2 trillion estimated for 2004 by Forrester Research.

This lesson will give you a general overview of the business-to-consumer process. In the first Step-by-Step, you'll see how to locate the goods and services you want to purchase. As you experience online shopping, think about how it compares to the kind of shopping you've done before.

Tracking Consumers

A *cookie* is a file of information about you that some Web sites create and store on your hard drive when you visit the site. Then when you return to the site, it can pull up the information from the cookie file on your computer, so that you don't have to enter your identifying information again.

Some companies use cookies to keep track of your navigation through the site. By doing this, the company can determine your preferences and even personalize the site for you the next time you visit. For example, an online clothing catalog might note that you are interested in hiking boots. The next time you visit, the site can retrieve this information about you from the cookie and immediately show you its best deals on hiking boots and hiking-related products, such as backpacks.

> **Hot Tip**
>
> You will learn more about consumer issues and security later in this book. For now, keep in mind that they are both important. The phrase *caveat emptor*—let the buyer beware—applies to online shopping just as it does to any other purchase you make.

S TEP-BY-STEP 6.1

1. The easiest way to begin online shopping is to go to your search engine and look for its shopping category. Click the **Shopping** category in AltaVista, Google, and Yahoo to see how they are organized.

   a. Which search engine's category list seems to group links in the most logical way? Why do you think so?

   _____

   _____

   b. Do the opening pages in each search engine's Shopping category have links to specific stores? Do you think the store had to pay to be listed?

   _____

   _____

STEP-BY-STEP 6.1 Continued

c. Do these Shopping categories allow you to conduct a search, or do you have to follow links? Which seems more efficient to you?

_____

_____

d. Which one of these search engines seems easiest to use? Why?

_____

_____

2. Internet shopping services will search online stores for the price and availability of an item you specify. Some of these require you to become a member or to download software. One that doesn't, and is easy to use, is **www.shopguide.com.** Go there and search for basketball shoes. Figure 6-3 shows some of the results you might get. Notice the symbols beside each site. These symbols can help you understand what a site offers. What benefits do you get from an online shopping service that you don't get from a direct online search?

_____

_____

FIGURE 6-3
Shopguide.com search results

> ▶ Location: ShopZone / Sports & Leisure / Sports Shoes / Basketball Shoes

| Apparel & Accessories | ▼ | **go** |

▶	**Wilson Sporting Goods Co** (more info)	❶ 🖥 ▤
	Sports Bags, Sports Hats, Basketball Shoes, Golf Shoes, Running Shoes, Tennis Shoes, Golf Bags, Golf Balls, Football, Basketball, Hockey, Soccer, Volleyball, Racquetball and Squash.	
▶	**cooleysport** (more info)	🛒 🖥 🔎 🛍 ☎ ▤
▶	**eastbay.com** (more info)	🛒 🖥 🔎 🛍 ☎ ▤
▶	**finishline.com** (more info)	🛒 🖥 🔎 🛍 ☎ ▤
▶	**footaction** (more info)	🛒 🖥 🔎 🛍 ☎ ▤
▶	**footlocker** (more info)	🛒 🖥 🔎 🛍 ☎ ▤

STEP-BY-STEP 6.1 Continued

3. Online malls serve the same purpose that physical shopping malls do: they give you access to a large number of stores in one convenient place. Hundreds of Web sites bill themselves as online malls, as you will see if you search for one. To see how they work, visit Mall Down the Hall, shown in Figure 6-4, and search for a portable CD player that you can plug into a car tape player.

a. What steps did you have to follow to get where you were going?

_____

_____

b. Was this an easy process for you? Explain.

_____

_____

c. What features of a physical mall would you like to have when you shop online? Did the clickable floor plan at this site help you?

_____

_____

FIGURE 6-4
Mall Down the Hall

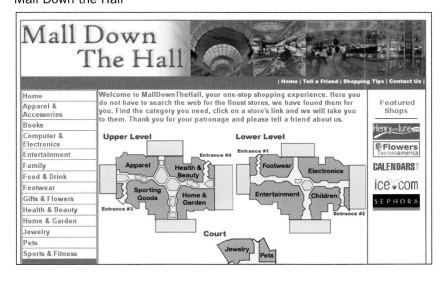

STEP-BY-STEP 6.1 Continued

4. How can online shopping provide the customer service you could get in a physical store? Imagine that you want to buy a gift and have decided on perfume. You certainly can't smell the fragrances online, so how will you make a choice? Almost all shopping directories have a category for fragrances or beauty, where you are likely to find these products. Visit **www.fragrancenet.com**, shown in Figure 6-5.

    a. What information can a shopper find at the **Fragrance Finder**? Does this provide enough information to compensate for your being unable to see (and smell) the merchandise and talk with a sales clerk?

    _____

    _____

    b. What information do you get when you click a specific fragrance?

    _____

    _____

    c. Under what circumstances would you buy this way?

    _____

    _____

5. Compare and contrast shopping online to shopping at a physical mall.

Extra Challenge

How do you feel about having shopping services or search engines do the browsing for you? Are there instances in your life when you would appreciate being able to shop online? Are there times when you would prefer to wander through a store?

FIGURE 6-5
Home page for FragranceNet

Find the Good Life on the Internet

Have you ever needed to buy flowers in a hurry? You may have forgotten a family birthday, or wanted to send a congratulatory bouquet or express sympathy. If you need to send flowers to someone in another location, you probably don't know the name of a reliable florist there. And although you could visit a local florist to look through pictures of arrangements, choose one and arrange for it to be delivered, you can do all of these things with much less difficulty online.

You can also use the Internet to locate service providers. Lawn care services, party planners, plumbers, and rental agencies want you to use their Web sites; many advertise so that you can find them easily.

If you've bought entertainment tickets recently, you know that most of these sales are done electronically through ticket services. You can jump into that role yourself and save money by buying tickets online.

As you complete this Step-by-Step and examine sites that provide flowers, services, or tickets, think about what they provide and how they provide it to the customer. Some of these Internet businesses are online branches of existing physical businesses; others are solely online.

S TEP-BY-STEP 6.2

1. Every search engine with a shopping category lists Flowers as one of the titles in the category. Figure 6-6 shows part of what appears at Yahoo.

FIGURE 6-6
Yahoo's Flower links

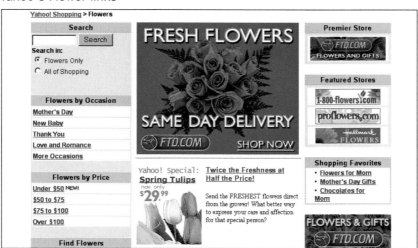

STEP-BY-STEP 6.2 Continued

Visit the Yahoo Flower category, or one from another search engine, and scroll through the list of links. Based on the descriptions shown, note four features of the floral companies that appeal to you as a consumer.

a. _____

b. _____

c. _____

d. _____

2. Go to **www.1800flowers.com**. Customers can contact this company by telephone, at retail locations in large cities, or interactively. To see how the selection process works, find **Business Gifts** in **Everyday Celebrations** and locate a plant that costs around $50.

   a. What does the site provide that would help you choose a plant?

   _____

   _____

   b. Click the **Member Benefits** tab at the top of the page. If you sent flowers frequently or wanted to be reminded of special occasions, how could registering with this site be helpful to you?

   _____

   _____

STEP-BY-STEP 6.2 Continued

3. Food items also appear in many search engines' shopping lists. Begin your examination of this kind of Internet shopping by looking at the Web site for Dean and Deluca, a gourmet food business, shown in Figure 6-7. Read about the company's newsletter.

a. Why does it make good business sense for Dean and Deluca to send an e-mail newsletter to subscribers?

_____

_____

b. Follow the links to read the descriptions of the pastas. Do these sound like the pastas you find in your local grocery store? Why can an online shop offer more variety?

_____

_____

FIGURE 6-7
Dean and Deluca

4. Gourmet food sites might appeal to you for a special occasion, but probably aren't the best way to stock your pantry with everyday items. One online company that is trying to do just that is Netgrocer. Like many superstores, Netgrocer offers household items, pet supplies, baby goods, and health and beauty items in addition to food. Go to the Netgrocer page and look at its categories. Read Netgrocer's help topics to find the answers to these questions:

a. Does Netgrocer have perishable items, such as milk and fresh fruit?

_____

b. How do Netgrocer's prices compare to your local grocer's?

_____

_____

STEP-BY-STEP 6.2 Continued

c. Where does Netgrocer get its items?

_____

_____

d. How long does it take for items to be delivered?

_____

e. What would Netgrocer have to do to entice you to buy dog food online rather than from your neighborhood supermarket?

_____

_____

5. Hundreds of Web sites sell tickets to concerts, sporting events, and theme parks. You can contact the event site directly for ticket information, or you can contact a ticket clearinghouse. Some sites specialize in hard-to-find tickets or resale of tickets. But for a good source, go to the Ticketmaster site. Here, you can search for a particular artist or event, or even search just to see what is coming to a particular location. Figure 6-8 shows the results from searching for basketball tickets in Indiana. Use the search-by-event feature to locate performances by an artist of your choice. Click the state nearest to you to find details. Explain how this information helps Ticketmaster sell more tickets.

_____

_____

6. Why do you think online businesses choose to operate this way? Why do some customers choose to buy this way?

_____

_____

Extra Challenge

Do you think that people who use the Internet are more likely to spend money for flowers, gourmet food, and entertainment? Which do you think is higher: the proportion of the general population who send fresh flowers, or the proportion of Internet users who send fresh flowers (by any method)? Does your answer help explain why so many retailers of these kinds of products have an online presence?

FIGURE 6-8
Ticketmaster search results

Configure a Dream Car or Computer

It is not surprising that computer manufacturers make it easy for their buyers to configure systems and buy online. After all, that is their business. It may surprise you, though, that you can shop for a car online. Car manufacturers' Web sites will help you understand models and options, but won't sell a car to you. Figure 6-9 shows the Research, Design, and Price page at the Saturn Web site. The center shows you how to find the car you want and how much it will cost. The site reminds you, though, that you can't definitively figure the value of a trade-in online, nor can you take a test drive. To actually purchase the vehicle, you will have to go to a dealer.

FIGURE 6-9
Saturn's Research, Design, and Price Center

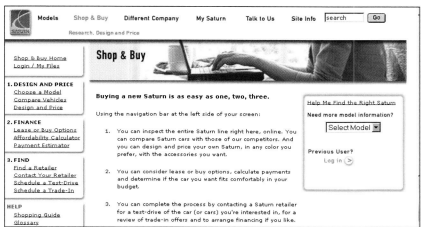

Computer manufacturers, however, let you configure and order your computer from the Web site. Of course there are differences between the products. A computer does not have to be titled, does not cost nearly as much as a car, and can be delivered by a shipping service. In this Step-by-Step, you'll see how to configure both a computer and a new car.

STEP-BY-STEP 6.3

1. To see how manufacturers' sites let customers plan a purchase, visit the Dodge Web site and click **Build Your Dodge**. Pass the cursor over the vehicle silhouettes until you find a car or truck model that is interesting to you. Click your choice to select it. Work your way through the choices for models, colors, and features until you have built your chosen vehicle. Do not ask for a dealer quote unless you are serious about buying the vehicle you have configured.

STEP-BY-STEP 6.3 Continued

a. Were you able to get the information you needed by clicking the information icon? Did this help you?

_____

_____

b. Would you use this kind of service as preparation before visiting an auto dealer? Dodge is not the only manufacturer to provide this kind of service. If you have not purchased a car, talk to someone who has and ask whether or not this would be helpful.

_____

_____

c. Return to the Dodge home page and use **Find a Dealer** to locate the dealer closest to you. Click the link to the dealer. Figure 6-10 shows the page for Palmer Dodge Hyundai West in Indianapolis. Place a check mark before each item below that you can do from your dealer's site.

_____ Link to the manufacturer

_____ Find the dealership location and hours

_____ Find out about rebates

_____ See a new car inventory

_____ See a used car inventory

d. What else would you, as a prospective customer, like to see at the dealer's site?

_____

_____

FIGURE 6-10
Palmer Dodge Hyundai West

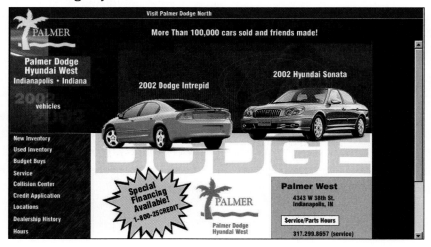

STEP-BY-STEP 6.3 Continued

2. To see how to configure a computer, visit the Web site for Dell computers. This site offers computers for consumers, for business, and for public purchases, such as government and schools.

a. From a business standpoint, why does it make sense for Dell to send these three groups of buyers to different parts of its site?

_____

_____

b. In the Consumer group, click **Home and Home Office**. Buyers who know what they want can move directly to the Start Shopping section, but for this step click **Computer Finder** under Purchase Assistance at the left of your screen. Configure a notebook computer with these choices: price under $1500, Pentium 4 Processor, processor speed at least 1.2 GHz, 384 MB of memory, and a 20 GB hard drive. How many models are available with these specifications?

_____

c. Adjust the price until at least three models are available. At what price level does this happen?

_____

d. Click **View Your Results**. You will see features of each model that satisfies your criteria. To see a more detailed list, click the small box under Compare for three models of your choice. Select **Compare**. The result is a complete list of specifications, shown in part in Figure 6-11. Is the amount of information shown appropriate for someone who is ready to buy? What do you see on this site (in addition to the phone number) that could offer a buyer additional information about these specifications?

_____

_____

FIGURE 6-11
Dell notebook comparisons

STEP-BY-STEP 6.3 Continued

3. Compare the car configuration process with the computer configuration process. List four differences in the processes that are the result of differences in the products.

a. _____

b. _____

c. _____

d. _____

Making the Purchase

Extra Challenge

New-car buyers can now see dealer costs online from sites such as Kelley Blue Book (*kbb.com*). In the past, a buyer needed to know someone in the car business or do extensive leg work to find invoice prices. How has the availability of this information influenced the way dealers quote prices to customers? If you were running a car dealership, how would you prepare your sales force to work with customers who brought Web site printouts when they came to buy a car?

As you complete your shopping and decide what you want to purchase, it is time to place the items you've selected into your shopping cart and proceed to the checkout counter. This is what buyers are accustomed to doing in stores, and the same process is repeated for most online purchases. Here, the *shopping cart* is a virtual one that keeps track of the quantity, price, and features of the items you have selected. As you add items to the shopping cart, the site may ask you if you want to keep shopping or proceed to checkout. The site may suggest additional items or accessories to go with what you have chosen. Like a friendly sales clerk, the Web site guides you through the sale.

Once you have filled your shopping cart, it is time to proceed to checkout. It is important to understand the security precautions in place at the site. You certainly don't want to provide any personal information or your credit card number unless you are absolutely sure that the information is protected. In this Step-by-Step, you will examine the purchasing process at a variety of locations.

S TEP-BY-STEP 6.4

1. Visit **www.amazon.com**, shown in Figure 6-12. Before starting to shop, examine the tabs across the top of the page and the links shown under Browse. Notice that Amazon recognizes a customer through a cookie and personalizes the site based on what that customer has ordered before.

FIGURE 6-12
Amazon.com home page

a. When Amazon was founded, its only product was books. What similarities do the other products have to books?

_____

_____

b. Click the **View Cart** link at the top of the page. Your shopping cart should be empty. Select **DVD** in the Search window and click **Go**. Search for the DVD of the movie *Citizen Kane*. Choose the special edition title and click **Add to Shopping Cart**. Look closely at the next screen that appears. The display for the contents of your shopping cart is small, and a large portion of the screen is covered with other choices that you are encouraged to consider. Why does Amazon show these other titles?

_____

_____

STEP-BY-STEP 6.4 Continued

c. Click **Proceed to Checkout**. You won't go beyond the first screen in the checkout cycle, but read the **Safe Shopping Guarantee** and other security information on this page. As the order progresses, the shopping cart icon travels across the top of the page. Look at Figure 6-13, which shows the screen where payment information is entered. The closed padlock at the bottom of the screen indicates that the transaction is secure and your information is protected. What option is available for customers who don't want to give a credit card number?

FIGURE 6-13
Amazon check out

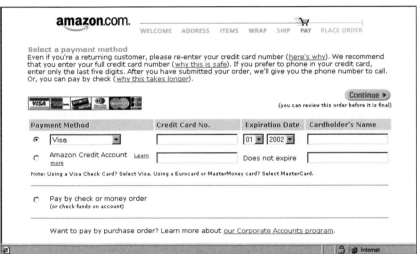

STEP-BY-STEP 6.4 Continued

2. Buying clothes online requires different kinds of choices than buying books or movies. In this step, go to the Gap Web site to see how to order khakis. Click the link for either **Men** or **Women**, and click **Pants**. Investigate the available options and click the link for a style you like. Figure 6-14 shows the choices that are available for one style.

   a. Are there sizes or colors available online that you wouldn't find in a store?

   _____

   b. What features are provided on the site to help shoppers put the right size in their shopping bag?

   _____

   c. Can a customer return an item that doesn't fit? How is this done?

   _____

FIGURE 6-14
Gap shopping

3. A different kind of purchase takes place at a site such as **www.netflix.com**. Go to this site.

   a. What do consumers buy at this site?

   _____

STEP-BY-STEP 6.4 Continued

b. Scroll down to the bottom of the screen and click **About Us**. How many customers currently subscribe to this site? Compare the rental process at this site with what you find at your local video rental store. What are the advantages of using Netflix?

____

____

4. There are many online sources for purchasing contact lenses. One of these is Lens Express. Find this site and click one of the contact lens brands displayed. Choose the **Buy** button and click **Continue** for a **New Customer** and proceed to the order form.

a. What information is required before a customer can complete an order for a prescription item?

____

b. Most of the sites that sell contact lenses claim that their prices are much less expensive than those at local providers. How can these companies sell the products for less?

____

c. Researchers track how many customers abandon their shopping carts without completing the purchase. Forrester Research estimates that 65% of all shopping carts were abandoned in 2001. Figure 6-15 shows the survey that appears when a Lens Express cart is abandoned. How does this information help the company improve its sales and service?

____

FIGURE 6-15
Survey for abandoned shopping carts

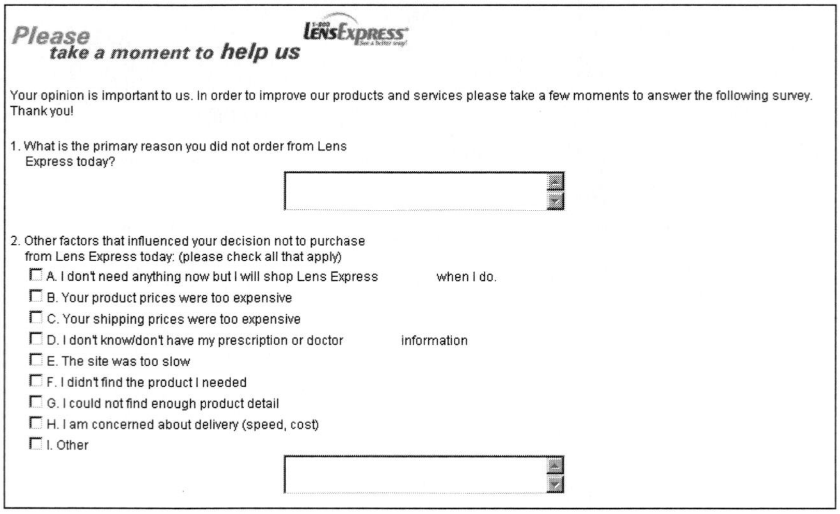
Please take a moment to help us

Your opinion is important to us. In order to improve our products and services please take a few moments to answer the following survey. Thank you!

1. What is the primary reason you did not order from Lens Express today?

2. Other factors that influenced your decision not to purchase from Lens Express today: (please check all that apply)
- ☐ A. I don't need anything now but I will shop Lens Express when I do.
- ☐ B. Your product prices were too expensive
- ☐ C. Your shipping prices were too expensive
- ☐ D. I don't know/don't have my prescription or doctor information
- ☐ E. The site was too slow
- ☐ F. I didn't find the product I needed
- ☐ G. I could not find enough product detail
- ☐ H. I am concerned about delivery (speed, cost)
- ☐ I. Other

STEP-BY-STEP 6.4 Continued

5. Once a purchase is completed, how is the merchandise sent to the customer? The final phase of the checkout usually asks the customer to designate whether standard or expedited delivery is needed, presents the total amount of the bill including shipping charges and any taxes, and asks the customer to confirm the order. It is customary for the seller to send an e-mail confirmation to the buyer after each completed order. Figure 6-16 shows an excerpt of a typical message, and Figure 6-17 shows the associated UPS tracking notice that was updated after delivery was made. Why is it important for a customer who has ordered something like a new computer to be able to track its delivery?

_____

6. In what ways are online purchases easier, or more convenient, than in-store purchases? Which do you prefer, and why?

_____

_____

_____

FIGURE 6-16
E-mail order confirmation

```
Total Merchandise:  $70.00
Tax:            $3.50
Shipping:       $10.00
Shipping Tax:    $0.50
-----------------------------
Total:          $84.00

Your package has been shipped via UPS.  Your tracking number is 1Z0RA1790308354906.  You can
use the URL below to track the package online.

http://wwwapps.ups.com/etracking/tracking.cgi?
submit=Track&TypeOfInquiryNumber=T&InquiryNumber1=1Z0RA1790308354906
```

FIGURE 6-17
Item tracking

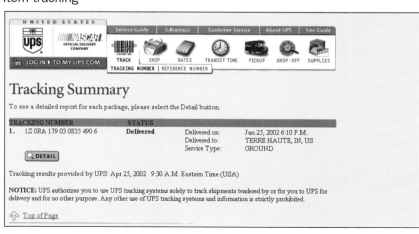

Sold to the Highest Bidder!

Internet users are finding a new way to shop online. An online *auction service* allows anyone to offer an item for sale to the highest bidder. Like other auctions, buyers learn about the merchandise, place a bid, raise their bid if necessary, and eventually either buy the item or drop out of the bidding. For years, art, antiques, and livestock have been sold at auction. Now with online auction services, you can bid on just about anything that anyone wants to sell. You'll find everything from baseball cards to boats. Figure 6-18 shows one of the more popular auction sites.

In this Step-by-Step activity, you'll visit several of the auction services. You'll learn how to offer an item for sale and how to bid. You'll also learn how auction companies make their money and see how payments are made.

FIGURE 6-18
Home page for eBay.com

STEP-BY-STEP 6.5

1. Over 100 companies offer online auction services. One of the best known is eBay. Founded in 1995, eBay currently has over 42 million registered users. In the year 2000, $5 billion worth of goods were traded on eBay. Go to the eBay site. Under Categories, choose **Video Games**. Under Platforms, locate **Xbox**. Choose one item that is of interest to you.

   a. What is the item?

   _____

   b. What is the current auction price?

   _____

   c. How many bids have been made?

   _____

STEP-BY-STEP 6.5 Continued

    d. When does the auction expire?

    _____

    e. Click the underlined link for the item name to see more details about the auction. Does it appear as though this seller uses eBay frequently? What do you see on this screen that makes you trust / cautious about doing business with this seller?

    _____

2. To help prospective buyers and sellers use the site effectively, eBay offers a tutorial for new users. Return to the home page and click the **Buying Tips** button in the New Users area. Choose **Getting Started: Guided tour and tutorials**. Having seen an auction in progress in Step 1, would you take the time to read or listen to these tutorials, or would you be tempted to jump right into the bidding? What prevents a new user from jumping right into the bidding?

    _____

    _____

3. Is there a charge to place a bid on an item? Is there a charge to place an item up for auction? To learn about charges, click **Help**, then **Seller Guide**, then **Listing Your Item**, then **Fees**. What does it cost to list an item with an opening value set at $100?

    a. What does it cost to list a passenger car on eBay Motors?

    _____

    b. Is this the only fee that is charged? Scroll down to read about Final Valuation fees. Why is it important for both the seller and buyer to understand the cost of conducting an auction transaction?

    _____

    _____

4. Yahoo established its auction site on September 14, 1998. Open Yahoo, and click **Auctions** in the Shop section. Select the **Quick Tour** under Getting Started. Read through the **Overview** page. As you see, you do not have to register in order to browse through the listings. How do the instructions at this site compare to what you read at eBay?

    _____

    _____

5. Use the Yahoo Auction search to see if you can find the same sort of item you examined in Step 1. If not, then use the links to work your way toward a similar item. Click on an item name to read more about it.

    a. What is the current bid for your item?

    _____

STEP-BY-STEP 6.5 Continued

    b. When does the sale end?

    _____

    c. Do you think this is a good price, and would you place a higher bid to win the item?

    _____

    d. How does this site and this method entice you to bid on this item?

    _____

    _____

6. Once an auction has concluded, the buyer and seller need to exchange payment and the item. It is up to the seller to provide shipment, but to alleviate payment problems, there are companies that serve as clearinghouses for credit card transactions between buyers and sellers. eBay provides the eBay Payments service.

    a. Return to the eBay home page and click **eBay Payments** near the bottom of the screen. What are the benefits to the buyer for using this service? What are the benefits to the seller? Are buyers and sellers required to use this service for all items sold on eBay?

    _____

    _____

    b. PayPal is another payment service for auction participants. Go to the PayPal Web site and read about the service. How is payment sent? What does it cost to use the service? In addition to auction participants, describe others for whom this could be a useful service.

    _____

    _____

7. Give three reasons why you would or would not use an online auction service.

    _____

    _____

    _____

Extra Challenge

John is interested in the U.S. Civil War and he frequently attends re-enactments. He has sold several Civil War memorabilia on eBay. What benefits could John receive from selling items this way rather than at re-enactments? What additional responsibilities would he have?

SUMMARY

In this lesson, you learned:

- You can locate goods and services for purchase online.
- You can comparison-shop and configure big-ticket purchases.
- You can place a secure order for a consumer product and track its delivery status.
- You can participate in an online auction.

VOCABULARY *Review*

Define the following terms:

Auction service	Drill down	Shopping cart
Cookie		

REVIEW *Questions*

TRUE / FALSE

Circle T if the statement is true or F if the statement is false.

T   F   1. The best way to shop online for a new bicycle would be to conduct a Web search using the word *bicycle*.

T   F   2. When you configure a new car online, you can select from among all the available options, see how much your car would cost, and find a dealer who has that particular model in stock.

T   F   3. The ability to comparison-shop easily and quickly is one of the benefits of B2C e-commerce.

T   F   4. Once you place an item in an electronic shopping cart, you are obligated to purchase it.

T   F   5. An auction is active until the seller decides to end it by accepting the current bid.

WRITTEN QUESTIONS

Write a brief answer to the following questions.

1. You have ordered books about music theory from an online bookseller, and the next time you return to the site, you are amazed to see that a music theory book is featured in a display. Should you be surprised? Why or why not?

2. Name three important things to consider if you are ordering clothes online.

3. How has the Internet changed the way customers bargain with car dealers?

4. How do auction sites make money?

5. How do consumers pay for items they buy online?

PROJECTS

 PROJECT 6-1

Choose several items and compare their prices in your local store to their prices at two different online locations. Check prices for a dozen roses, a pair of your favorite jeans, and a copy of *Hamlet*. Be sure to include delivery costs. Was one source consistently priced lower than the others? Why do you think this is so? What else are you paying for at each location?

PROJECT 6-2

Use a search engine to find the site for a truck rental company. Investigate what it would cost to rent a truck large enough to move two rooms of furniture from Phoenix to San Diego. Does the site help you determine the truck size that you need? Can you determine how much it would cost to rent the truck? Can you reserve the truck online?

 TEAMWORK PROJECT

With your group, investigate Personal Digital Assistants (PDAs) from Palm and Handspring. Choose one model from each manufacturer. Price each model at four retail sites and one auction site. Find information on the Diabetes Palm. Search Amazon for a book that would tell you how to make the best use of your PDA. Recommend a purchase and determine what it would cost, including shipping, for the PDA of your choice and an application book.

CRITICAL *Thinking*

 ACTIVITY 6-1

Imagine that you are shopping for a tent to take on a camping vacation. How has the Internet changed the way you can shop now versus the way you would have shopped five years ago? Explain the differences in about 100 words.

 ACTIVITY 6-2

Some of the sites you've visited in this lesson ask the purchaser to provide much more information than is necessary for purchasing the product and arranging for delivery. If you were running an online store, what would you like to know about your customers, and why? Do you think it is reasonable to ask this information of your customers? Answer these questions in about 100 words.

B2B: BUSINESS-TO-BUSINESS

OBJECTIVES

Upon completion of this lesson, you should be able to:

- Find sources for business purchases.

- Explain how virtual marketplaces and portals enhance B2B.

- Describe the benefits of using the Internet for internal business.

- Explain the importance of logistics and distribution systems to management of the supply chain.

Estimated Time: 2 hours

VOCABULARY

Electronic Data Interchange (EDI)

E-procurement

Intranet

Portal

Virtual marketplace

Vortal

Business Connections

In Lesson 2, you learned about the supply chain, a process that ensures the appropriate quantity of materials or products reaches the correct destination at the right time. For many businesses, supply chain management would be difficult without the Internet. The Internet enables more effective communication, timely responses, and the wide exchange of information—all activities that decrease inventory and improve cost effectiveness. Figure 7-1 shows how the supply chain is incorporated into the mission statement for the American Coffee Corporation.

FIGURE 7-1
American Coffee Corporation mission statement

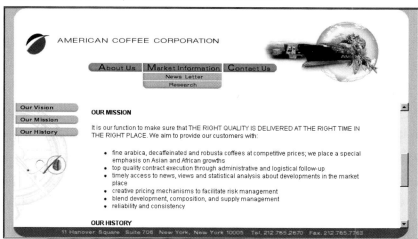

You may recall a television commercial that provided a humorous look at what can happen when the supply chain is not managed well. In the commercial, executives are watching an ad campaign for the company's G.I. Joe-type action figure. The music and voice-over track the soldier through mud and battle, but the film shows him dressed in prom dresses and other frilly costumes. At the end, the puzzled executives are told that there was a slight problem with the supply chain—the army uniforms didn't arrive on time from the manufacturer in China. The point of the commercial is to show the important role that logistics and distribution, as parts of the supply chain, play in business.

To manage the supply chain, an organization must make decisions that have the potential to improve every aspect of its business.

In beginning a business, facilities must be located and suppliers determined in such a way that the procurement of goods and materials is as efficient as possible. To *procure* in business means to obtain, or get access to, goods. *E-procurement* is Internet-based automation of obtaining or accessing goods. These decisions address transportation issues, capacity, quality, and financial matters such as taxes and tariffs.

When the production stage is reached, the business must decide what to make, what to buy, and where to do each of these. For tax reasons, companies sometimes find it more cost effective to begin production in one country and finish it in another. The tax savings may offset shipping costs and tariffs.

Managing the inventory of work-in-process and finished goods, in particular, has enormous potential for cost savings. Most companies try to minimize the amount of inventory they have, thereby needing less physical space and fewer employees, as well as reducing the financial resources tied up in inventory.

Through the entire chain, the logistics of transportation and distribution must be managed. Raw materials have to be in place where and when they are needed, but finished goods must also get to the customer at the right time. To make this happen, each component of the supply chain must use the same demand forecasts, or estimates of the number of items needed.

The Internet has played a vital role in improving supply chain management by helping manage the flow of information. Communication, visibility, and business integration are all improved when each part of the supply chain has the same information. The Voluntary Interindustry Commerce Standards Association has established standards for conducting Internet commerce, developing collaborative planning and forecasts, and other activities. The Association's Collaborative Planning, Forecasting, and Replenishment (CPFR) standards outline how companies should share demand data and collaborate to resolve differences, leading to higher accuracy, lower inventory, and quicker response times.

Electronic Data Interchange (EDI) refers to the electronic exchange of business information. When catalogs can be viewed, orders placed, invoices prepared, information exchanged, and payment received—all electronically—accuracy is improved and time and paper are saved. If all partners use the same standards, tremendous efficiencies can be achieved.

In this lesson, you will see how companies use the Internet to help manage the supply chain. You'll visit manufacturers to see how they do business electronically, you'll look at electronic marketplaces, and you'll see solutions for distribution. In the first Step-by-Step, you'll look at the procurement stage and see how business purchases are made.

STEP-BY-STEP 7.1

SCANS

1. To procure the materials needed in manufacturing, one business can work directly with another one. Figure 7-2 shows the customer information system requirements for Applied Extrusion Technologies. To see how procurement works, use your search engine to find the Web sites for the businesses listed below. In each case, determine whether you can see an online catalog, whether custom orders are possible, if access to ordering is restricted by password to those companies with established accounts, and how payment is made. Suggested links to follow are shown for each business.

FIGURE 7-2
Applied Extrusion Technologies customer information system

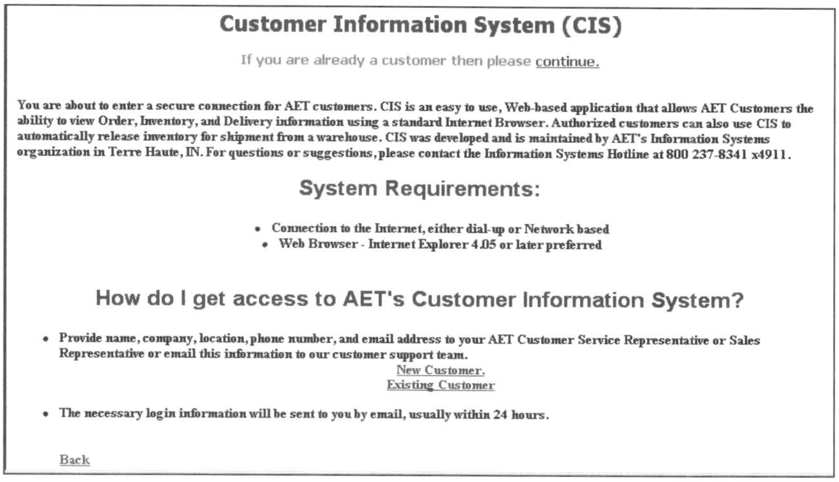

> ### Customer Information System (CIS)
>
> If you are already a customer then please <u>continue.</u>
>
> You are about to enter a secure connection for AET customers. CIS is an easy to use, Web-based application that allows AET Customers the ability to view Order, Inventory, and Delivery information using a standard Internet Browser. Authorized customers can also use CIS to automatically release inventory for shipment from a warehouse. CIS was developed and is maintained by AET's Information Systems organization in Terre Haute, IN. For questions or suggestions, please contact the Information Systems Hotline at 800 237-8341 x4911.
>
> ### System Requirements:
>
> - Connection to the Internet, either dial-up or Network based
> - Web Browser - Internet Explorer 4.05 or later preferred
>
> ### How do I get access to AET's Customer Information System?
>
> - Provide name, company, location, phone number, and email address to your AET Customer Service Representative or Sales Representative or email this information to our customer support team.
>   <u>New Customer.</u>
>   <u>Existing Customer</u>
> - The necessary login information will be sent to you by email, usually within 24 hours.
>
> <u>Back</u>

a. C. R. Laurence manufactures a wide variety of industrial products. For information about ordering, click **About CRL**, then **CRL Policies**, then **Ordering Information**.

_____

_____

b. At Southwire, purchasing information is found in the Quick Hits list under How to Buy.

_____

_____

c. At Abbey Color, click **Abbey Shopping Mall** to see the online sales process.

_____

_____

d. The Mason Box Company (**www.custompackage.com**) provides its **Order Online** link as well as its toll-free fax number on the Web site opening page.

_____

_____

STEP-BY-STEP 7.1 Continued

2. What does a business do when it has excess inventory? If this inventory could be useful to another business, both could benefit. Before the Internet, it was difficult for a business that wanted to buy excess inventory to have timely information regarding the inventory of a business that wanted to sell it. Now, however, there are sites that allow businesses to buy and sell everything from used equipment to unused raw materials to production overruns. To see how this kind of site works, visit **www.liquidation.com**, shown in Figure 7-3.

FIGURE 7-3
Liquidation.com

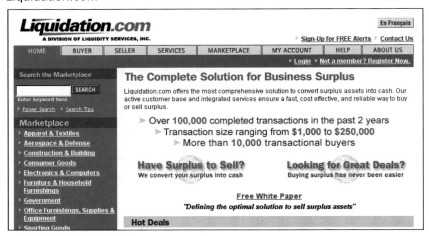

a. Click **Have Surplus to Sell?** Does it seem sensible to you that surplus would be sold in an auction format? Why would a business appreciate the anonymity promised by this site?

_____

_____

b. Return to the home page and click Looking for Great Deals? What does this site do to ensure that buyers will pay and sellers will deliver as promised?

_____

_____

c. Return to the home page and select a category that interests you from the list in the Marketplace. Figure 7-4 shows information for the liquidation of 10,000 cell antennas. Examine an auction that is underway. Describe the item, the quantity, and the current bid for the lot price. What kind of business might be interested in purchasing the lot?

_____

_____

STEP-BY-STEP 7.1 Continued

FIGURE 7-4
Liquidation auction information

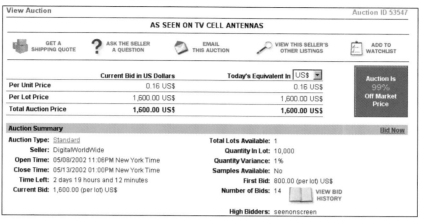

3. If you owned a business, how would you use the information you learned in this Step-by-Step?

_____

_____

_____

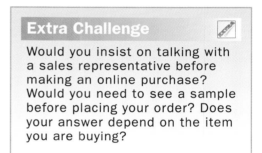

Extra Challenge

Would you insist on talking with a sales representative before making an online purchase? Would you need to see a sample before placing your order? Does your answer depend on the item you are buying?

Virtual Marketplaces

W orking directly with a supplier makes sense when a business has an established relationship or needs to meet certain specifications. When a business is interested in obtaining a commodity such as steel, or makes repeated routine purchases for supplies, purchasing efficiency may be improved if the business works through a ***virtual marketplace***, an Internet ***portal***, or a ***vortal*** (vertical industry portal). A virtual marketplace links purchasers and suppliers online; a portal is a central access point for related information, and a vortal provides specialization and encourages collaboration. Figure 7-5 shows information from SciQuest, a site that links 1.5 million scientific products from 750 suppliers in one Web site. In the following Step-by-Step, you'll visit portals and vortals to learn how they can enhance B2B e-commerce.

STEP-BY-STEP 7.1 Continued

FIGURE 7-5
SciQuest

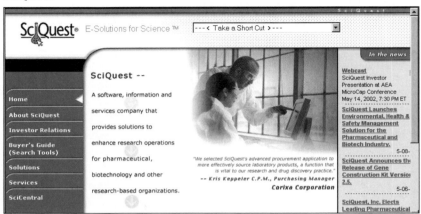

S TEP-BY-STEP 7.2

1. Begin by locating the Web site for SciQuest. Go to the site, and read **About SciQuest**.

  a. What does SciQuest offer businesses in addition to being a source of scientific equipment?

  _____

  _____

  b. Click the **Buyer's Guide** and search for safety goggles. How many suppliers appear? How many pages of choices appear? If you were buying a large quantity of safety goggles, how would you determine which model to buy?

  _____

  _____

2. Next, visit **www.amphire.com**, a site for the food service industry. The opening page is shown in Figure 7-6.

FIGURE 7-6
Amphire home page

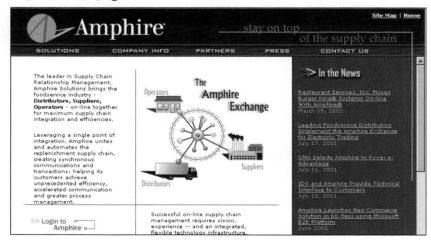

STEP-BY-STEP 7.2 Continued

a. Click **Solutions** and read what Amphire offers on the **Sell-side**. If you were a distributor and wanted to reach restaurant owners, what could having a storefront with Amphire do for you?

_____

_____

b. Next read about solutions for the **Buy-side**. If you were in charge of purchasing for a school cafeteria, what could Amphire do for you?

_____

_____

c. Click **Company Info** and read **About Amphire**. List three benefits of using a solution like this.

_____

_____

_____

3. MetalSite bills itself as "The Force in Metals e-Commerce." Visit this site and click **MetalSite Home**. Choose **Buyer Connection**. Is there a charge for buying through MetalSite? Can you order online?

_____

4. Market Mile is a different kind of site for e-procurement. Go to this site and read **About Us**. What kinds of products does Market Mile feature?

_____

_____

5. Procurement for higher education (institutional purchasing) is available through HigherMarkets, shown in Figure 7-7. Go to this site, click **Solution**, and read about the services offered. Do you see a catalog, order form, or shopping cart on the HigherMarkets site? How is this e-procurement site different from SciQuest?

_____

_____

FIGURE 7-7
Higher education procurement

STEP-BY-STEP 7.2 Continued

6. Now that you have seen examples of portals and vortals, learn more about their features and their future.

    a. Begin by going to **www.webopedia.com**. Search for an explanation of *vortal*. What is typically present at a vortal site?

           _____

           _____

    b. Visit **www.vortalbuilding.com,** the Web site of a company that helps clients create vortals. Go to this site and click **What is Vortal?** What is the difference between the target audiences for a portal and for a vortal?

           _____

           _____

    c. Now click **Why Vortal?** and read the information you find. According to this site, what four components make a vortal functional?

           _____

           _____

7. For B2B, how is using a vortal an improvement over using Yahoo or another general portal?

        _____

        _____

> **Extra Challenge**
>
> If you examined the vortal sites carefully, you saw that they not only assist purchasing but also offer software solutions. What are the problems that need solutions? In later lessons, you'll look more closely at how enterprise-wide solutions are established.

Internal Business

Many large businesses use the Internet to enhance communication between branches in widespread locations, to help their customers reach them, or to connect their agents in the field to corporate resources. Dealers for a heavy equipment manufacturer could use the Internet to order parts, retrieve service bulletins, and consult with experts. If the manufacturer is half a world away from the dealer, the customer service made possible by this connection will provide immediate benefits.

Some companies have *intranets*, private networks that restrict access to employees or authorized groups only. For example, an insurance company might have an intranet that connects its agents to the home office. Insurance policy information could be transmitted electronically, yet customer privacy would be maintained.

Businesses also use the Internet for human resources interactions. You saw in Lesson 3 that the hiring process can begin online with electronic job postings and submission of resumes. Businesses also use the Internet to distribute policies and procedures to employees and to make training information available.

Privacy considerations prevent you from examining intranets or other restricted sites, but you can see how a university uses the Internet to reach its employees and students. In this Step-by-Step, you will study online processes at Indiana State University. The home page is shown in Figure 7-8.

STEP-BY-STEP 7.2 Continued

FIGURE 7-8
Indiana State University home page

STEP-BY-STEP 7.3

1. Begin by locating the home page for Indiana State University. In this Step-by-Step, you will view processes for students.

   a. Click the **Apply Online** link. Click **Undergraduate Students** and read the instructions. Why is it helpful to a prospective student to be able to print application forms from home? Scroll down to **Let's Go to the Form**. How does it help the university to receive applications electronically?

   _____

   _____

   b. Return to the home page and click **Current Students**. Click **MyISU Portal**. You will not be able to enter the portal without a username and password, but you can see the kind of information that is available. As a student, how could you benefit from having access to information grouped in this way?

   _____

   _____

2. To see how employees interface with their employer, return to the home page and click **Faculty and Staff**.

   a. Under Employee Resources, click **Staff Benefits**. This is the office that deals with insurance, retirement, and other employment issues. In the links at the left, click **Advanced PCS**, the university's

STEP-BY-STEP 7.3 Continued

prescription drug provider. How is connecting to this site from their employer's site helpful to ISU employees in tracking their prescription orders and history?

_____

_____

b. Back at the Faculty and Staff page, under Academics, click **Office of Academic Affairs**. Click **Faculty and Staff Resources**. Click **Forms Available Online**. Click **Nomination for Promotion**. If prompted, check that you want to **Open the file from its current location**. This form is a Word document and is not submitted electronically. Even so, why is it useful to have the form available online?

_____

3. Return to the ISU home page and click **Current Students**. Under Technology Services click **Help Desk**. Under Email click **Setting up the portal to POP other email accounts**. Read the instructions. Do you think these instructions are sufficient to enable a student to complete this task? How does it benefit the university to provide this information online?

_____

_____

4. How are intranets beneficial to employees? Why are they important for companies?

_____

_____

> ### Extra Challenge
>
> In order for employees to use their company's Web site for training or human resources purposes, navigation of the site has to be straightforward. The ISU site has recently been redesigned, and there is a site survey for users to provide feedback. How can a business determine the effectiveness of its site?

Logistics and Distribution

Effective purchasing, quality production, and efficient inventory management are all essential in today's competitive environment. Unless a business can receive what it needs at the right time and correctly distribute its products to its customers, it will not be successful. The Internet and the advent of bar coding systems have enabled businesses to manage the information associated with the distribution function. Whether it is the grocery store scanner system that alerts a distributor that the store's supply of peanut butter is running low or the tracking system that enables both the recipient and the shipper to follow the delivery progress of a package, the Internet is a fundamental instrument in the sharing of business supply information. In this Step-by-Step, you will see examples of logistics and distribution systems.

STEP-BY-STEP 7.4

1. Caterpillar is a business that makes yellow heavy equipment items such as road graders and bulldozers. Go to the Caterpillar site, shown in Figure 7-9. Click **Services**, and then **Cat Logistics**.

FIGURE 7-9
Caterpillar home page

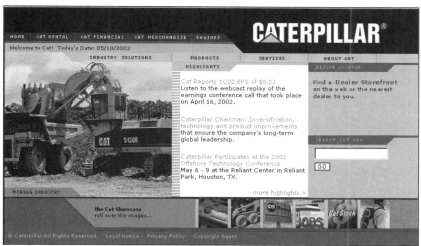

a. What part of the supply chain does Cat Logistics cover? Why does Caterpillar have a separate subsidiary to manage logistics?

_____

b. Click the link for **Press Releases** and find the release from November 1, 2000. What does this tell you about the way Cat Logistics has leveraged its expertise to service other businesses?

_____

2. Package delivery businesses have developed solutions to improve logistics. To see how this works at UPS, go to the UPS home page and click **Business Solutions**.

a. What does UPS offer in addition to package delivery?

_____

b. Click **UPS AND E-COMMERCE**. Click the link to **www.ec.ups.com** at the bottom of the page to reach the e-commerce site. Click **Solutions**, and then click **UPS Online Tools**. Click the link for **UPS Shipping** to learn about Web-based shipping. Scroll down the page to read how to add Web-based shipping to a site. Why do businesses that use this feature have to ship a minimum number of packages each day and use an internal site?

_____

STEP-BY-STEP 7.4 Continued

3. Next, go to the FedEx site and if necessary select your country. Close any security alerts that open. Click **eBusiness Tools**. You should see the Simplify My Shipping page. Under My role is choose **Business Owner/President** or any other role you think is interesting. Next, choose an organization **Between 100 and 500 employees**. Click **Continue Analysis** and answer the questions that appear. Click **Next** and continue providing answers until your shipping solution appears. How does the process of answering these questions help a business think about its entire delivery system?

_____

_____

_____

4. How is the distribution process different today for a shoe manufacturer than it was twenty years ago?

_____

_____

_____

SUMMARY

In this lesson, you learned:

- You can locate goods for business purchases online.
- You can find virtual marketplaces and portals that are dedicated to providing B2B resources for a specific market or industry.
- How a business can use the Internet to exchange information with its employees and customers.
- How a business can use the Internet to improve the distribution of its products.

VOCABULARY *Review*

Define the following terms:		
Electronic Data Interchange (EDI)	Intranet	Virtual marketplace
	Portal	Vortal
E-procurement		

REVIEW*Questions*

TRUE / FALSE

Circle T if the statement is true or F if the statement is false.

T   F   1. To manage the supply chain effectively, it is important that all component businesses share the same estimates for demand, as well as the same understanding of the schedule.

T   F   2. If your business needed to find a new source to purchase specialized machinery, it would make sense to search first for a portal for your industry.

T   F   3. The ability to exchange information without paper, reduce redundancy, and be in touch with trading partners anywhere at any time are benefits of B2B e-commerce.

T   F   4. A business that wants to exchange sensitive company information with its employees would avoid using an intranet.

T   F   5. Individual retail consumers are excluded from purchases on B2B sites.

WRITTEN QUESTIONS

Write a brief answer to the following questions.

1. Most online business-to-business purchases require the purchaser to register. Frequently, a sales contract must be made before the transaction can occur. Why is this important?

2. Give three reasons why a business would find a portal useful for procurement.

3. If your business sold chemicals to the paint industry, what could you do to increase business-to-business sales?

4. How can a business find a market for excess inventory or unwanted equipment?

5. How can using the Internet to post company policies and procedures help a business save paper and ensure that all employees have access to the latest information?

PROJECTS

 PROJECT 7-1

If you were starting a pizza restaurant, how could you use the Internet for your business? At a minimum, you would need ingredients such as flour, cheese, and sauce; equipment such as pans, knives, plates, glasses, and silverware; furnishings such as tables, chairs, and linens; and office supplies. Which of these could you find and purchase online? Find a supplier for each of these categories. Make a chart of the categories, with a supplier for each. Include the supplier's URL.

 PROJECT 7-2

Not all business-to-business purchases result in a physical item that must be shipped. Some purchases involve information that can be transmitted in a file. For example, your business might want to purchase market research data from one of the companies you studied in Lesson 1, or purchase credit information on prospective customers. Using Yahoo's B2B links, find three companies whose product would be delivered electronically. List each URL and the company's product, and provide an example of the kind of business that would buy this product.

_____

_____

_____

  TEAMWORK PROJECT

Jim Newton likes to play softball. For years, he has played in summer leagues, on intramural teams, and on a team at work. Every team Jim's played on has bought T-shirts and hats with the team name on them. Jim has a closet full of old team shirts and hats.

Jim is now looking for a business opportunity. He and two partners think that they have the time and resources to start a small business. They have decided to combine their sports knowledge and their business knowledge to start a team apparel store. Their plan is that the store will stock licensed college and pro sports logo items and will custom-print shirts and hats for local school and league teams. They've decided to name the store Good Sports.

Jim and his partners are experienced Internet users, and they'd like to take advantage of online business-to-business opportunities. The first site they visit as they begin to investigate how they can purchase supplies for the printing side of their business is the Fruit of the Loom Activewear site, a portion of which is shown in Figure 7-10.

FIGURE 7-10
Fruit of the Loom Activewear

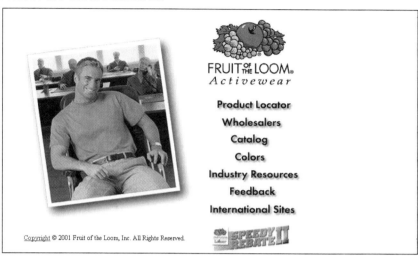

With your team, investigate what Fruit of the Loom offers to small businesses such as Jim's. Prepare a report recommending a basic T-shirt and sweatshirt for Good Sports to use for printing. Be sure to tell Jim which colors are available in each style shirt. Include in your report the names and addresses of three wholesalers that carry this product and are located close to Jim, who lives in northern Florida. Examine new product development, and make a suggestion for another product that Jim should consider ordering for his store.

CRITICAL *Thinking*

 ACTIVITY 7-1

B2B e-commerce is by far the larger part of the total e-commerce picture, yet most Internet users think of consumer purchases rather than business purchases when they think of e-commerce. Why do you think this is so? Explain your reasons in about 100 words.

CONSUMER ISSUES

The Savvy Online Buyer

Whether you are buying for yourself or for your company, you want to know before you buy that the online merchant will deliver what it promised. As a buyer, you want to be certain that the product or service is as described, that your purchase information is secure, and that you have some recourse if you are dissatisfied with the purchase. You should also be able to determine if the information you provide when you complete an online registration form will be shared with other companies. It is critically important to be aware of these issues when you are buying or offering information online.

With its wide access to information, the Internet can help you become a better consumer. You don't have to be an online buyer to find online help with consumer issues. The Internet can give you access to product safety information, to consumer news, and to product ratings. You can see if a product is subject to a *recall*, which is the manufacturer's request to return a product because of severe risks to health or safety. You can also use the Web to learn the specifications and prices of items you want by comparison-shopping electronically before you make a purchase decision.

> **Did You Know?**
>
> Because e-commerce can provide excellent solutions for consumers with special needs, businesses need to consider accessibility during Web site design. In Lesson 13, you will learn how to incorporate features that adhere to accessibility standards.

All of the major search engines provide links to topics of interest to consumers. When you search for the word *consumer* with Google, you find over 14 million references! Figure 8-1 shows a portion of the consumer page for FirstGov, the U.S. government portal you learned about in Lesson 2. Notice that several of these links deal specifically with e-commerce or online privacy. By following the links found here and at other sites, you can learn how to find all kinds of product information and become a savvy online buyer.

FIGURE 8-1
Consumer information at FirstGov

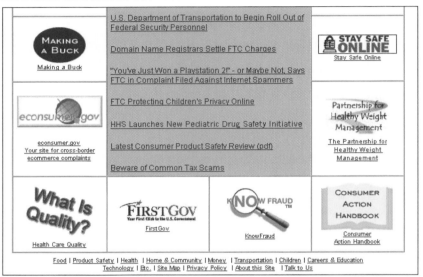

Technology Careers

Advising online stores about tax issues and developing privacy statements for Web sites are two of the tasks that commonly fall to Internet lawyers. A business with an online presence—and today that means many businesses—must be certain to adhere to technology laws. A large corporation needs to have lawyers in its legal department who understand issues of privacy and access, and smaller companies need to retain the same kinds of expertise. The relatively new specialty of Internet law attracts attorneys that are experienced Internet users, that can develop electronic contracts, and that understand the policies, procedures, and regulations of e-commerce. Those with some technical experience can provide even more benefits to their clients.

You can find links to Internet law through your search engine. You'll also find sites devoted to helping law offices make the most of the Internet. If you are interested in a career in Internet law, you might want to start your search for information at the American Bar Association's Web site. Harvard Law School's Berkman Center for Internet and Society offers an Internet Law Program for lawyers and other professionals that combines online instruction and discussion with a five-day intensive session in Cambridge.

Safeguarding Security and Privacy

Privacy and security are not new topics. In Lesson 6, you learned to look for a closed lock or other security symbol before you provide a credit card number or other secure information online. In this Step-by-Step, you'll take a closer look at privacy policies and visit a site that guarantees security.

STEP-BY-STEP 8.1

SCANS

1. You've visited sites that offer services and sites that sell products. Go now to the four sites listed below and examine each home page for a statement of privacy. This is usually found through a link near the bottom of the home page. You may need to look under **Legal Information**. Describe briefly what each site tells you about security, privacy, and responsibility.

   Monster _____

   _____

   Quicken _____

   _____

   Amazon _____

   _____

   Dell _____

   _____

2. Monster offers services. Amazon and Dell sell products. Quicken does both. How do the security and privacy statements of these sites reflect their business?

   _____

   _____

3. Not all sites have security and privacy statements, and some companies are better than others at upholding what they say they will do. How can you be confident that a site will operate according to appropriate guidelines? One way is to look for accreditation by an agency that evaluates online operating principles.

   "Building a framework for global trust™" is the slogan of TRUSTe, an organization founded in 1996 to certify the privacy and security operations of Web sites. Go to the **TRUSTe.com** home page and look under **For Consumers.** Click on **Learn More** under **TRUSTe's Privacy Seal.** Read about how TRUSTe protects privacy. Then read the **FAQs** under **For Consumers, For Businesses,** and **Consumer Education**.

   a. What are the two basic principles of the TRUSTe program?

   _____

   _____

STEP-BY-STEP 8.1 Continued

b. What are the four privacy principles of fair information practice?

_____

_____

c. What does "Click-to-verify" mean, and how does it guarantee safety?

_____

_____

TRUSTe participants come from all areas of e-commerce and display the trustmark on their home page or within their privacy statements. Figures 8-2 and 8-3 show the TRUSTe trustmark at an Internet site and a corporate site. If you examine the list of TRUSTe licensees, you'll see eBay, Lending Tree, NetFlix, and other sites you have visited in earlier lessons.

FIGURE 8-2
The TRUSTe trustmark at AOL

FIGURE 8-3
The TRUSTe trustmark at television station WRTV

4. When B2C first began, consumers were very wary about providing credit card information online. Retailers have incorporated highly sophisticated security measures to protect their customers, but some consumers still feel that entering a credit card number online is less secure than giving it to a sales professional over the phone at a catalog retailer or handing the card to a server in a restaurant. There is no doubt that some Web sites have not incorporated adequate privacy and security information, but most reputable retailers have. To understand what a consumer should look for, go to **www.smarterkids.com**, an online children's toy store, and click **Security** at the bottom of the page. Read the security statement.

STEP-BY-STEP 8.1 Continued

a. If someone else uses your credit card at that site to order $150 worth of merchandise, what is the most that your bank can require you to pay? With the SmarterKids guarantee, what is the most you would have to pay?

_____

b. Click the **Privacy** link at the bottom of the page and read about **Cookies**, **Log Files**, and **Sharing**. List three reasons that the business offers for keeping information about its customers. Do the explanations provided on the site provide enough reassurance to you as a consumer?

_____

_____

_____

c. Drop down to the **Security** section. What is the difference between http:// and https://?

_____

_____

Speaking Up

Just as the Internet enables companies to reach an ever-expanding number of Web consumers, it also enables these users to react online to their experiences. A buyer can contact the company's customer service department by e-mail and expect to get a quick response. There are professional organizations and Web businesses that gather ratings information from users and publicize the results online. In extreme cases, users with complaints about a product or service have launched their own Web pages to air grievances, making it simple for search engines to help others find the site and add their opinions.

In the next Step-by-Step activity, you'll look at some of the avenues available to you if you want to make responsible comments about a product or service.

Extra Challenge

Would you make an online purchase from a company you had never heard of if it displayed the TRUSTe symbol? Would you purchase from an established company's Web site if it did not offer you a privacy statement whose terms you could accept?

Hot Tip

You can register to get rid of junk e-mail by visiting the Junkbusters site.

Did You Know?

There are Web sites that support ethical financial behavior. You can report problems with Internet banking to the FDIC and see a broker scorecard at Gomez. You can find other online avenues for complaints at the Netcheck Commerce Bureau and your state's Attorney General or consumer affairs sites.

STEP-BY-STEP 8.2

SCANS

1. The Federal Consumer Information Center sponsors the Consumer Action Website. Go to **www.pueblo.gsa.gov/crh/respref.htm** and click the link for **Cars**.

   a. Read the section about car repairs. Did you find advice that was new to you? What was it?

   _____

   _____

   b. Click the link for **Shop At Home**. Scroll through the page until you reach the **Smart Shopping Online** section. You will see references to sites mentioned in this lesson. In addition, what does this site tell you about providing private information in e-mail messages?

   _____

   _____

   c. Consumers can use the listings in the **Useful addresses, phone numbers, and websites.** frame at the left side of the page to locate contact information for corporations, government offices, and consumer organizations. If you had a question about using a household product made by Procter & Gamble to clean a vinyl floor made by Armstrong, whom could you contact?

   _____

   _____

   d. In many cases, the corporations in this list include the URL of the corporate Web site. What does this list provide that the corporate site does not?

   _____

   _____

STEP-BY-STEP 8.2 Continued

2. You can submit your own review of a book to *Amazon.com* or of a product to Consumer Review. Each of these sites sells items and encourages its visitors to post reviews. Figure 8-4 shows some of the golf clubs that have been reviewed by users at the Consumer Review site. Visit this site and read the submitted reviews of a product you know well.

FIGURE 8-4
Golf clubs reviewed at Consumer Review

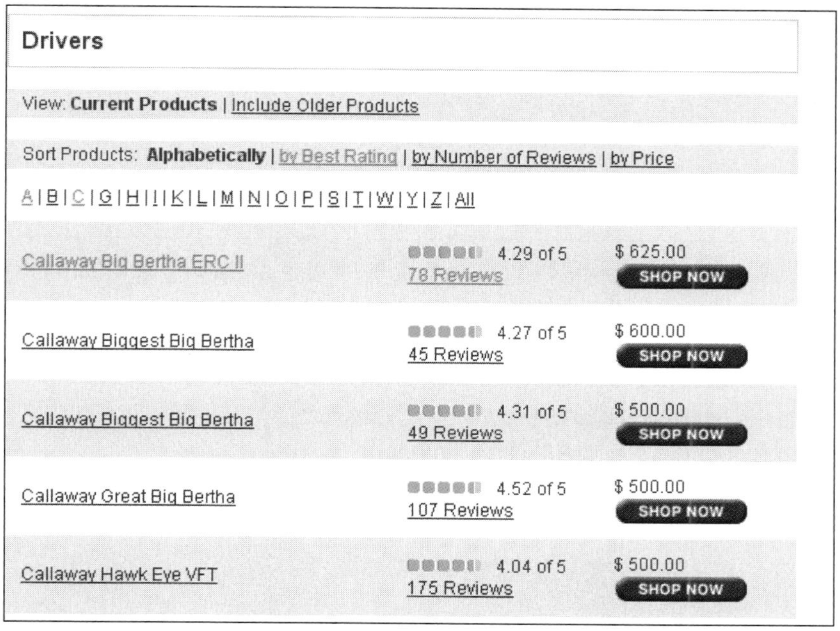

Drivers		
View: **Current Products**	Include Older Products		
Sort Products: **Alphabetically**	by Best Rating	by Number of Reviews	by Price		
A|B|C|G|H|I|K|L|M|N|O|P|S|T|W|Y|Z|All		
Callaway Big Bertha ERC II	◼◼◼◼◻ 4.29 of 5 78 Reviews	$ 625.00 SHOP NOW
Callaway Biggest Big Bertha	◼◼◼◼◻ 4.27 of 5 45 Reviews	$ 600.00 SHOP NOW
Callaway Biggest Big Bertha	◼◼◼◼◻ 4.31 of 5 49 Reviews	$ 500.00 SHOP NOW
Callaway Great Big Bertha	◼◼◼◼◻ 4.52 of 5 107 Reviews	$ 500.00 SHOP NOW
Callaway Hawk Eye VFT	◼◼◼◼◻ 4.04 of 5 175 Reviews	$ 500.00 SHOP NOW

a. Do you agree with the reviews you read? Why or why not?

_____

_____

b. Are any of the reviews moderate, or do they all express strong opinions?

_____

_____

c. Do you think that people who are dissatisfied are more likely to write a review than those who are happy?

_____

_____

d. How seriously should buyers take unscientific ratings like these?

_____

_____

STEP-BY-STEP 8.2 Continued

e. If you were the manufacturer of this product, how much attention would you pay to reviews like these? Why? What action would you take if you found a negative review of your product?

_____

_____

3. If a serious situation of fraud occurs, users can make a report through the **Know Fraud** link at the FirstGov consumer site or through the National Fraud Information Center's Internet Fraud Watch site. Figure 8-5 shows a description of the site. Go to the site at **www.fraud.org/welcome.htm**, and click **Online complaint form**. Scroll through the form to see the kind of information a user would report.

a. Why do you think the form has special instructions for problems encountered during online auctions?

_____

_____

b. Why does the form urge a user to be clear and concise when writing a **Summary of Events**?

_____

_____

c. Why would the Internet Fraud Watch want your credit card company but not your credit card number?

_____

_____

Extra Challenge

How has the Internet changed the way companies and consumers can exchange information about products and services? List three positive factors and three negative factors that can be traced to Internet technology.

FIGURE 8-5
The Internet Fraud Watch home page

Making Comparisons

Binary Compass, a company that prepares marketing research for other companies, is the creator of BizRate.com, an independent shopping and rating system for online stores. Binary Compass was founded in June 1996, with a mission "to facilitate widespread acceptance of electronic commerce by providing both consumers and merchants important information about one another." BizRate not only helps its visitors with comparison-shopping but it also gathers information from online customers and makes that information available to the public. Figure 8-6 shows some of the categories of BizRate information.

FIGURE 8-6
The *BizRate.com* home page

How does BizRate gather the information? If you order a toy from a participating online toy merchant, BizRate will contact you and ask you to complete a survey about your satisfaction with all phases of the online purchase. The retailer has been accepted as a gold star merchant, agreeing to allow BizRate access to its customers. Member merchants receive customer comments and can purchase other marketing research reports from Binary Compass Enterprises. In the following Step-by-Step, you'll examine the shopping and rating information found at *BizRate.com*.

S TEP-BY-STEP 8.3

1. Go to **www.BizRate.com** and click the link for **Jewelry and Watches**. Find a watch that you like and click **Compare prices and stores**. What information appears on this screen and how does it help the shopper?

_____

_____

STEP-BY-STEP 8.3 Continued

2. Click a smiley face in the SmileyScale rating for a store that sells the watch you have chosen. Look first at the Store Ratings Summary. Which of these four scales would be most important to you if you were ordering a watch? List your top two and explain why you chose them.

_____

_____

3. Click **See Detailed Store Ratings**. Click the link for **Store Information** in the Store Details box. This information is objective, however the ratings that appear are subjective assessments by customers. Is the combination of kinds of information important to you as a customer? If only five people had evaluated the site, would you place as much faith in the ratings?

_____

_____

4. Return to the BizRate home page and click **Store Ratings Guide** near the top of the page. Click the link to see all of the stores for a category of interest to you. Click the arrow in the **Sort This Table** box to sort the table by **Would Shop Here Again**. Examine the ratings of the top-rated store in the category, and then compare them to the ratings of the most poorly-rated store in the category. Note: Stores at the end of the list are not rated, so you will have to scroll through the list to find the lowest-rated store. Were all of the ratings worse in the second case, or was there one factor that led to the downfall of the worst store? If this were your store, how would you feel?

_____

_____

Wise Consumerism

When some people hear the word *consumer*, they automatically think of publications like *Consumer Reports* that provide ratings on consumer products. Others think of issue-oriented campaigns for product safety or fair pricing. The Internet is home to online versions of a number of sites that serve exactly these purposes. In Step-by-Step 8.3, you looked at ratings of merchants; in this Step-by-Step you'll see how to find ratings of products.

Did You Know?
Are you stuck with a car that you call a lemon? Legally, a *lemon* is a car with so many problems that the manufacturer repurchases it. Vehicle Identification Numbers of lemons have to be reported to the state. You can check to see if your clunker is really a lemon by submitting its VIN to the Carfax Lemon Check. This check is free. The company also sells information about your car's history.

STEP-BY-STEP 8.4

1. Begin your Web tour by visiting the online version of *Consumer Reports* magazine, shown in Figure 8-7. To read ratings of products, you must purchase a subscription to the online magazine. But there are features you can access without subscribing. Buying guides for products and links to selected articles, such as "Online Shopping: Then and Now," and topics from the current month's issue are available. Go to the site, choose a featured article that is interesting to you, and read it.

FIGURE 8-7
Consumer Reports Online

a. Why do you think the magazine chose to include this article?

_____

_____

b. Do you think that after reading it a person would be more interested in subscribing to the magazine? Explain.

_____

_____

STEP-BY-STEP 8.4 Continued

c. Visit two other large consumer sites. Go to **www.consumerreview.com**, shown in Figure 8-8, and **www.consumerworld.org**, shown in Figure 8-9. How would you use these two sites if you were buying a portable CD player?

_____

_____

FIGURE 8-8
ConsumerREVIEW

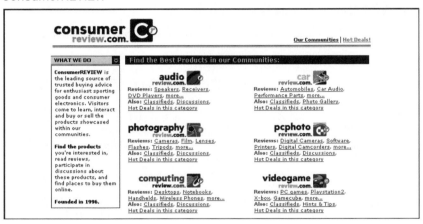

FIGURE 8-9
Consumer World

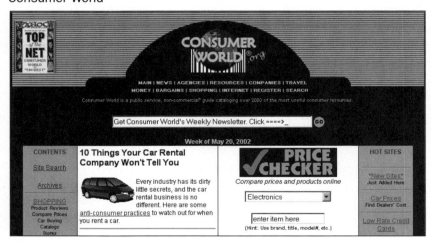

STEP-BY-STEP 8.4 Continued

2. The immediacy of the Internet makes it particularly useful for posting safety bulletins. In the United States, the Consumer Product Safety Commission is charged with reducing the risk of injury and death associated with the use of consumer products. This agency sets standards, evaluates products, and educates the public about safety hazards.

   a. Go to **www.cpsc.gov**, shown in Figure 8-10, and click the button for **Recalls/News**. What kinds of information did you find there?

   _____

   _____

FIGURE 8-10
The Consumer Product Safety Commission

STEP-BY-STEP 8.4 Continued

b. Some online stores also have links to safety information. Figure 8-11 shows information from the ToysRUs Recall Center at *Amazon.com*. How else could you find general information about product recalls? One way would be to do a general search for *product recall* with your search engine. Do this, and record below the names of three companies that have posted recalls of their products.

_____

_____

_____

FIGURE 8-11
Product recall information at the Amazon/ToysRUs site

c. Other than to comply with the legal requirements to post recall notices, why would a corporation use the Web for this purpose?

_____

_____

STEP-BY-STEP 8.4 Continued

3. When you visit company sites on the Internet, you may see the Better Business Bureau Online icon displayed. Figure 8-12 shows the icon on the BBBOnline site. Go to **www.bbbonline.org** and click **For Consumers**. Click the link for the **standards for ethical online business practices**. Click **FAQs** under **Reliability Seal**. What is the Reliability Seal and how is it different from the TRUSTe trustmark?

_____

_____

_____

> ### Extra Challenge
>
> _Consumer Reports_ reminds visitors over and over again that they accept no advertising. Other consumer sites put their advertisers on the home page. What effect do you feel these strategies have on the attitudes of the consumers who visit these sites?

FIGURE 8-12
BBBOnline site

BBB A Better Business Bureau® Program   For Consumers   For Businesses

BBBONLINE®   Other BBB Sites >

▼ **Consumer Information**

Safe Shopping Site

**Search Privacy
Participants**

FAQs

Consumer Benefits

**Report Misuse of
BBB**OnLine** Seals**

BBB Services

Other Resources

File a Complaint

▸ **BBB**OnLine** Programs**

▸ **BBB**OnLine** Information**

© 2002 Council of Better
Business Bureau, Inc.

Welcome to BBBOnLine's Safe Shopping Site

Use our safe shopping site to locate companies that are members of their local Better Business Bureau, pledge to meet the BBBOnLine Reliability **standards for ethical online business practices** and have agreed to resolve complaints using the BBB's dispute resolution program or a similar program. Companies must live up to these promises or lose the right to remain in our program.

Safe Shopping Site

Before engaging in an online transaction, look for the BBBOnLine Reliability seal.

Company/Keyword: [   ]

State/Province (VA): [   ]   Zip/Postal Code: [   ]

[Search]

▸ **Browse BBB**OnLine**'s Safe Shopping Site alphabetically**. (10954 web sites)

▸ **Locate a BBB**OnLine** Privacy Program Participant** (693 web sites)

feedback@cbbb.bbb.org | **Privacy Policy** | **Site Map** | **About Us**

SUMMARY

In this lesson, you learned:

■ How to evaluate the security and privacy of a site you visit.

■ You can access information about products and companies.

■ How to view customer evaluations for online businesses.

■ How to find product comparison and safety information online.

VOCABULARY *Review*

Define the following terms:
Lemon   Recall

REVIEW *Questions*

TRUE / FALSE

Circle T if the statement is true or F if the statement is false.

T   F   1. Security and privacy policies are important only if the Web site is making a sale.

T   F   2. The federal government, state attorney general offices, and local Better Business Bureaus can all provide consumer information.

T   F   3. Online merchants can earn the right to display icons that vouch for their trustworthiness.

T   F   4. If a consumer has a bad experience with an online merchant, there is nothing the consumer can do.

T   F   5. A lemon is a car that has been recalled.

WRITTEN QUESTIONS

Write a brief answer to the following questions.

1. Why is it important that your personal information remain secure online, even when a sales transaction is not conducted?

2. Where would you look for a company's statement on user privacy?

3. What would you look for at a corporate site if you had a problem with the company's product?

4. What does the BizRate company do?

5. If you were buying a large-screen television and needed to know how the features and prices of different models matched up, what kind of site would give you the information?

PROJECTS

 PROJECT 8-1

You are hosting a baby shower for friends who will make the world's most protective parents. The other guests know how concerned the parents will be, so they want to make sure their gifts are safe for the baby. They've asked you to check for rating information and product safety bulletins for pacifiers, strollers, baby carriers, and educational toys. They'd also like you to recommend an online store for baby things. Using BBBOnline, BizRate, and any other online resources, determine the products in these four categories that the other guests should avoid. Find three online stores that carry baby merchandise and that you would feel comfortable recommending.

  TEAMWORK PROJECT

Your team has been hired to recommend a cell phone plan for your consulting client. Use the Internet to comparison-shop. Determine a customer profile (business? individual? family?) and the amount of usage (weekday? weekend? evening?). Find the five best plans for your customer. Don't forget to investigate to see if there are any complaints about the phone companies or plans you recommend.

CRITICAL*Thinking*

 ACTIVITY 8-1

In this section, you've visited many online stores to see how they work, and you've learned some of the strategies buyers should follow when they shop online. In about 100 words, develop and explain *your* five principles for online purchasing.

BUYING ONLINE

REVIEW *Questions*

TRUE/FALSE

Circle T if the statement is true or F if the statement is false.

T   F   1. If you are shopping for a new car you can configure the model you want at the manufacturer's Web site.

T   F   2. You must use a credit card to make a purchase from an online retailer.

T   F   3. If a retailer provides tracking information to a customer, it is possible to determine the progress of the shipment and when it will be delivered.

T   F   4. Online auction sites are the online presence of corporate auction houses that sell expensive art and antiques.

T   F   5. To place a bid through an auction site, an individual must first be approved by the auction site.

T   F   6. The best way for a business to find a needed raw material, such as steel, would be to enter the word *steel* in a search engine.

T   F   7. B2B transactions include the exchange of data as well as the execution of purchases.

T   F   8. Logistics and distribution are parts of the supply chain that can be aided by the Internet.

T   F   9. In order to judge the reliability of an online retailer, look for the symbol of one of the organizations that evaluates sites.

T   F   10. Before submitting credit card or other secure information online, read and understand the site's security provisions.

MATCHING

Match the description in Column 2 to its correct term in Column 1.

Column 1

____ 1. eBay

____ 2. TRUSTe

____ 3. PayPal

____ 4. BizRate

____ 5. comparison-shop

____ 6. configure

____ 7. auction

____ 8. supply chain

____ 9. portal

____ 10. recall

Column 2

A. Company that awards reliability ratings to Web sites

B. Determine model specifications

C. Sale in which buyers offer larger and larger bids for merchandise

D. The collection of related companies and processes for manufacturing

E. Web site that provides an entry point to sites of common interest

F. Method to provide a payment interface between buyers and sellers

G. Examine features, prices, and availability of similar items

H. Manufacturer or agency has customers return items to be fixed or replaced

I. Popular auction site

J. Web company that collects and publishes consumer evaluations

PROJECTS

 PROJECT 3-1

After a vacation in the mountains, your family has become excited about building a vacation home in the woods. You volunteer to check the Web sites of log home manufacturers to begin to collect some information. Use your favorite search engine to look for the corporate sites of at least four manufacturers of log homes. Set up a grid that will allow you to comparison-shop among them. In the grid, list each manufacturer and the URL of its Web site, whether or not floor plans and model specifications are available online, whether pricing information is available online, whether you can buy directly from the manufacturer or have to go through a dealer, where you can find the nearest dealer or see a model home, and what kind of professional standards or consumer evaluations the manufacturer exhibits.

 PROJECT 3-2

As coffee lovers, you and two friends have decided that your town has room for another coffee shop and the three of you are the ones that can make it successful. You have leased property in a good location, have completed all of the legal work needed to open your business, and have found an excellent supplier for coffee beans. What you need to do now is find furniture and supplies. Using the B2B links at your favorite search engine, find sources for tables and chairs, paper goods (cups, napkins, utensils), cleaning supplies, and coffee brewing equipment. Choose one of the suppliers you found, and investigate what is required to do business with that company electronically. How are orders placed? Will you work with a salesperson? How is payment made? What kind of customer service is available?

 PROJECT 3-3

What is required before a business can display the TRUSTe trustmark, belong to the Better Business Bureau Online, or participate in BizRate? Investigate each of these from the perspective of an online office supply company and summarize the requirements.

SIMULATION

 JOB 3-1

Evan Peters is making great progress gathering inventory for his online store. He now knows more about the products he will sell and he is putting the finishing touches on his business plan. He knows, however, that to attract customers he will not only have to provide excellent service, but he will also have to price his items competitively. Evan could stroll through his local electronics superstore to check the retail prices for the merchandise that he is planning to sell, but he decides it would be much simpler to comparison-shop online. A friend has told him about the *MySimon.com* site and after visiting it, Evan decides that it would be a good source for price information.

Go to **www.mysimon.com,** or a similar site that offers price comparisons. Locate a cell phone, a color printer, a PDA, and a digital camera. Record the manufacturer and model number of each, and find the best price and source for each one. Then go to the Web site of an electronics superstore and see if you can find the price of the same item. Which site would be most useful for Evan to visit as his business expands and he needs to update prices?

 JOB 3-2

Gloria Fernandez, a Florida real estate agent, has a problem. The signs that her company places in the yards of listed properties need to be replaced, and the company that made the existing signs has gone out of business. Gloria wants to incorporate a new graphic design and to buy signs that have an attachment that allows the agent to include paper flyers with more information on the property. Using the search technique of your choice, help Gloria find a B2B source that will not only manufacture the signs but also offers graphic design consultation. Consider the ease and reliability of doing business electronically with this company. Do you feel comfortable recommending this company to Gloria?

DOING BUSINESS ON THE WEB

Unit 4

Estimated Time for Unit: 6 hours

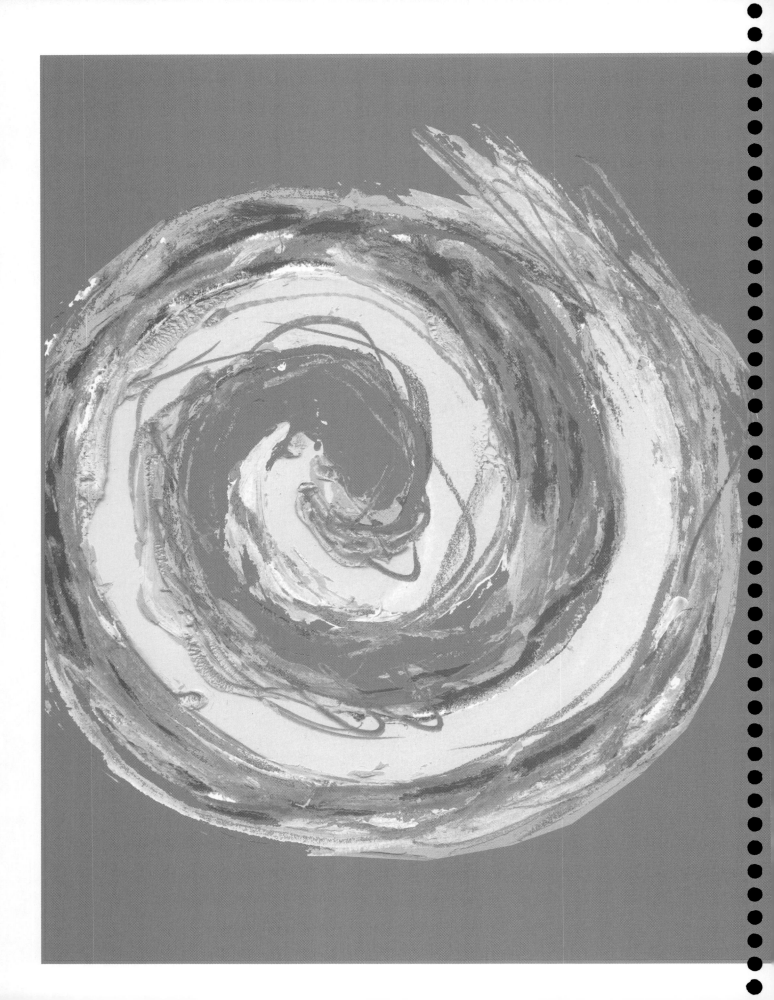

INTERNET MARKETING

Doing Business on the Web

In Units 1-3, you learned about e-commerce from a consumer's perspective. In this unit, you will begin to see e-commerce from the business's point of view. You will learn why and how companies use the Internet for business purposes.

Your work in this section will take you through the typical business marketing cycle. In this lesson, you will examine how your company can provide presale service, accept orders electronically, deliver some goods electronically, and provide post sale follow-up and customer service. You will see how a shipper can track packages electronically using the Internet. You will configure a customized personal computer through a Web page.

Businesses have found that e-mail based newsletters provide an inexpensive way to deliver their messages directly to the consumer. Lesson 10 includes a thorough discussion of digital advertising, including use of targeted advertising and banner ads. You will learn how an advertiser can achieve both richness and reach with Internet advertising. You will find out how to promote your Web site, including how to get it into the search engine listings.

If you're planning a visit to another country—or looking to open a business facility in another country—the Internet can help you learn the customs of that country. You can visit Web sites of global companies and access information originating in other countries. Lesson 11 covers the global perspectives of the Internet and electronic commerce.

> **Net Tip**
>
> For a good presentation of reasons to do e-commerce, see "20 Reasons to Put Your Business on the WWW," by Stormy Knight, at *www.net101.com/reasons.html*.

Marketing Through a New Medium

Companies have been marketing products to consumers through traditional media—TV, magazines, billboards, etc.—for decades. Marketing managers take advantage of the characteristics of each medium in implementing their marketing plan. Now marketers have a new medium with its own unique qualities: The Internet.

Marketing products to consumers is a four-phase process:

1. Providing presale information.

2. Taking the order.

3. Delivering the product.

4. Providing post-sale customer service.

The Internet offers some unique advantages for marketers in each phase of the marketing process.

Presale

Let's say that you are the owner of a small company, and you would like to start using the Internet to grow your business. The first thing you must do to market to your customers is advertise your products. On the Internet, your main advertising tool is a Web site with lots of product information. Because customers look for vendors through search tools like Yahoo or Lycos, make sure your Web site is located in the search tool catalogs. Another advertising possibility is to send e-mail messages to targeted customers with a Web link to your Web site. You can also place ads at other companies' Web sites, with links to your own site.

Taking the Order

Once customers reach your Web site, they can browse through your online catalog to locate the product they want. You might want to catch their eye by featuring sale items on your home page. Once customers make their product selection, your Web site can take their order or direct them to your telephone number or to your retail store. Most electronic commerce sites encrypt or code personal information, such as a credit card numbers, for security.

Delivering the Products

After customers place their orders, they can track the progress of their orders by visiting the customer service section of your Web site. If you sell products such as software, maps, or research data, you could even deliver the product itself through the Internet.

Postsale

After your customers receive their products, they might want to learn more about the product or ask a question about its functions. To give your customers good service after the sale, you could place common questions and answers on your Web site. You could also provide directions for returning or exchanging the product at your site. To answer more technical questions, you could include a link to the manufacturer's Web site.

Gathering feedback from your customers is always important for helping you improve your products and marketing effort. To gather feedback, you could include a follow-up questionnaire on your Web site to find out about your customers' satisfaction with your company's product and service.

As you can see, the Internet offers several valuable marketing opportunities in all phases of the marketing process. Doing business online is less costly than interacting with customers at a retail store or through a catalog operation. It is also an inexpensive way to distribute your product information and gather information from and about your customers. With information you gather about customer interests, you can use the Internet to create a unique message tailored to those individuals that are most likely to be interested in your product.

Phase 1: Presale

The Internet offers many opportunities for conveying your advertising message to your customers. You can set up an electronic showroom for your customers to browse. Your site can make it easy for customers to order product literature, comparison-shop, or "test drive" your product's features. You might even offer free sample products. Not only is online advertising cost per customer much less than with printed catalogs, but also you can provide multimedia features in your online product displays.

You can also gather information about potential customers. A Web *hit counter* is an electronic device that keeps track of the number of customers that visit your site during a particular time period, and provides limited identity information about them. You can learn what Web pages visitors have navigated and even what Web sites they came from when they arrived at your site. In fact, some advertising rates are based on the number of people that click on an ad taking them to that advertiser's Web page.

By offering giveaways to entice customers to fill out a brief electronic survey, you can update your customer database and mailing list. Once the customers are in your database, it is easy to send periodic e-mail messages about special offers. Your message can refer customers to your storefront Web site with a built-in hyperlink. Unlike radio and television advertising, you can target messages to a particular consumer.

> ### Did You Know?
> An *embedded hyperlink* is a link between one object and another that, when clicked, opens your browser and loads the linked document or Web site. Some e-mail programs automatically create or "embed" a hyperlink when you type a URL. All your e-mail receiver needs to do is click on the embedded hyperlink to go to the linked site. This is a great way to encourage potential customers to visit your Web site.

Let's take a look at some of the types of advertising you can use to let your customers know about your company and products. You will learn more about Internet advertising in Lesson 10.

STEP-BY-STEP 9.1

1. A *banner ad* is a boxed advertisement that appears on a Web page and usually has a hyperlink to the advertiser's own Web site. You can use a banner ad to target customers with a particular interest in your type of products. To see how this works, open Yahoo and search for "basketball" as the keyword.

   a. What banner ad or sponsored link does Yahoo display on the page of matches to basketball Web sites?

   _____

   _____

STEP-BY-STEP 9.1 Continued

    b. Why do you think this advertiser chose to place a banner ad or sponsored link on this page?

_____

_____

    c. How does this banner ad target customers that might have an interest in the advertiser's product?

_____

_____

  2. Now search Yahoo using the keywords below. What product did the banner ad feature on the list of search matches? What customer interest does each ad target?

SEARCH KEYWORD	ADVERTISED PRODUCT	TARGETED INTEREST
a. Hawaii		
b. computer		
c. newspaper		
d. wireless		
e. family		

  3. Many companies use sweepstakes or giveaways to gather information about customers for future targeted mailings. Figure 9-1 shows the results of clicking the Sweepstakes link at the OfficeMax Web site. If OfficeMax is no longer offering giveaways, search for this text's home page at _www.course.com/ downloads_ to find a link to a site that is offering them. Follow the links to the sweepstakes details.

    a. How is the company gathering information about its customers through the sweepstakes?

_____

_____

    b. What kind of information is it collecting that will help the company market itself to customers?

_____

_____

    c. What incentives is it offering to customers to encourage them to provide this information?

_____

_____

STEP-BY-STEP 9.1 Continued

FIGURE 9-1
OfficeMax sweepstakes page

4. Many Web sites keep information about customers in a small text file called a "cookie" located on the customer's own hard drive. As you learned in Lesson 6, a cookie allows the Web site to identify a previous visitor and quickly display information about that customer. Figure 9-2 shows the home page of *Amazon.com*. Notice that the name of one of the authors of this text, Bruce J. McLaren, and links to his account appear on the page. When McLaren registered at Amazon, he provided the requested information about himself, and the site stored the information in a cookie on his hard drive. Then when he returned to the site, the site retrieved this information from the cookie and used it to personalize Amazon's Web page for him. In this case, Amazon "knows" what books he has previously ordered and automatically displays similar titles that he might wish to consider.

   a. Go to the Amazon Web site at **www.amazon.com**, and read about "Your Account." If you wish, follow the instructions to create an account. In what ways will Amazon personalize the Web site for you?

   _____

   _____

STEP-BY-STEP 9.1 Continued

b. What kinds of information about you do you think the company would store on the cookie to personalize the site for you?

_____

_____

_____

_____

c. How does personalizing benefit the company?

_____

_____

_____

_____

Hot Tip

Generally speaking, it is unwise to create a cookie on a computer in a public area, such as a library or school computer lab. Any one of a number of users could use that computer and gain access to your private information. So only personalize a Web site when you are working at your own machine.

Extra Challenge

Are you likely to click an embedded hyperlink in a company's e-mail to visit its Web site and view its products? When would you consider a particular e-mail "junk" and not read it? What would you do in an e-mail to encourage customers to visit your company site?

FIGURE 9-2
Amazon.com online store with personal information

Phase 2: Taking the Order

O nce your customers have made a selection, you must give them a painless way to order it. Some Web sites are designed to funnel customers to a salesperson at a retail store or on a toll-free telephone line. This approach may work best for complex products because customers are likely to have questions about such products. Even with simpler products for which online ordering is easy, you might want to provide an option for customers to talk to a salesperson. For people that are uneasy about providing credit card or other personal information online, talking to a live person might spell the difference between making and losing the sale.

> **Net Tip**
>
> Gateway has another way to communicate with potential customers. Their eSales system lets the customer engage in an online chat session with a live Gateway sales agent. This way the person can ask questions while looking at the configuration information from the Gateway Web site.

Of course, customers have to pay for the goods. For ordering online, you can provide a secure Web site that scrambles credit card numbers so that others cannot read them. The closed lock in the status bar of Figure 9-3 indicates a secure transaction; an open (or missing) lock means a normal session. Also, the URL in the address bar of a secure site will begin with "https" rather than "http." Your Web site must verify that the credit card number is authentic and that your customer has sufficient credit to pay for the transaction. You'll learn more about electronic payment systems in Appendix C.

FIGURE 9-3
Secure transaction in Internet Explorer browser

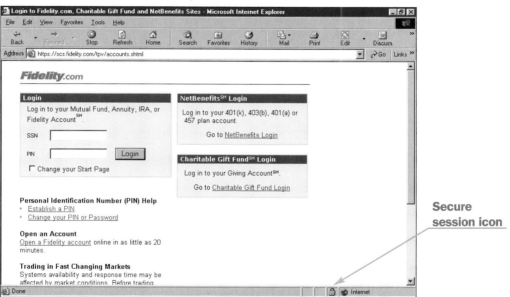

To make electronic ordering easy for your customers, your Web site can display a form on the screen. In Lesson 6, you saw an electronic shopping cart used at *Amazon.com* and other online stores. Customers use the electronic shopping cart to "hold" their orders until they are ready to check out, just like the shopping cart in a grocery store. A cookie keeps track of customers' selections as they shop. Then the selections appear on their order form when they are ready to check out.

The order form should also provide shipping information. Customers can specify the type of shipping and enter a shipping address and an e-mail address. Many companies send an e-mail message to confirm receipt of the order and to give an estimated shipping time. For out-of-stock products, another e-mail message can notify the customer when the product is ready to ship.

> **Did You Know?**
>
> The process of scrambling credit card information for security purposes is called *encryption*. You'll find out more about encryption in Appendix C.

> **Hot Tip**
>
> Never enter your credit card number or other sensitive information unless your browser displays the secure transaction indicators.

S TEP-BY-STEP 9.2

SCANS

1. Connect your browser to the PC Connection Web site pictured in Figure 9-4. Search the catalog for "virus." Pick one antivirus product. What kinds of information does the catalog give for that product? What other information about that product would you like to see in the PC Connection online catalog?

_____

_____

FIGURE 9-4
PC Connection home page

STEP-BY-STEP 9.2 Continued

2. Add the antivirus product to your shopping cart. Select another kind of product and add it to your cart. Then click the **View/Checkout** button, as shown in Figure 9-4. Notice that the selections are conveniently listed and totaled. Now click the **Buy (Secure)** button. *Unless you want the products, don't fill out or submit the order form!*

a. What kinds of information does the order form collect?

_____

_____

b. How can this information help the business to market products to this same customer in the future?

_____

_____

3. Visit the CDNOW Web site and look for an album by Faith Hill or your favorite artist. What information does the CDNOW online catalog provide for that album? What other information would you like to have as a consumer?

_____

_____

4. Go to the Gateway Web site at **www.gateway.com**. Click the link for **Home Notebooks**. Select one of the models, and click the **Customize** button. Configure an entry-level notebook computer for a college-bound student. Be sure to click **update total** if you made changes to the standard configuration. Notice that the configuration sheet shows both the Web ordering link and the telephone number to speak to a salesperson. Would you prefer to purchase this product through the Internet or by a toll-free telephone number? Why?

_____

_____

Extra Challenge

You have looked at several online catalogs in this Step-by-Step. From what you have seen, what characteristics make an online product catalog effective? How would you improve upon the ones you've seen?

Net Business

Amazon.com single-handedly created a new kind of virtual company—one that doesn't really exist in the physical sense. The company has minimal actual inventory and no storefronts, but it does have a huge product catalog and the ability to get books shipped to customers very quickly. *Amazon.com* uses its own and other book distributors' warehouses, and clever information systems that pick the closest shipping point to a customer. But not all the marketing for *Amazon.com* is done on the Internet. It uses television advertising to draw customers to its Web site. Why do you think *Amazon.com* was instantly successful in e-commerce? Why do you think some people would prefer not to purchase a book or compact disc from an online company?

Phase 3: Delivering the Products

Most products and services cannot be delivered electronically over the Internet, so this marketing phase of online commerce usually means tracking the progress of goods that are shipped by conventional means. Of course, products like software can be delivered instantly over the Internet by downloading the files.

One of the most popular products delivered online is information, such as custom newsletters, specialized news stories, personalized stock prices, legal cases, and the like. For information products, the Internet saves customers significant time because they don't have to visit the library or wait until the information is printed and mailed. Refer back to Figure 9-3, which is a Web page from Fidelity Investments. Financial sites like this deliver information in the form of stock quotes, financial news, and educational materials about investing.

> **Did You Know?**
>
> Music files are huge and must be compressed to travel quickly over the Internet. *MP3* is a compression format that has revolutionized the way high-quality digital music can be delivered over the Internet. MP3 stands for the MPEG 1, level 3, standard for compressing music and speech. You can identify MP3 filenames by their extension "mp3." See *www.mp3.com* for information about MP3 music titles.

Many e-business Web sites sell tickets for events or take reservations for hotel rooms, rental cars, campground spaces, and rental boats. Some airlines use only eTickets so nothing is actually delivered, except the ticket number; all of the information is maintained on the computer's database and the customer presents identification at the gate. The customer usually receives a confirming e-mail message that can be printed for reference.

Some companies promote their products by delivering free samples over the Internet. For example, CDNOW offers free audio samples of the music it sells, so you can hear it before you buy it. Let's take a look at some of the products now being delivered electronically.

S TEP-BY-STEP 9.3

1. Suppose you are planning to do some hiking and need U.S. Geological Survey topographical maps. Visit the MapMart Web site at **www.mapmart.com** shown in Figure 9-5. Follow the **Scanned Topo Maps** link to the map download section for your community.

   a. What image file formats are available?

   _____

   _____

   b. What is the price for twelve 1-meter black and white maps?

   _____

   _____

   c. How long does it take to download a sample map with a 28.8 modem?

   _____

   d. How much does a state bundle for Maine cost?

   _____

FIGURE 9-5
MapMart Maps

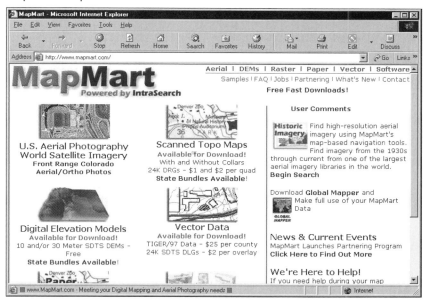

STEP-BY-STEP 9.3 Continued

2. In Lesson 4, you learned about the kinds of information that some financial sites offer subscribers. At some financial sites, you can get specialized financial research reports delivered online by becoming a member. Figure 9-6 shows online growth fund prices from Fidelity Investments. You can also subscribe to popular periodicals online. Visit Business Week Online to see how to order an online subscription. What does the subscription cost? How would the online magazine differ from what is delivered to your physical mailbox?

FIGURE 9-6
Fidelity Investments growth fund prices

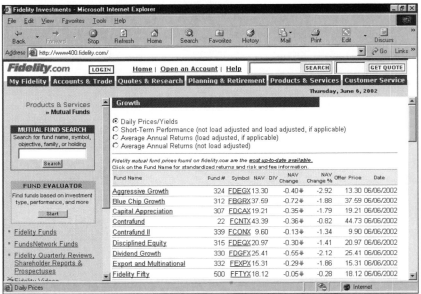

STEP-BY-STEP 9.3 Continued

3. Both UPS and FedEx have extensive online Web sites for providing customer service. The FedEx tracking page is shown in Figure 9-7. Visit the UPS site and locate the nearest drop-off point for your package. Use your home or school address.

a. Why is it better for the customer to use the Web site rather than other ways of finding this information?

_____

_____

b. List three other services for shippers at the UPS Web site.

_____

_____

FIGURE 9-7
FedEx tracking page

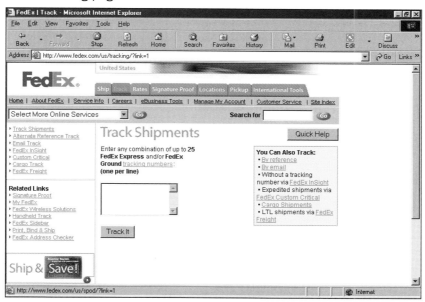

4. Suppose you have purchased a U.S. Robotics V.90 modem and want to upgrade it to the new V.92 standard. Visit the USR Web site at **www.usr.com**, and learn how you can upgrade your modem by simply downloading a software patch. Would you rather upgrade your current modem by downloading a patch or buy a new V.92 modem that contains the new capability? Why?

_____

_____

> **Net Fun**
>
> Some radio stations have placed their broadcasts on the Web. Sporting events are especially popular for fans. Visit the Yahoo Broadcast site at *broadcast.yahoo.com* and select a radio station to hear. What other types of information can you hear from this site?

STEP-BY-STEP 9.3 Continued

5. The Hilton Hotel company offers a frequent-traveler program called Hilton HHonors. Not only does the traveler accumulate points for staying at a Hilton property such as Hampton Inns or Embassy Suites, but can also earn bonus points for reserving rooms online. Go to the **HiltonHHonors.com** Web site to learn more about this program. Which hotels are eligible for this program? How many bonus points are earned when you book a room online?

Extra Challenge

Using a FedEx or UPS package tracking number, you can track a package's shipping details from pickup to delivery at the company's Web site. From the perspective of the shipping company, why would you want to offer an online package tracking service? How does this online system benefit your company?

Phase 4: Postsale

Marketing doesn't end with the delivery of the products. After the sale, you need to provide customer service. E-mail and a friendly form on your Web site are easy tools for communicating with your customers. When customers order a book from Amazon.com, they receive, several weeks later, a friendly letter from the company president, thanking them for their order and suggesting other books by the same author or on a similar subject.

Often after customers receive their products, they have questions about product features or how to use the products. Rather than fielding all customer questions by phone, you could post an online FAQ list. A *FAQ (frequently asked question)* list provides answers to common customer questions. In many cases, your customers can find out what they want to know from the FAQs, and you don't have to pay the cost of having enough employees to handle every customer question personally.

Sometimes customers misplace their instruction manual or configuration guide. You can deliver a replacement to them as quickly as browsing the Web and printing it out. Not only is this less costly than working through a human customer service agent, but it is also quicker and certainly less trouble than faxing the missing documents.

PDF (portable document format) is a file format generated by the Adobe Acrobat program that makes it possible to download and read files on different computers. To read PDF files on any machine, users need the Acrobat Reader program. This program can be downloaded free from the Adobe Systems Web site at *www.adobe.com* or at many sites that feature PDF documents. Using PDF, companies can make even complicated technical drawings available for customers to download, view, and print out. For example, Figure 9-8 shows technical information about installing a microwave oven, delivered as a PDF file. PDF files can be very large, so downloading them can take longer than other types of files.

FIGURE 9-8
Microwave installation sheet in PDF

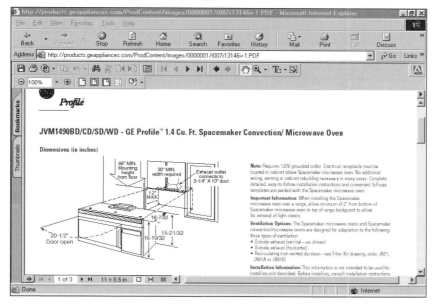

You can also use your online customer database for additional product surveys and questionnaires delivered via e-mail, often with a link to an easy-to-answer Web site form. Your customer database serves as an e-mail listing for sending promotional messages, starting the marketing cycle again.

STEP-BY-STEP 9.4

1. Maxtor is a manufacturer of popular hard drives for personal computers. Maxtor drives are frequently used to upgrade a computer to a larger hard drive, purchased after the original. Open the Maxtor Web site at **www.maxtor.com**. Switch to the **Product Support** page. In the second Desktop Drives ATA combo box, select **DiamondMax Ultra ATA** as shown in Figure 9-9. What kinds of support services are available at this Web site?

_____

_____

FIGURE 9-9
Maxtor Product Support home page

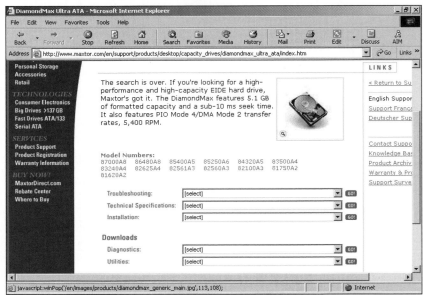

2. Suppose a customer needs to return a Maxtor drive for repair. Investigate the information that must be included with the packing slip. Why is it important for Maxtor to have this information?

_____

_____

 Net Ethics

Some customers use the Internet to locate products of interest, and then visit a local store to examine the products carefully and ask questions of the salesperson. Is it ethical for them to turn around and order the same product from a Web site, depriving the local store of its revenue for that item?

STEP-BY-STEP 9.4 Continued

3. Assume you are selling a non-technical product, such as a compact disc or book, via e-commerce. Brainstorm with a friend about the sorts of post-sale customer service features you could add to a Web site or accomplish through electronic mail. List three ways these postsale-efforts could be used as the pre-sale phase of someone's *next* purchase:

_____

_____

_____

4. If you worked in a Rubbermaid customer service office, would you prefer to talk to a customer on the phone or through e-mail? What are the advantages and disadvantages of each?

_____

_____

_____

Extra Challenge

Think of a situation in which a thoughtful customer service representative solved a problem for you after you bought a product, and convinced you to buy another product from that company. How can the Internet be used to provide good customer service?

SUMMARY

In this lesson, you learned:

- Your customers can find out about you and your products through Internet advertising.
- You can sell products through online catalogs and order systems.
- You can track and deliver products using the Internet.
- You can give your customers post-sale services electronically.

VOCABULARY *Review*

Define the following terms:		
Banner ad	FAQ (frequently asked	MP3
Embedded hyperlink	question)	PDF (portable document
Encryption	Hit counter	format)

REVIEW *Questions*

TRUE/FALSE

Circle T if the statement is true or F if the statement is false.

T F 1. Web site sweepstakes can be used to develop a mailing list of information about potential customers.

T F 2. A banner ad often has a hyperlink that takes the viewer to the advertiser's own Web site.

T F 3. Although orders can be taken over the Internet, the product purchased must be delivered by a delivery service like FedEx, UPS, or the US Postal Service.

T F 4. A cookie is a text file that provides information about a previous visitor to a particular Web site.

T F 5. A FAQ is a file format generated by the Adobe Acrobat program that makes it possible to download and read a file on different computers.

WRITTEN QUESTIONS

Write a brief answer to the following questions.

1. Why would a company use an online sweepstakes giveaway through its Web site?

2. What types of products would be difficult to sell through the Internet? Why?

3. Why should you have an e-mail program that supports embedded hyperlinks?

4. How can companies use cookies to personalize their Web pages?

5. Why is PDF useful for distributing files through the Web?

PROJECTS

 PROJECT 9-1

Go to the Dell Computers Web site and analyze the way Dell accomplishes the four phases of marketing presented in this lesson. For each phase, record what the site shows or asks you to do. What are your reactions? Would you, as a customer, feel comfortable buying this way? If you were a Dell marketing manager, how would you improve the site to market your products more effectively?

 PROJECT 9-2

Catelynn is driving from St. Louis to New York City for a summer internship job interview. She needs to stay in a hotel along I-70 near Columbus, Ohio. Because she has a Hilton HHonors card, she wants to stay in a Hampton Inn. Use the Hampton Inn Web site to search for hotels in this area.

1. List the Hampton Inn hotels in the area. What is the address and telephone number for the property closest to I-70?

    _____

2. Select the hotel closest to I-70. Select a date, and then find the cost of a King Standard room with a AAA discount. How much is saved with the AAA discount?

    _____

3. How much notice is required to avoid a penalty if Catelynn cancels the reservation?

    _____

4. How does the online reservation feature help Hampton Inn manage its information more efficiently?

    _____

PROJECT 9-3

Go to the "20 Reasons" Web site cited in the Net Tip at the beginning of this lesson and read through the set of reasons why a company would want to do business on the Internet. For each of the following service companies, pick the three most important reasons for each to do business on the Internet and explain why. Would you recommend that any of these types of firms *not* do business on the Internet? Why?

1. Hotel/marina in a resort area (**www.moorsresort.com**)
    A. _____
    B. _____
    C. _____

2. Real estate company (**www.beverly-hanks.com**)
   A. _____
   B. _____
   C. _____

3. Web development company (**www.seventy-twodpi.com**)
   A. _____
   B. _____
   C. _____

  TEAMWORK PROJECT

Each member of your team should examine the home page of a different sort of online seller. You might include an apparel company (The Gap), a computer company (Gateway), a consumer products company (GE), a services company (Marriott), and a gourmet coffee company (Starbucks). Each group member should write down at least five features that the site uses to market to consumers. Also analyze how each feature contributes to the company's marketing efforts.

Compare your lists. Although these sites offer diverse products, what similar features do they have? How are they different? Why do you think these differences exist? Make a presentation that summarizes your findings.

CRITICAL*Thinking*

 ACTIVITY 9-1

How do you feel about cookies? Is this an invasion of privacy? On a separate piece of paper, write a 100-word summary that a business could use to justify its use of cookies to a user who thinks cookies are invasive.

DIGITAL ADVERTISING

OBJECTIVES

Upon completion of this lesson, you should be able to:

- Subscribe to e-mail services and discuss how to use e-mail effectively for advertising your business.

- Describe types of banner advertising on the Web and discuss the benefits and drawbacks of each type.

- Discuss ways to promote your company Web site and get your site in a search engine's catalog.

Estimated Time: 2 hours

VOCABULARY

Alt-text lines

Animated GIF ad

Cooperative ads

CPM (cost per thousand)

Demographics

Dynamic ads

E-mail ads

HTML-enhanced e-mail

Mailing list service (LISTSERV)

Pixel

Pop-under ads

Pop-up ads

Portal sites

Reach

Richness

Rotation ad

Spam

Static ad

Web spider

Richness and Reach on the Internet

Advertising traditionally requires a tradeoff between richness and reach. *Richness* is the degree to which the ad content can be designed for a specific market segment. *Reach* refers to how many people view the ad. Television as a medium has great reach, in that many people view TV ads, but the ads are the same for everyone. A personalized letter or a sales call have great richness, in that the message can be tailored specifically to the needs of the person addressed, but it reaches only that person. In the past, advertising could have either richness or reach, but not both.

The Internet age brings a new way of communicating with potential customers. Most companies doing e-commerce advertise their products through targeted e-mail and banner ads that appear when customers search for certain keywords. Ads can have both richness and reach. Creating and placing these messages in banner ads and e-mail is a way to draw customers to the company's Web site.

Demographics are characteristics of human populations, such as age, gender, income, and ethnic background. Advertisers collect demographic information to help them target their ad messages to particular groups of customers. For example, if your company sells baby clothes, your advertising would be most effective if you could send it to just parents with babies.

You can collect demographic information for your customer database through various methods, including surveys, sweepstakes giveaways, product registrations, or even buying the information from other companies. Along with typical demographic information, such as age and gender, you would probably also want to collect e-mail addresses and interests. Once you have captured your customers' information in your database, you can target your advertising message to particular customer groups. For example, if you run a sporting goods store, you can write an e-mail message promoting your camping equipment to all customers between the ages of 18 and 30 that like to camp. Your message will have richness, because it is specifically tailored to customers with an interest in what you are selling. It also has reach, because you can send an e-mail to many customers at once.

In this lesson you will examine various types of advertising and learn ways to promote your company's Web site so that it will appear in search engine lists of potential sites when someone searches.

> **Net Fun**
>
> Many companies generate interest in their Web sites by offering contests and sweepstakes. Check out the Sweepstakes-Online Web site to see what contests are being offered each day.

E-mail Marketing

The most common type of Internet advertising uses electronic mail messages sent to individuals whose names and other information is maintained in a database. *E-mail ads* are inexpensive, easy to send, and hard to ignore in the recipient's inbox. The ads describe the company's products and services, and usually include one or more links to the company's Web site.

You can add customer names to your company database in several ways:

- Purchase the names from another company

- Have customers add their names and information through online surveys when they visit your Web site

- Pick up the names when customers make a purchase

- Pick up the names when customers enter a sweepstakes

- Acquire the names in normal "bricks and mortar" (not e-commerce) business transactions

E-mail ads can be complete as sent or can contain an embedded hyperlink to a Web site. In fact, most e-mail ads are linked to a Web server with much more information. Many of the e-mail messages work best with *HTML-enhanced e-mail* programs, which are capable of displaying messages with embedded HTML commands that link to Web pages. Eudora, Netscape's Messenger e-mail client, Outlook Express, and Microsoft Outlook all support HTML e-mail. HTML e-mail contains graphic images, fonts, and colors and resembles a Web page. You will learn more about HTML in Lessons 12 and 13.

> **Net Tip**
>
> Your e-mail message is not properly configured to handle HTML-enhanced e-mail if it contains text that looks like this: *Savings on popular products like HP, Canon, Epson, Compaq and Lexmark!* http://www.flowgo.com/ page.cfm?lk=26808<a href="http://www.flowgo.com/ page.cfm?lk=26808"> AOL Link</a>

Figure 10-1 shows an e-mail ad from Staples, notifying customers of weekly specials and linking to the company's Web site for full details. This ad also contains a special sale for first-time online buyers. What type of customer do you think Staples is targeting in this e-mail ad?

FIGURE 10-1
Staples e-mail advertisement

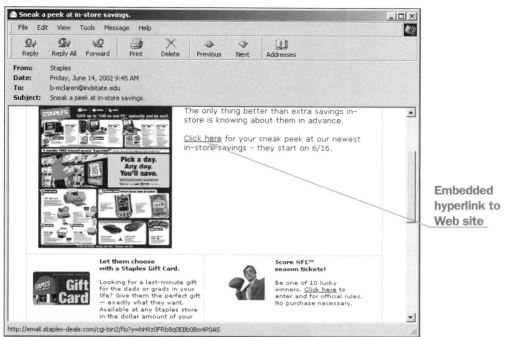

Embedded hyperlink to Web site

You can electronically group customer e-mail addresses in your database according to common demographic characteristics. For example, you could group together all customers who have purchased ski equipment from your sporting goods store or expressed interest in skiing in a survey. Then when you have a sale on ski accessories, you can send an e-mail to these customers, and not send it to other customers who have not shown an interest in skiing.

Another way to target specific customer groups with an e-mail ad is to advertise with an Internet mailing list service. A *mailing list service* is an automated e-mail system on the Internet, maintained by subject matter. Internet users subscribe to the service if they are interested in the service's subject, such as sports news, reports of snow conditions in the mountains, or any of thousands of subjects offered this way. New users generally subscribe by sending an e-mail with the word "subscribe" in it, and then automatically receive all e-mail reports sent to the list of subscribers. Such a service is often called a "*LISTSERV*" after the popular software used to maintain mailing lists. Such a service is also called a discussion group because participants can discuss issues online.

Did You Know?

Because members of mailing lists might want to discontinue the service at some time, virtually every e-mail message to subscribers has a section at the end that explains how to remove your name from the mailing list. This is known as unsubscribing from the mailing list.

For your sporting goods store, a mailing list service identifies potential customers for you and gives you a way to reach them. People who have subscribed to receive reports about snow conditions in the mountains would likely be interested in your ski equipment. If you advertise with this mailing list, then your ski equipment ad will be placed on the e-mail reports that go to the list's subscribers. Again, you get the benefit of both richness and reach in your e-mail ad.

Spam is unsolicited e-mail that is sent to many addresses at the same time. Most people consider spam to be junk mail and it tarnishes the image of the sender. E-mail marketing experts recommend creating high quality e-mail messages as well as giving the recipient a way to opt out of the message database. Numerous software publishers have created anti-spam software that helps protect against unwanted incoming e-mail messages. The *www.fraud.org* site contains useful information from the National Consumer's League about such e-mail fraud.

Did You Know?

Many online companies agree to a privacy code that says they will not share customer information with any other organization without the explicit permission of the customer. They ask subscribers at the time of registration whether they will allow their names or e-mail addresses to be used outside that organization. Customers can change that election at any time.

STEP-BY-STEP 10.1

1. One popular mailing list service is InfoBeat. Its e-mail reports are free, and the ads pay for the cost of providing the service. InfoBeat delivers customized e-mail messages to thousands of subscribers each day. Go to the InfoBeat Web site, shown in Figure 10-2. Name three mailing list subjects available at this site. What types of products might a retailer promote to each mailing list?

MAILING LIST SUBJECT	PRODUCTS TO PROMOTE TO THIS LIST
a.	
b.	
c.	

FIGURE 10-2
InfoBeat home page

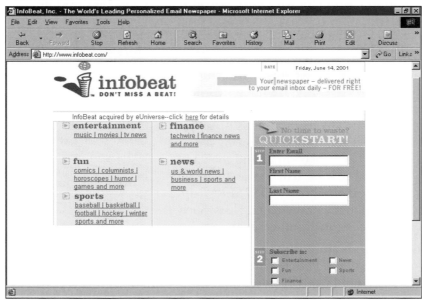

STEP-BY-STEP 10.1 Continued

2. From the InfoBeat home page, select the **Entertainment** service. Describe the entertainment services available at this section. What advertisers might be interested in using this section for promoting their products?

_____

_____

3. Subscribe to the TV News service at InfoBeat. You must have a valid e-mail address to subscribe. Figure 10-3 shows a portion of the InfoBeat Finance e-mail newsletter.

FIGURE 10-3
InfoBeat's Finance e-mail newsletter

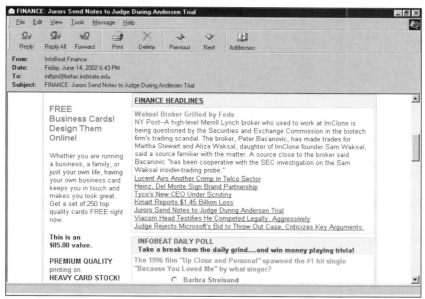

a. Print a copy of an actual e-mail message from this service when it arrives in your e-mail inbox. What advertisement(s) appear in the message you received?

_____

_____

b. Does your e-mail program support the embedded hyperlinks to the advertisers' sites?

_____

c. Does your e-mail program support HTML mail? How can you tell if it does not support HTML mail?

_____

_____

4. Follow the directions to unsubscribe if you no longer want to receive the messages from Infobeat.

STEP-BY-STEP 10.1 Continued

5. Now visit the Cross pen Web site at **www.cross.com**.

    a. What advantages does the customer have for registering at the site?

    _____

    _____

    b. View the Cross privacy policy contained in the **About Cross** link. How do customers indicate whether they wish to receive e-mail announcements of special sales?

    _____

    _____

6. Open the Exact Target Web site at **www.exacttarget.com**. Click the **Products** link and then click **Connect link**.

    a. How could a company wishing to do an e-mail marketing campaign use this e-mail marketing software?

    _____

    _____

    b. What reports does this software provide for a company that uses this software to generate an e-mail marketing campaign?

    _____

    _____

> ### Extra Challenge
>
> Web marketing companies like BullsEyeEmail offer mass e-mail services to corporations. Why would a company want to use the services of a firm like this? How could a college benefit from having regular e-mail messages go out to prospective students?

Banner Advertising

Banner ads appear on Web pages usually as a rectangular image. Most banner ads contain a link to the advertiser's Web site for the viewer to click. Unlike print advertising, banner ads can not only grab the customers' attention, but also in seconds they can supply customers with detailed information about the ad's contents—right on their own computers!

> ### Net Fun
>
> If you have a Yahoo ID, you can establish alerts at Yahoo. Yahoo will send you an e-mail message when there is breaking news in the categories you select.

Static ads are advertisements that always appear in a given location on the Web page, similar to an ad in a magazine or newspaper. These ads appear regardless of the key words used to arrive at the site. Advertisers pay rates based on the number of hits on the Web page containing the ad, with a bonus if the viewer clicks on the ad. Check out the URL of a hyperlink in a Web banner ad, and you will usually see extra codes at the end that tell the advertiser where the user came from and/or where to search. The advertiser can use this information to make decisions about future advertising placement. Ad rates for some ads are based on how many hits came from a specific location. Figure 10-4 shows a banner ad at the *New York Times* site. When the pointer is over the banner ad, as in the illustration, the hyperlink shows in the status bar. Notice the extra information at the end of the URL.

FIGURE 10-4
Hyperlink for banner ad

Animated GIF banner ad

Hyperlink for banner ad with ad information

Some banner ads are animated, drawing your eye and increasing the likelihood that you will click on the ad to find more information. These *animated GIF (graphic interchange format) ads* are often much larger and take longer to load than do nonanimated ads. Although not depicted in the restricted environment of the printed page, the ad in Figure 10-4 is animated on the Web, flipping between two different messages.

Companies choose to advertise on Web sites that draw the types of people who would most likely be interested in their products. A computer hardware company's Web site might contain ads by software firms that produce products that run on those computers. In some cases, companies have reciprocal agreements that allow each to put advertisements on the other's Web site. These *cooperative ads* are pairs of ads placed in complementary sites. Viewers at one site would likely be interested in products at the other site. For example, the PC Connection home page highlights computers made by a certain manufacturer. When you get to that manufacturer's Web site, you will find PC Connection listed first among the online sellers.

Search engine sites are often called *portal sites*, because they are natural starting points for users. A portal site contains links to other sites, acting as a doorway or portal. Because popular sites like Yahoo and MSN are in the top three sites for Web activity, they are popular among advertisers that want to capture more viewers.

Did You Know?

The Jupiter MediaMetrix Web site compiles lists of the most popular Web and digital media properties based on unique visitors. They show U.S. and global rankings. In April 2002 the top three sites were the AOL/Time Warner network, MSN/Microsoft sites, and Yahoo sites.

In the last lesson, you saw how entering subject keywords in a search engine brings up an advertisement related to that subject at the top of the search results. These ads are called *dynamic ads*, because they only appear when users select a particular subject. Advertisers prefer dynamic advertising, because they know the viewer is already interested in topics that pertain to their products.

One way to improve the effectiveness of your advertising message is to use alt-text lines with the ad. *Alt-text lines* are short text phrases that appear in an image's location while the image is downloading. Larger images take longer to download, particularly when the user has a phone line connection to the Internet. The alt-text lines are replaced by the image when it has finished loading. But for Internet users who have a text-only browser, the alt-text lines are the only way to display information about a graphic image. Figure 10-5 shows alt-text lines in the CNN site. Moving your mouse over an image will also display its alt-text line for a short time.

FIGURE 10-5
CNN site with alt-text line in image locations

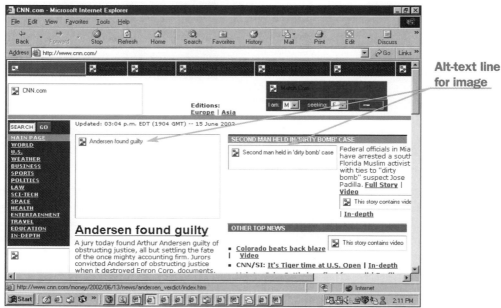

Banner ads are sold by size, measured in pixels. A *pixel* (PIX [picture] ELement) is the smallest element on a computer display screen. The most popular ad size is full-banner, which is 468 pixels wide by 60 pixels high, or about six inches wide and one inch high. Other common sizes are 392 pixels by 72 pixels (5 inches by 1.2 inches), 234 pixels by 60 pixels (3 inches by 1 inch), 125 pixels by 125 pixels (1.6 inches by 2.1 inches), and 120 pixels by 240 pixels (1.5 inches by 4 inches). Because of the geometry of a computer monitor, pixels do not measure the same way horizontally and vertically. Roughly, 78 pixels equal one inch horizontally and 60 pixels equal one inch vertically. CASIE (Coalition for Advertising Supported Information and Entertainment) is an advertising industry organization that established standards for Web ad size and for measuring the viewing audience for online ads.

Advertising rates are usually based on *CPM*, or cost per thousand impressions. On the Web, the number of impressions is the number of hits, or times the page has been accessed. CASIE recommends that a third party, rather than the site owner, measure the number of hits a Web site receives. MediaMetrix is one of the leading companies that measure Internet audience. Nielsen Media Research, which has been rating television programs for many years, also tracks the clicking activities of online users.

The more targeted the audience, the more expensive the ad rates. To minimize the cost of advertising, two or three companies might share a rotation ad on a given Web page. A *rotation ad* is a banner ad that rotates between advertisers. Each time the page is loaded or refreshed, the advertiser changes. Usually the sponsors of the rotation ads are named at the bottom of the Web page.

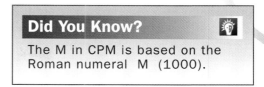

Did You Know?

The M in CPM is based on the Roman numeral M (1000).

One popular portal site charges $24–$38 CPM for general rotation ads that appear at the top of pages on the site. Advertisers can reserve keywords for a certain period of time at a rate of $70–$85 CPM. A reserved keyword means that whenever the viewer searches for that keyword, one advertiser's ad appears. Advertisers receive daily reports about hits on their ad sites.

Each Web site has its own advertising rates. As a potential advertiser, you can negotiate with the provider for favorable rates. You can lower the CPM cost by agreeing to a longer advertising contract. Figure 10-6 shows the Excite Network RateCard site. Each type of banner ad is shown with the CPM rate. Because dynamic ads can target potential customers with relevant interests, they sell at a premium rate. Advertisers may compete for a prime spot in a popular Web site like Yahoo or ESPN.

FIGURE 10-6
Excite Network RateCard

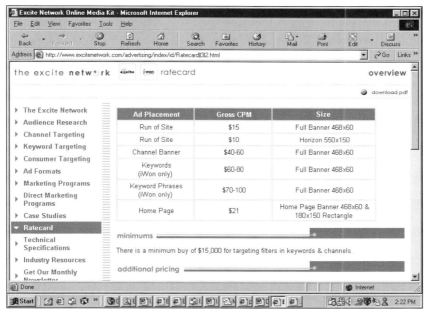

Pop-up ads are ads that appear in a different browser window on top of the base Web page that remains open in the background. *Pop-under ads* appear underneath the current Web page and are viewed when you close the main browser window. A pop-up or pop-under ad can grab a viewer's attention more than a normal banner ad within a Web page, and therefore earns a premium advertising rate. To remove the ad from view, users must close the extra window by clicking the Close button, probably causing the ad to remain in users' minds longer than other types of ads. Figure 10-7 shows the pop-up ad for AOL at *www.netscape.com*.

FIGURE 10-7
AOL pop-up ad at Netscape Web site

ZDNet's Anchordesk site incorporates a kind of advertising called a sponsored link at the bottom of some of its pages. These hyperlink ads are text-only and less expensive than banner ads with images. Figure 10-8 shows some of the sponsored links on the Anchordesk Web site.

FIGURE 10-8
Anchordesk sponsored link ads

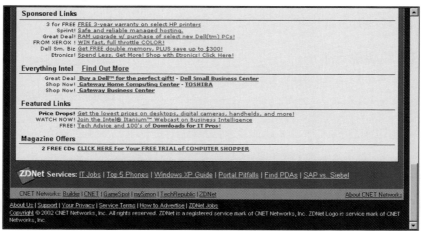

S TEP-BY-STEP 10.2

SCANS

1. Go to the CNN Web site. What banner ads appear on this home page? Don't forget to scroll down to the bottom.

_____

_____

2. Go to the Excite Web site and look up information about advertising at this site. The online media kit is found at **www.excitenetwork.com/advertising**, shown in Figure 10-9.

Hot Tip 🎯

With Internet Explorer and Netscape Navigator browsers, you can save an image file on your hard drive for use on your own Web pages. Right-click on the image. Then select Save Picture As or Save Image As and provide a name for the file. Remember that images from copyrighted sites can only be used with the owner's permission. The copyright information usually appears in the fine print at the bottom of the page.

FIGURE 10-9
Excite media kit page

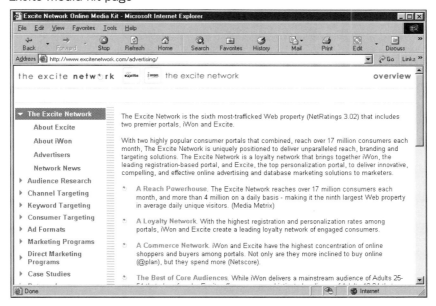

a. What is the basic rate for full banner ads?

_____

b. How much do keywords cost?

_____

STEP-BY-STEP 10.2 Continued

    c. What is a keyword package, and why would an advertiser want a package of keywords?

_____

_____

    d. What other Web sites appear in the Excite network?

_____

_____

    e. What is the market coverage of the Excite network?

_____

_____

3. Go to the Mapquest site. Examine the current ads there.

    a. What companies are represented in the ads?

_____

_____

    b. Key **Los Angeles** in the City box and **CA** in the State box. Click the **Map It** button. What ads appeared there?

_____

_____

    c. Would advertisers that purchase ad space on the Los Angeles page be more or less likely to find customers interested in their products?

_____

_____

 Net Ethics

    Some companies have a check box to let customers choose whether they want their names shared with other companies. Others, such as Office Max, use a pledge of privacy for all information gathered about a customer at a Web site. For an example of a privacy pledge, go to the Office Max site and follow the links for **Privacy Policy**. What is the responsibility of a company to protect customers' identities once they get into the company's database?

STEP-BY-STEP 10.2 Continued

4. Suppose you are planning to purchase advertising keywords at a major portal site that supports a company offering the following products. Select three keywords for each product and list them in order of decreasing importance.

a. Camping gear

_____

b. Sunglasses

_____

c. Lawn mowers

_____

d. Gourmet coffee

_____

e. Tax preparation service

_____

5. Go to the Quicken Web site and wait at least 10 seconds. Then check to see if a pop-under ad has appeared underneath the Quicken browser window. If so, what product is featured, and why would it be associated with viewers of the Quicken Web site?

_____

_____

6. Visit the Jupiter MediaMetrix Web site and list the top three U.S. Web sites based on unique visitors for the most recent time period available.

_____

_____

> **Extra Challenge**
>
> Do you think banner ads will maintain their advertising effectiveness? In 2002, CPM rates were declining after a peak in 2000.

Promoting Your Site

You need to deliver your message to potential customers. Most companies doing e-commerce try to lure buyers to a Web site. So how do you get that URL out to the world? Consider the following:

- Make your business name part of your URL. For example, see *cnn.com*, *www.unitedway.org*, and *www.washingtonpost.com*.
- Include your URL in e-mail messages sent to prospective customers.
- Place a banner ad on another popular Web site that potential customers are likely to visit.
- Submit your URL to the major portals, such as Yahoo, Excite, Lycos, InfoSeek, and Google. When customers search using keywords relevant to your business, your site will come up in the list of Web sites that match their search criteria.
- Advertise your Web address in other media, such as print, television, and radio.
- Include your Web address on your business cards, stationery, and other documents.

■ Advertise your Web address on billboards, trucks, and other places visible to potential customers.

■ Use a paid service to promote your Web site.

■ Hire an advertising agency to promote your site.

■ Do nothing and hope that the search engines' Web spiders will find your site and catalog it. The search engine sends out a ***Web spider*** or robotic search tool that constantly examines sites around the Web and adds them to a search engine's catalog or index.

It is particularly important to make sure that your Web site contains appropriate keywords that Web spiders can pick up. Select good descriptive words that will be programmed into the home page file by a Web developer. Make sure the title of your site is a good description of the site. The site title appears in the title bar of the browser when customers visit your site and is frequently listed in the search engine search results. The location of your title bar depends on your browser: Some title bars are at the top of the screen and others are at the bottom. A Web developer can place the title text into your site's home page file. We will discuss creating a home page in Lessons 12 and 13.

S TEP-BY STEP 10.3

SCANS

1. To get an idea of the kinds of titles used in Web sites, visit the following sites and write down the title from the title bar of your browser. Is each one a good description of the site?

a. www.ge.com

_____

_____

b. www.real.com

_____

_____

c. www.indystar.com

_____

_____

Technology Careers

A Web developer creates the computer files necessary to maintain a Web site. Most advertising firms now offer Web development services to their clients. In fact, some print advertising materials can be converted for use in Web pages. Although a Web developer must have some programming skills, artistic talent is also a necessary skill. Lessons 12 and 13 will focus on the details of developing Web pages.

STEP-BY STEP 10.3 Continued

d. www.nike.com

_____

_____

e. www.intel.com

_____

_____

2. Suppose you are building a Web site for your retail sporting goods store. Use a search tool such as Google to find the Web sites of three sporting goods stores. How did you find the sites? What keywords would you submit to a search engine to make your store's site easy to find?

_____

_____

3. Refer to the *USA Today* Web site, shown in Figure 10-10. In your opinion, are the banner ads at the bottom of the Web site effective? Which ones are most interesting to you, and why? Open the current *USA Today* page and compare those ads to the ones in Figure 10-10.

_____

_____

FIGURE 10-10
USA Today Marketplace banner ads

STEP-BY STEP 10.3 Continued

4. Visit the Northwest GIF Shop shown in Figure 10-11, a repository for free animated GIF files, at **www.oregoncoast.com/northwestgifshop**. Click some of the free GIF files. Also search Google using the keywords "animated GIF" to find other GIF sites. List the names of three animated GIFs that would enhance the Web site for your sporting goods store. How would you use each one?

FIGURE 10-11
Web site for free GIF files

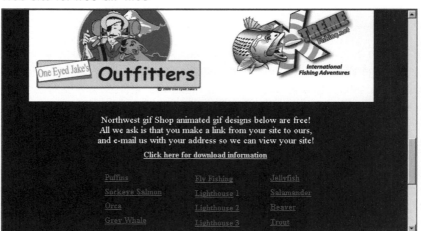

a. GIF 1: _____

   Use: _____

b. GIF 2: _____

   Use: _____

c. GIF 3: _____

   Use: _____

d. Why would you want to use animated GIFs in your business Web site? What are some possible disadvantages of using animated GIFs?

_____

_____

5. Visit the Yahoo page and click on **How to Suggest a Site** at the bottom of the page.

   a. How can you tell if a site is already in Yahoo?

_____

_____

   b. How does Yahoo distinguish business sites from noncommercial sites?

_____

   c. What is the cost to list your business page via Yahoo Express?

_____

   d. Should a business site be listed in a regional Yahoo catalog?

_____

STEP-BY STEP 10.3 Continued

6. Submit-It is a paid service that promotes Web sites. It will send your Web site's URL to over 400 search engines and other online indexes for one fee, increasing the likelihood that someone will come across your site when searching. Open the Submit-It site at **www.submit-it.com**, shown in Figure 10-12.

FIGURE 10-12
Submit-It Web site

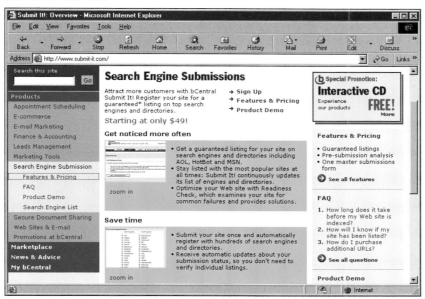

a. How could Submit-It help you promote your sporting goods store?

_____

_____

b. What is the cost for this service to announce one or two URLs?

_____

Net Business

Nielsen NetRatings provides the same kind of viewer behavior measurements for Web visitors as it does of television viewers. Participants are selected randomly to be Nielsen subjects. They receive a CD-ROM and instructions to install the monitoring software on office and home computers. While they surf the net, the software will record subjects' keystrokes and clicks, and then send this information over the Internet to the Nielsen organization. From these subjects, Nielsen is able to predict with confidence the _total_ audience at various Web sites. This information can be used to establish advertising rates.

STEP-BY STEP 10.3 Continued

c. How long does it take to get your Web site into the search engine databases?

___

SUMMARY

In this lesson, you learned:

■ Your customers can subscribe to e-mail services and you can use e-mail effectively to advertise your business.

■ You can describe types of banner advertising on the Web and discuss the benefits and drawbacks of each type.

■ You can promote your company Web site and get your site in a search engine's catalog.

VOCABULARY *Review*

Define the following terms:

Alt-text lines	HTML-enhanced e-mail	Reach
Animated GIF ad	Mailing list service	Richness
Cooperative ads	(LISTSERV)	Rotation ad
CPM (cost per thousand)	Pixel	Spam
Demographics	Pop-under ads	Static ad
Dynamic ads	Pop-up ads	Web spider
E-mail ads	Portal sites	

REVIEW *Questions*

TRUE/FALSE

Circle T if the statement is true or F if the statement is false.

T   F   1. E-mail marketing is effective for most companies because of its richness and reach.

T   F   2. Most e-mail systems are able to display HTML e-mail.

T   F   3. Banner advertising rates are quoted in CPM, cost per million impressions.

T   F   4. Entering sweepstakes online is often a way to begin receiving unwanted e-mail messages.

T   F   5. It is possible for one company to rent names and e-mail addresses from other companies.

WRITTEN QUESTIONS

Write a brief answer to the following questions.

1. How do the names and e-mail addresses for customers get into a company's database?

2. Why are portal sites popular places for advertising?

3. Why do advertisers have to pay more for keyword or dynamic advertising?

4. In the advertising business, what is CPM?

5. What does a Web spider do for a search engine site?

6. Why is it important to select appropriate keywords and titles for your Web pages?

PROJECTS

 PROJECT 10-1

Suppose you are in the business of selling and repairing lawn mowers and outdoor power equipment. What kinds of e-mail marketing campaigns might you plan for your business? Would you use different campaigns in different seasons? How would you find names and e-mail addresses for potential customers?

 PROJECT 10-2

Suppose you have been given funds to promote your business on the Tampa Bay Online Web site for this year. Click the **Advertise with us** link in the Welcome section at the top of the page. Explore that Web site's rate sheet, and discuss how you might allocate those funds to various types of banner ads. Which type of banner ads would you choose, and why?

 PROJECT 10-3

Suppose you are in the business of selling tickets to popular band concerts. Give your company a name. What keywords would you use to describe your Web site? Where would you put these keywords on your site? Why?

Think of ways to promote your Web site. What companies would you consider approaching to share cooperative ads? What major Web sites would you consider for placing your ads? Why? What are some other good ways to promote your kind of business? Explain why you chose these particular ways.

  TEAMWORK PROJECT

Assign each team member a type of online advertising for promoting your team's concert ticket business. Each person should write an advertisement for the business, designed to work well for the assigned ad type. Be creative! Find ways to capture your customers' attention and lure them to your site. Use the unique features of the Internet to help you promote your product.

The team should then prepare a presentation of your company's ads for the class. Your presentation should explain why each ad was designed as it was. How does each ad contribute to promoting your business? How does each ad use the capabilities of the Web to your business's advantage?

After all teams present their advertisements, discuss the features that seem to work best.

CRITICAL*Thinking*

 ACTIVITY 10-1

How would you go about creating an e-mail advertisement program for a company that sells sporting goods? What kind of information do you want to put in the e-mail messages? How is it different from a print ad for the same firm? How would you persuade people not to unsubscribe from these messages?

GLOBAL E-COMMERCE

Doing Business Anywhere, Anytime

Today, business is a global activity. *Multinational corporations* have branches, plants, and business partners all over the world. They may gather raw materials in one country, refine them in another, assemble them into finished goods in yet another country, and sell their finished products virtually everywhere. And although English is the dominant language in North America, the United Kingdom, and a few other countries, most multinational firms must be able to conduct business in many languages. As you will see in the activities in this lesson, larger firms offer versions of their Web sites in several languages, available by clicking a link. Some search engine sites have international versions that highlight sites in that particular country, often in the country's language.

The Internet lowers geographic barriers by supporting low-cost communication between suppliers, employees, business partners, and customers. You are likely to see television commercials that tout a tiny eastern European company's presence on the Internet. Through the Internet, it can sell products in the U.S. as easily as its larger counterparts can.

In fact, the Internet permits business partners to exchange information through e-mail and Web sites without ever meeting face to face. For instance, the authors of this book have never met (face-to-face) with any of the editorial or production staff associated with this book. Virtually all of our communications have taken place through e-mail, with attachments for document files. We use a file server to hold edited copies of the manuscript.

If you were an international businessperson, you could access critical information about other countries through the Internet. You could learn about the culture and business practices of a particular region, along with demographic statistics, transportation capabilities, industrial resources, and so forth. You could begin to develop business relationships before you ever set foot in the country.

Lowering Geographic Barriers

In the past, a company operated by creating products, running facilities that manufacture the products, a distribution system that delivers the products, stores that display the goods, and a sales force that promotes the products. In most cases, the company's customers were primarily from the same geographic region.

But the Internet is reducing the need for some of these traditional business activities. If your company has an e-commerce site on the Web, customers can reach you for free from just about anywhere. You don't need a retail store or salespeople to call on customers. You don't even have to accept sales orders in person any longer. Small companies can forgo these large expenses and use the Internet to compete with large corporations.

Net Fun

In the world's first International Piano E-Competition, contestants recorded their pieces on a Yamaha Disklavier piano in Minneapolis in front of some of the judges. The digital file containing each person's performance was transferred from the United States to Japan via the Internet where it was played on an identical piano before the remaining judge.

The Internet is truly global—there are Internet connections and Web sites on all seven continents. Table 11-1 shows country code domain names for a few of the countries that populate the Web. For instance, a URL ending in *.DE* refers to a site in Germany (Deutschland).

Currently, there are more than 240 country code domain names, and the number is growing all the time. The Internet Assigned Numbers Authority (IANA) Web site contains complete details about country codes.

TABLE 11-1
Country Code Domain Names

COUNTRY	DOMAIN NAME
Australia	AU
Brazil	BR
Canada	CA
France	FR
Germany	DE
Hong Kong	HK
Israel	IL
Japan	JP
Korea (Republic)	KR
Russian Federation	RU
Spain	ES
United Kingdom	UK
Zimbabwe	ZW

A URL that ends in *.com* refers to a commercial company or business. Though most of these firms are in the United States or Canada, many are located elsewhere in the world. Although the domain name does not necessarily have the country code at the end, in many cases it does, and the next-to-last word is often *co,* short for *company.* For instance, *www.thomson-directories.co.uk* is the URL for Thomson Directories Ltd., a company in the United Kingdom.

Figure 11-1 shows the home page for the Canon Web site. The large graphic images in the center are all animated GIF files, displaying different scenes. This site links to several Canon worldwide network locations and even has a link to a Japanese version in the text at the bottom of the page.

> **Did You Know?**
>
> Web pages are transmitted in blocks of data called *packets.* The packets are reassembled at the receiver's end into the complete Web page. The data packets often are delayed as they pass across different networks. It will take noticeably longer for a Web page to download to your computer if it is coming from another continent. Some companies set up a mirror site in another country, so that users in that country can download its Web pages more quickly. A *mirror site* is a Web site that contains a duplicate of the master site's contents.

FIGURE 11-1
Canon worldwide network home page

A company can translate the text on its Web site into a different language for users in other countries. The Netscape Web browser is available in 13 foreign languages. The English version can display many foreign characters.

S TEP-BY-STEP 11.1

SCANS

1. Go to the Canon Web site. Move your mouse pointer to the English and Japanese links at the left side of the home page. As you linger on each one, note its actual URL in the status bar at the bottom of your screen. What country code appears for each link? That code means that the page will be sent to your browser from that country.

STEP-BY-STEP 11.1 Continued

2. At the Canon site, select the **Americas** link.

a. What countries are available through this link?

_____

_____

b. Go to two of the Americas links. What main difference do you see?

_____

_____

c. Return to the Canon home page. What countries are available through the **Europe** link?

_____

_____

d. Why do you think Canon has so many different Web sites?

_____

_____

3. Suppose you are planning a trip to London and want to find lodging. Open the Lycos home page and click the link to go to its **United Kingdom** site. From the **www.lycos.co.uk** URL, you can see that this page is fed by a Web server located in the United Kingdom. Select **UK** next to the Search box and search for the keyword **hotel**, as shown in Figure 11-2.

FIGURE 11-2
Lycos UK home page

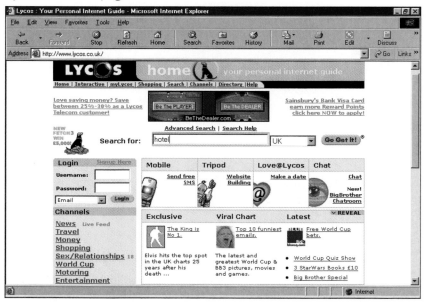

STEP-BY-STEP 11.1 Continued

a. What effect does this "UK" catalog setting have on your search?

_____

_____

b. Why would hotel owners want to have their Web sites in the Lycos UK version?

_____

_____

c. Do the hotel owners anticipate that people living outside the UK will use the UK version of Lycos? Why?

_____

_____

4. Search for the **Caterpillar** home page, click the **ABOUT CAT** button, and then click **CAT WORLDWIDE** as shown in Figure 11-3. Answer the following questions about Cat's global businesses.

FIGURE 11-3
Caterpillar home page

Cat Worldwide

a. What are Caterpillar's businesses?

_____

_____

b. What percentage of Caterpillar's annual sales is outside the U.S.? _____

c. How many dealers does Caterpillar have? How many countries does Cat serve?

_____

d. What Cat facility is in Grimbergen, Belgium? _____

STEP-BY-STEP 11.1 Continued

    e. How does this global Web site help Caterpillar sell tractors in Europe?

_____

_____

  5. Visit the portal site **www.freetranslation.com** for all sorts of language translation information available on the Web.

    a. What is the French translation for this sentence?

_____

    b. Why would a business want to use a site such as _freetranslation.com_?

_____

_____

> **Extra Challenge**
>
> How would a multinational company like Caterpillar use the Internet to do global e-commerce? For instance, comment on the navigation bars at the top of the Cat Worldwide page.

Asynchronous Worldwide Activities

Traditionally, a business transaction could occur only if the business and customer were in the same place at the same time. You would walk into a store, pick up the item you wanted, and pay at the cash register. You and the business were synchronized in time and place. To do business, the company facility would have to be near customers and open when the customers wanted to buy. If the company wanted to sell to a larger area, it would need multiple facilities.

Mail-order companies have taken advantage of the telephone to get around the problem of time and place, to some extent. Still, customer service employees must be available to take orders. Also, the companies have to get their catalogs into the hands of the customers, which is costly. Updating catalogs means repeat mailings. Some companies mail catalogs 20 times a year.

On the Internet, business activities can be *asynchronous*—not synchronized in time and place. Internet companies can accept orders whenever customers want to place them, and online catalogs are always up-to-date. Customers and sellers can transact business at different times and in different locations. An airline customer can check flight schedules and make reservations online at any time, not just when the airline reservations center is able to answer the phone call from that customer.

The activities in this Step-by-Step demonstrate the benefits of being able to do business almost anywhere at any time.

STEP-BY-STEP 11.2

1. Open the Northwest Airlines Web site pictured in Figure 11-4. Notice the Enroll in WorldPerks link at the lower right that is used to add customers to the mailing list. If you add your name to the list, sales and special promotion information will be sent to you via e-mail.

FIGURE 11-4
Northwest Airlines home page

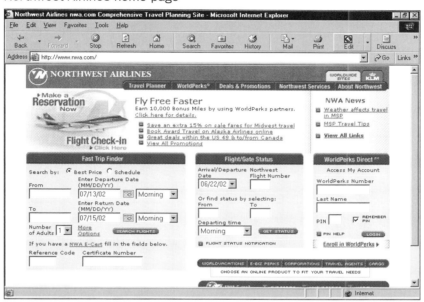

a. Why would someone want to subscribe to this service?

_____

_____

b. Using the Northwest Flight Schedule section, complete the table below for two flights between Minneapolis and Paris on a date at least three weeks in the future.

FLIGHT NO.	DEPARTS	ARRIVES	COST

2. Open an international airline Web site, such as Japan Airlines. Write down information about a flight between a city in the United States and one in the country of that airline.

FROM	TO	FLIGHT NO.	DEPARTS	ARRIVES	COST

STEP-BY-STEP 11.2 Continued

a. How can an airline's Web site be helpful in making international business travel plans?

_____

_____

b. Why should JAL provide an English language version of its Web site on the Internet?

_____

_____

Did You Know?

The blue navigation bar at the bottom of Figure 11-4 is called an *image map*. It is a picture that is separated into sections. Each section contains a link that when clicked will take users to different Web locations. Watch the browser's status bar as you move the cursor over various parts of the image map. When you click a section of an image map, the link associated with that (x, y) coordinate opens another Web page in your browser.

3. Visit the *XE.com* Universal Currency Converter site, shown in Figure 11-5. Use the currency converter at this Web site to convert $500US into the following currencies. Write down the amount for each currency.

a. British Pounds _____

b. Euro Dollars _____

c. Japanese Yen _____

d. Australian Dollars _____

e. Malaysian Ringitts _____

FIGURE 11-5
XE.com currency converter Web site

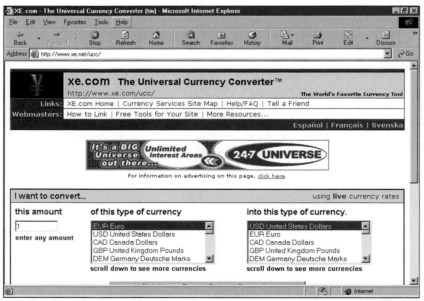

STEP-BY-STEP 11.2 Continued

4. Suppose you want to purchase American Express traveler's checks in local currency denominations for a trip to Shanghai, China. Visit the American Express Web site shown in Figure 11-6 and locate the address and telephone number of the American Express office in this city. What are the hours of operation at this office?

Extra Challenge

You used the Internet to plan a domestic trip in Lesson 5. How is the process of planning an international trip different from planning a domestic trip? What issues other than airline flights are important for international travel? How can you prepare for your international trip using the Internet?

FIGURE 11-6
American Express personal Web site

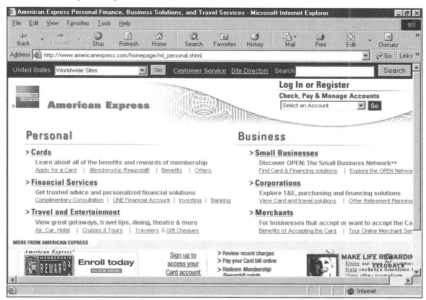

5. The Internet version of the World Travel Guide is available online at **www.wtgonline.com**. Select **United Arab Emirates** from the Middle East section, shown in Figure 11-7. Answer the following questions about this country, using business profile information found at this site.

a. What industry is the main provider for the country? _____

b. What country is the largest buyer of products from this industry? _____

c. What is the appropriate dress for business meetings? _____

d. What special office hours are observed during the month of Ramadan? _____

e. What language is largely spoken in business circles? _____

f. Why is it important for business people to learn about local customs practiced in other countries?

_____

_____

STEP-BY-STEP 11.2 Continued

FIGURE 11-7
World Travel Guide Web site

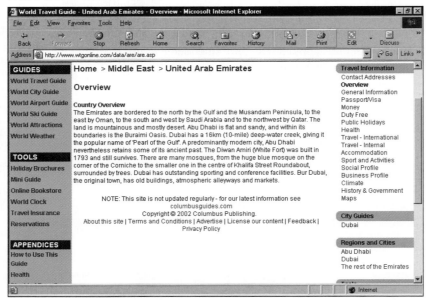

Online International Business Information

When you are planning to do business with someone from another country, there is a lot of research to do. Michigan State University operates CIBER–Center for International Business Education and Research. The CIBER home page is shown in Figure 11-8. CIBER's globalEDGE section contains links to many international business Web sites. For example, you might search there for:

■ Regional insights (business climate, political structure, history, and statistical data)

Net Tip

The U.S. State Department site offers many services for the business traveler, including passports, visas, and articles about travel to certain regions of the world. Check this site and look for warnings about travel to some parts of the world.

 Technology Careers

Do you enjoy working with technology and also enjoy foreign countries? As you saw from Step-by-Step 11.2, many organizations around the world have sophisticated Web sites. Some companies, such as Yahoo and Lycos, have openings in other countries. Most positions require that you live in that country. For instance, at this writing, Yahoo lists openings for a core surfer in Hong Kong, a head of agency sales in the United Kingdom, and an associate producer in Brazil. See Jobs at the Yahoo site. Google lists an adwords client services coordinator in France. See the Jobs, Press, Cool Stuff link at the Google site.

- Research (academic links, government resources, rankings, and lists)
- News and periodicals (global, regional, and individual publications)
- Trade (tutorials, trade law, portals, logistics, and company directories)
- Reference (standards and conversion, culture, living abroad, language)
- Money (stock exchanges, banks, and finance)
- Market potential indicators (compares emerging markets)
- Glossary of terms and acronyms

FIGURE 11-8
Michigan State CIBER international business resources

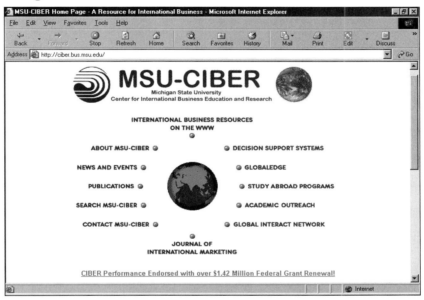

Much of the information maintained at the CIBER site is suitable for those individuals interested in pursuing international business.

In the Step-by-Step that follows, you'll assume that you work for World Ventures Limited, a company that does business around the globe. Your team needs to find answers to questions about commerce in a number of countries outside the United States.

> **Net Fun**
>
> People around the world watch CNN. Take a look at the CNN International site. You'll find news stories organized by region as well as the top stories. What other languages are available on this site?

STEP-BY-STEP 11.3

1. Using CIBER, find information about doing business with South America. Select **Brazil: Big Emerging Markets**. What is the telephone number of the Brazilian Central Bank in Brasilia? What language is spoken in Brazil? How long is a typical work week in Brazil?

_____

_____

STEP-BY-STEP 11.3 Continued

2. Check out the CIBER mailing list's hyperlink, and explain how to add yourself to *The Economist Newspaper's* Business and Politics summaries by e-mail. As an employee of World Ventures Limited, why would you want to subscribe to the world business summary news?

_____

_____

> **Net Tip**
>
> According to the Global Reach Web site, English is the most popular native language on the Internet, with about 58% of the entire online population. Following English is Spanish at 8.61%, German at 8.57%, Japanese at 7.7%, French at 3.7%, Chinese at 2.6%, and Swedish at 1.7%. Portuguese, Italian, Dutch, and Korean have about 1% each. This site also offers translation services to convert a Web site from one language to another.

3. Many international newspapers and business digests are available on the Internet. Visit the Inside China Today Web site, available through the Regional News section of CIBER, shown in Figure 11-9.

a. What does it cost to subscribe to the EIN daily briefs? "EIN" refers to the European Internet Network, a business information and online news service. _____

b. In what medium would you receive the EIN daily briefs? _____

c. Do you think this site is as sophisticated as U.S. or Canadian newspaper sites? Explain.

_____

_____

FIGURE 11-9
Inside China Today Web site

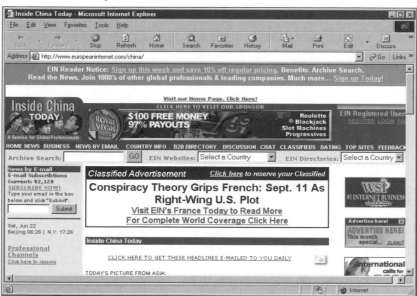

4. Suppose World Ventures wants you to relocate to Hawaii to pursue U.S.–Japanese ventures in the Pacific. Visit the Matson Navigation Company site shown in Figure 11-10.

a. How much would it cost to ship your personal automobile from the U.S. mainland to Honolulu?

_____

STEP-BY-STEP 11.3 Continued

b. Should you drain your fuel tank before you leave the car at the Matson port facility?

_____

c. What are the mainland ports of discharge (departure) for Matson auto cargo ships?

_____

d. If a Matson container ship leaves from Los Angeles on Saturday, when does it arrive in Honolulu?

_____

e. If the Web site was not available, how would you find out about transporting your car to Hawaii?

_____

_____

> ### Extra Challenge
>
> All the information that you retrieved in Step-by-Step 11.3 was available free of charge. If global information was available on the Internet only for a subscription fee, would you still prefer to research the Internet for global information? In other words, is having this information quickly important to you? Explain your answer.

FIGURE 11-10
Matson Web site

Intranets, Extranets, and the Internet

You have been working with the Internet for most of this textbook. The **Internet** is a network of public networks, generally available everywhere around the world. When information is placed on the Internet, it is usually considered public information and freely accessible.

But some companies want to make information available to employees only, not the general public. For this, a company can install an *intranet*, or internal network, as you saw in Lesson 7. An intranet is like a private Internet. Instead of being available to everyone, the intranet's cable that connects computers is only accessible inside the firm. Organizations put employee handbooks, company news and information, inventory status, internal job postings, FAQs, and other internal information resources on an intranet. Information can be updated and distributed easily over the intranet, so companies prefer this online information tool over sending information updates to employees manually.

For organizations in which all users are in one central location, it is fairly easy to create an intranet. But for international companies with widely dispersed locations, it is not possible to install a private cable. In this instance, the company can implement an *extranet*, an intranet that uses the Internet to transmit private information beyond the firm's physical space, or building. To keep the extranet private, companies install *authentication* software. It asks for a username and password before allowing a user access to the extranet's pages. With authentication, a business is assured that only authorized users with proper knowledge can gain access to a particular site.

One advantage of creating an extranet is the ability to take advantage of inexpensive Internet connections from virtually anywhere in the world to connect to the firm's intranet.

S TEP-BY-STEP 11.4

1. Open the Fidelity Investments home page. Then navigate to **Online Trading** by clicking that link at the upper left of the page. You should see the authentication box shown in Figure 11-11.

   a. Why do you think authentication usually requires two pieces of information instead of just one?

   _____

   _____

FIGURE 11-11
Fidelity Investments online trade authentication box

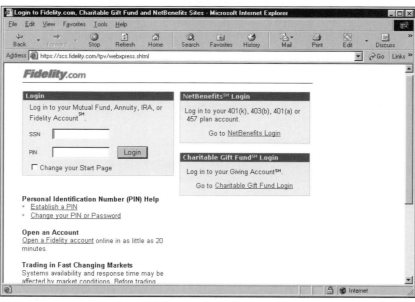

STEP-BY-STEP 11.4 Continued

b. Is the online authentication a program of an intranet or an extranet? _____

2. Suppose that a marketing organization maintains confidential price quote information on its intranet. Give at least three reasons why the company would want to have an extranet for use by the sales force.

_____

_____

3. The Mindbridge Company sells intranet technology to other companies via its IntraSmart software as shown in Figure 11-12. Click on the **Testimonials** link. From these organizations' testimonials, answer the following questions about uses of the intranet.

FIGURE 11-12
Mindbridge IntraSmart Web site

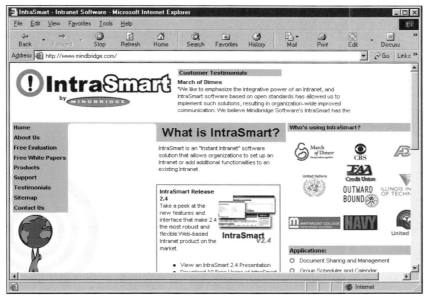

a. What benefit did the March of Dimes attribute to its intranet?

_____

_____

b. How did the Warwick Public Schools use its intranet?

_____

_____

c. Why would the Mindbridge company want to highlight its customers' successes on this Web site?

_____

_____

STEP-BY-STEP 11.4 Continued

SCANS

4. At the Mindbridge site, navigate to **www.mindbridge.com/getAway.htm** and read the *USA Today* article about intranets. Based on this article, answer the following questions. (*Hint: If you cannot find the article on the Mindbridge site, check out* **www.usatoday.com/life/cyber/tech/cth577.htm**.)

a. What percentage of companies use their intranet as a way of delivering information to corporate users?

_____

b. List three types of documents that Hallmark has placed on an intranet.

_____

_____

c. How does Texas Instruments use its intranet for new employees?

_____

_____

d. List three types of documents that could be placed on an extranet.

_____

_____

_____

Net Fun

Visit the CoolSavings Web site to see how you can print real coupons with your own computer. What characteristics of an extranet does this site possess? (Hint: Think about the security issues associated with the login box.)

Extra Challenge

Think about a company for which you have worked. What kinds of information would be appropriate and useful for this company to put on an intranet? Think about frequently requested items, or items that tend to change often for which a printed reference is needed. What sorts of information would not be appropriate for an intranet?

SUMMARY

In this lesson, you learned:

■ You can use the Internet to do business virtually anywhere in the world.

■ You can use the Internet to bring customers and sellers together, even though they are not in the same place at the same time.

■ You can find international business information on the Internet.

■ Your company can take advantage of its own "private Internet" to manage business around the world.

VOCABULARY *Review*

Define the following terms:

Asynchronous	Image map	Mirror site
Authentication	Internet	Multinational corporations
Extranet	Intranet	Packets

REVIEW *Questions*

TRUE / FALSE

Circle T if the statement is true or F if the statement is false.

T   F   1. There are about 100 country code domain names on the IANA Web site.

T   F   2. You can search some portal sites and restrict the search to a local region.

T   F   3. Asynchronous activities refer to transactions between individuals that occur at different times or places.

T   F   4. The U.S. State Department provides travel warnings on its Web site.

T   F   5. An extranet is an intranet that uses the Internet to transmit private information outside the organization.

WRITTEN QUESTIONS

Write a brief answer to the following questions.

1. Explain how the domain name for a particular Web site can identify the country where that site is located.

2. Why is having a mirror site particularly helpful for global companies with operations on more than one continent?

3. Why does a company place information in different languages on its Web site?

4. How does the Internet permit asynchronous business activities?

5. Explain how to convert U.S. dollars into foreign currency.

6. How can the CIBER site help someone that does business overseas?

PROJECTS

 PROJECT 11-1

Use the Internet to plan a one-week business visit to Malaysia. Find out how many U.S. Dollars are needed in exchange for 10,000 Ringitts. Leaving from Chicago, Illinois, find detailed round-trip flight information to Kuala Lumpur. What is the cost of your flight in U.S. dollars? What time does your flight leave Chicago, and when does it arrive in Malaysia? Be sure to give the correct *date* for each arrival—is it today or tomorrow? (*Hint: You will cross the international date line.*)

 PROJECT 11-2

You have been assigned the task to research the best possible site for locating a new manufacturing facility in Indonesia. Use the Internet resources to find out the local currency, the weather during October and November, the geographic regions, the major cities, the population, the head of the government, the gross domestic product (GDP), the major products or industries, and the inflation rate. In preparation for your visit to the capital city, find a hotel and learn its street address, telephone number, and a Web site address, if available. Give the name of a local newspaper and its Web address, if available.

  TEAMWORK PROJECT

Each member of the team should extend Project 11-2 by examining possible manufacturing sites in a different country. For variety, look for countries in different parts of the world such as Zimbabwe, New Zealand, Romania, and Chile. Write a report that compares the conditions in these countries. Where would your team recommend locating the manufacturing site? Why?

CRITICAL *Thinking*

 ACTIVITY 11-1

You have visited many different international e-commerce sites in this lesson, and have seen some that are available in different languages. Write a 100-word summary that describes the sorts of customer support problems that might occur due to language or cultural differences.

DOING BUSINESS ON THE WEB

REVIEW *Questions*

TRUE/FALSE

Circle T if the statement is true or F if the statement is false.

T F 1. In order for a site to qualify as an e-commerce Web site, it must offer something for sale on the site.

T F 2. HTML-enhanced mail can be a very effective way to display graphics, fonts, and hyperlinks to prospective customers.

T F 3. It is possible to deliver an e-commerce product directly over the Internet without using a package delivery company.

T F 4. Authentication is based on providing a username and a password.

T F 5. Encryption is used to protect sensitive information such as social security and credit card numbers.

T F 6. The PDF file format is a way to transmit musical and audio information over the Internet.

T F 7. The text files stored on the customer's computer that contain information about a Web interaction are called brownies.

T F 8. A pixel refers to a tiny dot on a computer screen.

T F 9. A Web spider refers to a Web site map for visitors that are lost.

T F 10. Unwanted e-mail messages are also known as spam.

MATCHING

Match the description in Column 2 to the correct term in Column 1.

	Column 1		Column 2
___	1. Spam	**A.**	E-mail message resembling a Web page
___	2. PDF	**B.**	Text message that appears in place of a graphic image
___	3. Cookie	**C.**	Method used to secure sensitive information
___	4. Alt-text	**D.**	Robotic search tool that discovers new Web pages for search engines
___	5. Intranet	**E.**	Private network accessible through the Internet
___	6. Encryption	**F.**	Unwanted e-mail message
___	7. Pop-up ads	**G.**	Second Web site that appears shortly after you open a Web page
___	8. Web spider	**H.**	Private network not accessible outside the boundaries of an organization
___	9. Extranet	**I.**	Text file containing identifying information from a Web transaction
___	10. HTML mail	**J.**	List of personal information, education, and experience

PROJECTS

SCANS **PROJECT 4-1**

MapQuest was the most popular mapping service on the Internet as of September 2001. Visit the MapQuest Web site and explore the **About MapQuest** link.

1. What are the basic services offered by the MapQuest Web site?

    _____

    _____

2. Explain why a business might want to advertise on MapQuest instead of a portal such as Yahoo or Lycos.

    _____

    _____

3. Discuss why a company such as Borders Bookstore might want to place a link to MapQuest on the Borders Web site. How could a company use the MapQuest mapping services for its own marketing purposes?

_____

_____

SCANS PROJECT 4-2

1. Using the FedEx Web site, explore the package tracking features available for Express shipments. Click the **Quick Help** link to learn about the information you can obtain about your package. For example, what do you need to key in about your package and what information is available?

_____

_____

2. Use the UPS Web site to learn about drop-off points for UPS shipments in your community. Enter your address and zip code, and search for UPS sites. Select the closest drop-off point. What are the pick-up hours, and how far is this point from your location?

_____

_____

SCANS PROJECT 4-3

1. Visit the Jupiter MediaMetrix Web site. What are the top five U.S. Web sites in terms of unique visitors?

_____

_____

2. Visit the Nielsen NetRatings Web site. What are the top five U.S. Web sites in terms of unique visitors?

_____

_____

3. How can you explain the differences between the rankings from these two sources?

_____

_____

SIMULATION

 JOB 4-1

Evan Peters has learned a great deal about running Evan's Trading Mart on the Web. He wants to put together a plan for his e-commerce business. With your knowledge of the four phases of marketing, what should Evan include in his plan for marketing?

 JOB 4-2

Gloria Fernandez, a Florida real estate agent, knows that many of her potential customers do not live in the Florida area. She is seeking the assistance of a marketing company to expand her customer list. What information do you think her potential customers might want to have about Florida vacation home rentals and sales? How should this information be made available to potential customers?

DEVELOPING AN ELECTRONIC COMMERCE WEB SITE

Unit 5

Lesson 12
Creating a Web Site

4 hrs.

Lesson 13
Developing a Web Site with Microsoft® FrontPage

4 hrs.

Estimated Time for Unit: 8 hours

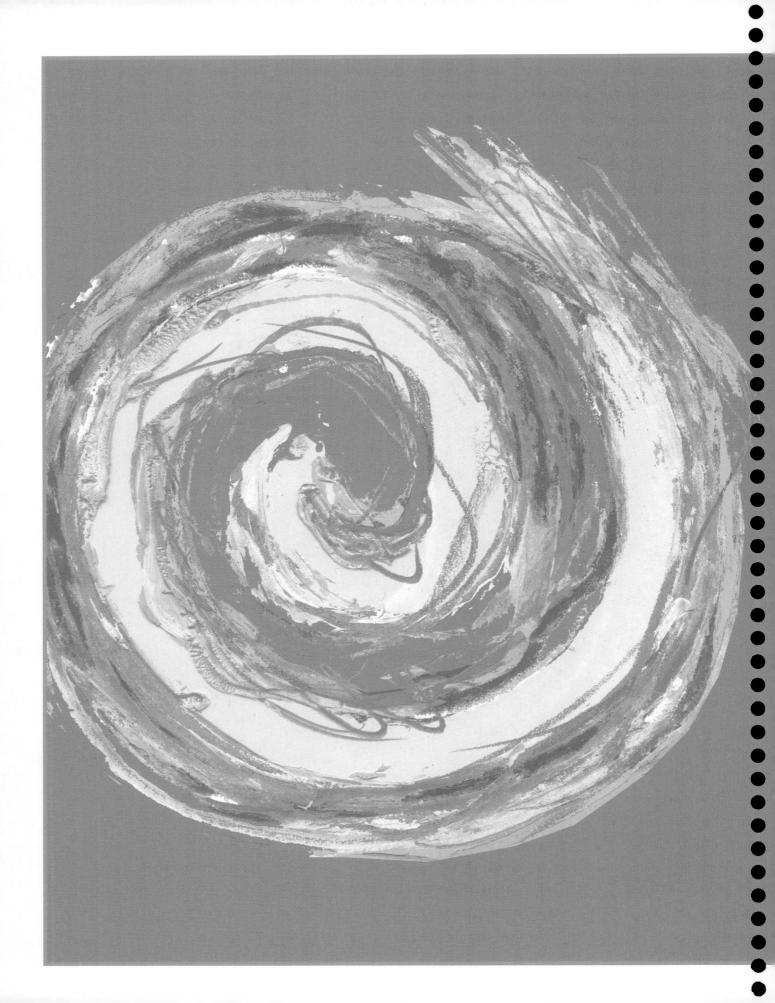

CREATING A WEB SITE

VOCABULARY

24/7

Clip art

Domain name

Domain registrar

File transfer protocol (FTP)

GIF

HTML (hypertext markup language)

HTML tags

JPEG

Top-level domain name (TLD)

Web editor

Web server

Webmaster

Your Electronic Commerce Web Site

This lesson discusses the components of an e-commerce Web site. You will learn how a business Web site works and the methods that are available to you for developing the site. You will even develop an online store in this lesson. Then you will learn how to register your domain name and submit your site's URL to the major Web browsers.

What You Need to Make Your Web Debut

Creating a Web site is actually much simpler than most people think. Of course, building an *effective* Web site requires a touch of artistic creativity and some energetic work to keep it fresh. Simple Web sites are straightforward to build and publish on a Web server.

Here are the components of e-commerce Web sites that you will learn about in this lesson:

■ Text files with embedded HTML commands

■ Images, usually .GIF or .JPG files

■ Web server hardware and software to hold the text files and images

- A connection to the Internet or an intranet

- Optional programs called scripts that contain instructions for the Web server

- A database server supporting the online catalog (optional)

- An internal search engine to locate information in the Web site (optional)

Many organizations hire a consultant or advertising company to design and build the site. These individuals are called Web developers. If you have the technical knowledge and some artistic talent, you can do it yourself. The online stores at Yahoo make it easy to build your own Web site, which Yahoo will host for a low monthly fee. Or, you can purchase Web package software that helps you create an e-commerce site by simply answering a series of questions.

As discussed in Lesson 10, you need to promote your site so that potential customers can find it on the Internet. We will look into ways to submit your site's URL to the major search engines, and other ways to let people know your site exists.

Components of a Web Site

Basically, a Web site consists of a few text files containing special HTML formatting commands and a Web server computer to host your site. The Web server runs special software that sends out the HTML files to users whose browsers request them. Your Web server will need a connection to the Internet or an intranet. An e-commerce site will also need software to process payments, such as credit cards. Let's take a closer look at each part of a Web site.

HTML Files

The language used to create most Web pages is *HTML (hypertext markup language)*. This simple language adds formatting tags to the basic text of the page. *HTML tags* are computer codes that tell your Web browser how to display information on your screen. HTML tags are used to indicate such features as bold, character size, font color, hyperlinks, and images. Each tag is sandwiched between angle brackets. For example, <B> turns on bold for a phrase. The text remains bold until the matching </B> tag turns bold off.

Thus <B>Organizational Department,</B> School of Business would display as:

Organizational Department, School of Business

Figure 12-1 shows a simple HTML file and the resulting Web page as viewed in a browser. To view an HTML file in your browser, use the File/Open command and then specify the path and file name, as in C:\sample.htm.

FIGURE 12-1
Sample HTML file and resulting Web page

Although it is possible to program Web pages manually using HTML tags, development software tools called Web editors can insert the tags for you, simplifying the task of coding home pages. There are many HTML primers available on the Internet. You'll take a look at one in the first Step-by-Step.

Image Files

As you have already seen throughout the Web sites featured in this book, most use graphic images to enhance the design of Web pages. These images come from a variety of sources, including clip art, photographs, and other software applications. *Clip art* is a collection of electronic drawings, pictures, and icons, created for use in Web pages and other documents. You can also purchase professional images from online sources, often simplifying the process of finding appropriate graphics for your site. Many Web sites contain free clip art that you can use at your own site. Check out *clipartconnection.com* for thousands of clip art files.

Web Editor

You can build your own Web site using Web editor software to create the HTML file. A *Web editor* looks like a word-processing program. In it, you can type the contents of your Web page and then select various formatting options. The Web editor program inserts the necessary HTML tags. You can choose such things as

- Font size and color
- Special formatting, such as bold, italics, underline, and blinking

- Bulleted and numbered lists
- Line alignment (left, center, right)
- Hyperlinks for text (and images) in your page
- Images
- HTML tables to create columns like those that you see in a newspaper

The advantage of a Web editor is the ease with which you can build the features of your Web page. Advanced features such as tables and forms are easy to create and place with Web editor software such as Microsoft FrontPage or Netscape Composer.

When you are finished designing, you can save the HTML file with *.htm* or *.html* as the file extension. Then you can transfer the file to the Web server using *file transfer protocol (FTP)*, a standard method for copying files from one computer to another over the Internet. We'll talk more about Web development in Step-by-Step 12.2 and in Lesson 13, where you will build a Web site with FrontPage, the most popular Web editor.

Web Server

A *Web server* is a computer that stores the HTML and graphic files that make up a Web site. When your browser requests a Web page stored at the server, the Web server sends the appropriate HTML and graphic files over the Internet to your machine for display on your screen. When an organization hosts a Web site, it stores the associated Web pages on its Web server. Specialized software on the Web server can track users and gather statistics about visits to your Web site.

Internet Connection

Unlike your personal computer's occasional modem connection to the Internet, the Web server computer needs to have a full-time Internet connection. That is, the server must be available *24/7* (24 hours a day, 7 days a week), whenever someone might request a Web page. Few companies host their own Web site unless they have a full-time connection, which can cost anywhere from $60 per month to $1,000 or more, depending on the size of the Web site, the connection speed, and the amount of data transferred.

Most Internet Service Providers (ISPs) offer a limited amount of Web space for hosting personal Web sites as part of the monthly fee. You can also find other sources to host your Web site. Most colleges provide free Web hosting space to their students for personal Web sites.

Internal Search Tool

Most large Web sites include an internal search tool that can be used to look for information on that site. They work just like the search engines that you can access at Yahoo and Google, with keyword searching capability. These search tools catalog new material as it is added to the Web site, constantly updating an index of relevant keywords in the search database. For instance, the University of Texas–El Paso uses a private version of Google for internal searches.

When someone visits a Web site and searches for a keyword, pages containing that word can be found quickly. Figure 12-2 shows a typical advanced search screen found at a large e-commerce Web site. Most e-commerce sites offer advanced search capabilities such as product category, manufacturer, product name, model number, price range, clearance items, and so forth.

FIGURE 12-2
E-commerce Web site showing advanced search capabilities

Database Server

Companies often store product catalogs and other useful information in electronic databases on a company server. When the company wants to add a product to the catalog or change a product's stock quantity, it simply makes the changes in the database. If the company Web site links to the database on the company server, then a Web customer can look up a product in the online catalog, and any changes will be reflected there. The company doesn't have to make the changes on the Web site, too. When a customer requests something in the catalog, the Web site simply calls up the company catalog database, retrieves the desired information, and formats it for display on the customer's screen.

STEP-BY-STEP 12.1

1. Open your browser and go to the University of Illinois Beginner's Guide to HTML, which is shown in Figure 12-3. The URL is **archive.ncsa.uiuc.edu/General/Internet/WWW**.

FIGURE 12-3
University of Illinois HTML online guide

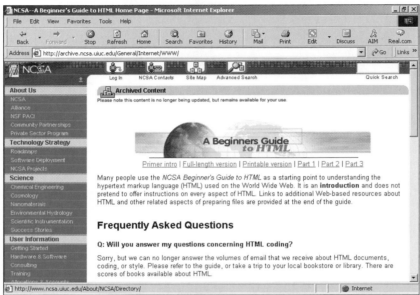

Open Part I of the guide and scroll down to the section on Markup Tags. What do each of the following HTML tags do?

a. <TITLE> _____

b. <H1> _____

c. <P> _____

d. </P> _____

e. <UL> _____

2. Open the Web site at **misnt.indstate.edu/mfbjm/firstpage.htm**. To see the actual HTML source code that creates this page, click the **View** menu and then **Source** (in Internet Explorer) or **Page Source** (in Netscape Navigator). You should see the source code shown in Figure 12-4. You can close the source code window by clicking the **Close** button in the upper right corner. (For a more detailed book about HTML programming, see Course Technology's *HTML Basics, Second Edition,* by Barksdale and Turner.) You'll have the opportunity to do more work with this Web page in Project 12-1.

STEP-BY-STEP 12.1 Continued

FIGURE 12-4
HTML source for Web document

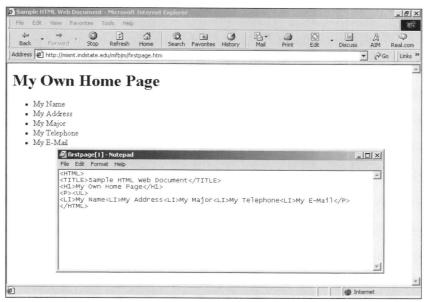

3. Go to Yahoo's clip art directory at **dir.yahoo.com/Computers_and_Internet/Graphics/Clip_Art/**. Find clip art images for the following subjects, and print a copy of each image: basketball, lawn mower, computer, family, textbook.

Once you have viewed an image in your browser, you can save a copy of that image by right-clicking the image and then choosing **Save Picture As** (in Internet Explorer) or **Save Image** (in Netscape Navigator) from the menu, as shown in Figure 12-5.

Net Tip

The University of Illinois was a pioneer in Internet development. Both Netscape Navigator and Internet Explorer descended from Mosaic, an early browser developed at the University of Illinois. The developers of Mosaic, graduate students at the university, co-founded the Netscape company in 1994.

Did You Know?

Caution: Many images you find online are copyrighted and cannot be used without obtaining permission from their owners. Organizations such as Indiana State University have specific rules about use of logos and other trademarks. Be sure to check first.

STEP-BY-STEP 12.1 Continued

FIGURE 12-5
Clip art with Save Picture As command

 Save Picture As

4. You must convert an image into a compatible electronic format before it can be used on the Web site. Most sites use the .GIF or .JPEG graphic file formats. *GIF* (Graphics Interchange Format) is the universal standard format for storing images for display in Web browsers. It is used for most lettering, small pictures, and animations. *JPEG* (for the Joint Photographic Experts Group, the photography committee that designed it) is the standard for compressing still images, such as photographs and art. JPEG files do not render lettering well. If you have a photograph or artwork, use a scanner to convert the image to an e-file. If you have a digital camera, it can capture an image and save it as a .GIF or .JPG file directly.

Did You Know?

The JPEG compression can reduce a 2 megabyte image file to 100 kilobytes or smaller. However, the compression loses some of the original image when it is displayed in your browser. The degree of compression is adjustable, providing a tradeoff between download time and image quality. The greater the compression you choose, the faster the image file will download, but the lower the image quality when displayed.

STEP-BY-STEP 12.1 Continued

5. To see what these HTML features look like on a Web page, open **www.buy.com**, shown in Figure 12-6.

FIGURE 12-6
Buy.com Web page

a. Notice the use of several font sizes. Which catch your eye? Why?

_____

_____

b. The page designer has used bold to emphasize certain items in this page, particularly in the welcome message in the center of the page. Which items appear in bold, and why?

_____

_____

c. Notice the many hyperlinks on this page. Some are the traditional blue underlined text phrases, while others are just blue. Move your cursor to one of the hyperlinks. What happens to the mouse pointer when it reaches a hyperlink?

_____

_____

The Web designer has used tables on this page to organize the material. Notice the use of individual cells near the top, beginning with Home and ending with Affiliates. The column at the left with the Price Mistake of the Day contains several cells in the table, one for each featured product. The main content in the middle with a white background is also one large cell in the table. The contents of this cell are built dynamically, possibly to vary for different types of visitors to this Web site.

STEP-BY-STEP 12.1 Continued

6. Open the Yahoo GeoCities site **www.geocities.com**, pictured in Figure 12-7. Click the **Sign up for a free web site** link at the left of the page and sign up for the free service. Then find the following information about this service:

a. How much space is available for your Web site in the basic program?

_____

b. What is the monthly GeoCities Plus membership fee? What additional services are available in GeoCities Plus?

_____

_____

c. What additional services are available in GeoCities Pro?

_____

d. Can you perform commercial activities such as advertising in the basic GeoCities home page space?

_____

e. Visit your own ISP's Web site and look around to see if it offers Web hosting space. Does it? If so, how much space are you allowed?

_____

_____

FIGURE 12-7
GeoCities site with free home page offer

STEP-BY-STEP 12.1 Continued

7. Open the **www.indstate.edu/it/user-serv/** site at Indiana State University. In the Search box on the left side, key the word **frontpage** and press **Enter**. The Web server will do an internal search, looking only at pages posted to this university's Web site. You should see results similar to those shown in Figure 12-8. How many articles appear in your search? Why is it useful to have an index of the documents available at this site?

FIGURE 12-8
Results of internal search for "frontpage"

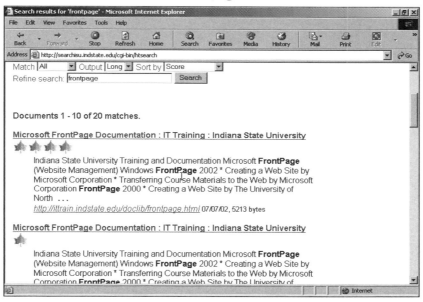

8. To see how data is retrieved from a database server, go to the Beverly-Hanks Real Estate site at **www.beverly-hanks.com**. Click the **Search Our Online Database** link in the middle of the opening page. Click the **Residential** property type button, and then choose **All** for Area/County to view a property selection form, as pictured in Figure 12-9. Using this form, customers can search for particular properties in the company's database. They can enter search criteria, such as square footage, price range, and number of bedrooms to call up just the properties they want to review.

STEP-BY-STEP 12.1 Continued

Fill in the form with your own criteria. Click the **Search** button to have the database server find properties that match your choices. When you see the search results, click the picture of one home to see the detailed information. List your property criteria below, and print the listing (including the photograph of the property) for at least one property that matches your choice.

FIGURE 12-9
Realtor Web site database query form

a. City: _____

b. Type: _____

c. Bedrooms: _____

d. Bathrooms: _____

e. Price Range: _____ to _____

f. Street: _____

g. How many properties matched your selections? _____

h. What is the address of one matching property? _____

i. This site also features a mortgage calculator. Click a property in your search results to select it. Then scroll down to the bottom of the screen and click the **Mortgage Payment** link. Using the default values in this form, what is the monthly payment for your property?

_____

Extra Challenge

Why is it a good idea to use a professional firm to host your company Web site? What are the disadvantages of hosting it on your own computer?

Methods for Developing a Web Site

In the previous Step-by-Step, you learned that Web sites are composed of HTML files and images. You will need a Web server to host your site and, in addition to building the site, you need to create and register a domain name for it. There are several approaches to creating the Web site: You can hire a Web developer, do it yourself, use an online store, or use Web-building software.

Outsource: Hire a Web Developer

Most organizations hire an outside expert to develop the Web site. The Web developer is often an advertising firm that already has expertise in developing and delivering marketing messages to customers. This firm is able to put together the contents of the site as well as physically prepare the HTML files. Other kinds of Web developers would know how to build Web pages but would not necessarily have the expertise to create an effective promotional message. With this type of developer, your organization would be responsible for developing the promotional message and the contents for the Web site.

Most consultants advertise on the Web by including links to their home page on the sites they create. Like many other business services, word-of-mouth may be the best way to learn about effective Web developers.

Some organizations contract on a per-hour basis, while others offer one price for the entire Web site. Updates are necessary, so don't forget to include this expense in your organization's budget.

Do It Yourself

Rather than hire a Web developer, you could build the site yourself. This alternative is similar to the first one except *you* would be the Web developer! Before you panic, remember that building the Web page HTML files is fairly straightforward once you have the ideas for what you want to say. To build your own site, you would need Web editor software, such as Netscape Composer or Microsoft FrontPage, and FTP software to publish HTML files on a Web server. To publish means to transfer a file from your computer's hard drive to a Web server using FTP. In Lesson 13, you will see how to develop a Web site with FrontPage.

Use an Online Store

A few services will create and maintain a complete online e-commerce Web site for you. The best known of these is Yahoo!Stores. Your entire store would be hosted by Yahoo, including online catalog, order entry forms, and payment processing. You could add products, descriptions, prices, and even pictures of your products to your store. The process is simple, and there is a tutorial to get you started with a sample store. Your Yahoo!Store would offer your customers an electronic shopping cart and online payment methods, and would provide you plenty of management reports.

STEP-BY-STEP 12.2

SCANS

1. Go to the Beverly-Hanks Web site shown in Figure 12-9. Follow the link near the bottom of the page to the developer's own Web site **(www.seventy-twodpi.com)** shown in Figure 12-10. List five of the roles this company performs as a Web developer, shown at the bottom of the home page.

_____

_____

_____

_____

_____

FIGURE 12-10
Web developer reference

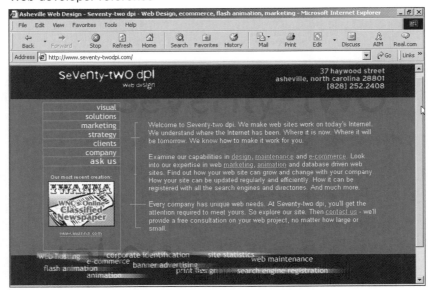

2. What should you consider in deciding whether to do it yourself or hire a Web developer to build your site? What skills do you need to be your own Web developer?

_____

_____

_____

STEP-BY-STEP 12.2 Continued

3. To access the Yahoo!Store as a shopper, go to **shopping.yahoo.com**. Figure 12-11 shows the Yahoo!Shopping site. Notice how the store categories resemble the Yahoo site opening page, listing categories with main headings and subheadings beneath them. In which Yahoo shopping category would you locate the following types of stores?

a. Sporting goods _____

b. Bicycles and outdoor recreation _____

c. Antiques and curios _____

d. Web development service _____

FIGURE 12-11
Yahoo!Shopping Web site

> **Net Tip**
>
> To run an online store using Yahoo!Store, you will need a computer with a Web browser and Internet access. You need a Yahoo!Store account and a merchant account with a credit card processor.

STEP-BY-STEP 12.2 Continued

4. To see how a Yahoo!Store operates, visit Harrington's of Vermont. If you can't find it in the Gourmet & Kitchen category, search for it with the Find Products search box. The opening page for this Yahoo!Shopping site is pictured in Figure 12-12.

The advantage of an online store through a service such as Yahoo is that everything is done for you once the store is created. You don't have to host the site or provide any hardware or software for the site. Yahoo stores the orders for you to check, or you can request the orders be e-mailed to you. Yahoo promotes your store along with its other online stores, and your URL can appear in Yahoo's main catalog and in other search engines.

FIGURE 12-12
Harrington's Yahoo!Store site

Locate the following information about Harrington's Yahoo e-commerce site:

a. How do you request a printed catalog?

_____

_____

b. What is the cost of the catalog? _____

c. Describe one of the current Web site specials and its cost. How much do you save by ordering from the Internet rather than from the catalog?

_____

_____

d. How does Harrington's determine shipping charges for an order?

_____

_____

STEP-BY-STEP 12.2 Continued

 e. What is the price of the smaller (6.5-7.5 lb.) spiral-sliced smoked party ham?_____

5. Go to the main Yahoo page and click the **Store Building** link near the bottom right of the page. Then click the **Y! Store Basics** link near the center of that page. You will then see the Yahoo!Store opening page pictured in Figure 12-13. Answer the following questions about Yahoo!Store:

 a. What is the cost per item to list them in your online catalog? _____

 b. What is the monthly cost for a small store? _____

 c. What is the per-transaction cost for operating the store? _____

 d. How is information protected when customers use a credit card?

 _____

 _____

 e. In what ways can the merchant receive orders from customers who want to buy from the Web site?

 _____

 _____

FIGURE 12-13
Yahoo!Store Basics page

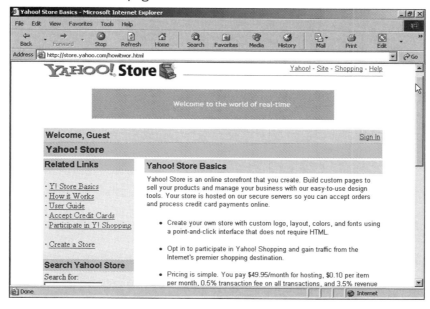

6. The project at the end of this lesson will ask you to create a Yahoo bicycle sample store. For now, you will choose a name for your store and go through the test drive at the Yahoo site. You'll use this work when you complete the project. Don't create two different Yahoo sample stores.

STEP-BY-STEP 12.2 Continued

Follow the **Set up a Test Store** link to create your own store. Figure 12-14 shows a portion of the account creation form for the free 30-day trial version of the Yahoo!Store. You will need to log in with your Yahoo ID or create a new ID if you do not have one. This ID permits you to receive e-mail at *yahooID@yahoo.com* and to use the Yahoo!Store service.

You will have to provide the following account information for your Yahoo store: Unique account name, full name of your store, account password (for management purposes), your name, your e-mail address, and your phone number. Then answer the remaining questions. Click the **Create my Yahoo!Store** button to start building your store.

Net Tip

When you create a sample store, it must have a unique account ID. Yahoo will tell you if you have chosen a name already selected by someone else. Remember that your test store is good for only 30 days. Save your account ID and password in a safe place, because you will need it later to enter products and get management reports for your sample store.

FIGURE 12-14
Account setup for Yahoo!Store

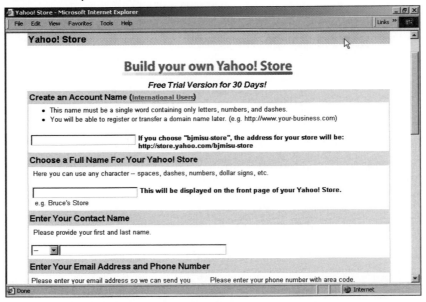

Carefully follow the instructions on the screen. You must agree to the store merchant service agreement before proceeding with the store. The test drive includes a five-minute guided tour that shows you how to create a store by adding categories, products, and so forth.

STEP-BY-STEP 12.2 Continued

7. There are many useful online tips for merchants who want to build a successful store. Access Yahoo's *10 Secrets of Selling Online* at **www.store.yahoo.com/vw/secrets.html**. Pick four secrets and write a brief description of the advice the author provides for each item.

a. _____

_____

b. _____

_____

c. _____

_____

d. _____

_____

Extra Challenge

Most experts say that a Web site must be continually updated to keep it fresh. Why do you think this is important, especially for e-commerce sites?

Use Web Package Software

You can buy Web package software that automates the preparation of the Web store, similar to the way Yahoo!Store does. The software asks you questions about products and services you plan to present in your online store. From the answers you provide, the software builds the database and the HTML files to support your store. Then you need to locate a host server for the Web site. Typically, this alternative also includes registration of your domain name, described in Step-by-Step 12.3. For example, see the ShoppingQ e-commerce system at *shoppingq.com.*

Technology Careers

A *Webmaster* is an individual within an organization who is responsible for developing and maintaining the Web site. The Webmaster's e-mail address is often listed at the bottom of a Web page as the contact for suggestions or complaints about out-of-date material or nonfunctioning links. The Webmaster must know HTML commands and have programming skills. The Webmaster will have access to the Web server that hosts the organization's Web site. Some companies outsource the Webmaster's duties to an outside Web developer.

Registering and Promoting Your Web Site

The ICANN Web site at *www.icann.org* is responsible for domain names and the registration process. A company that accepts domain name registrations is known as a *domain registrar.* The *domain name* is the last part of a URL that includes the organization's unique name followed by a *top-level domain name (TLD)* designating the type of organization that owns the site. Most organizations choose domain names that contain a form of the organization's name, to make the site's owner easy to identify from its address. For instance, the U.S. Senate domain name is *senate.gov,* Purdue University's domain name is *purdue.edu,* and the Coca-Cola domain name is *coke.com.* Some companies register more than one name: *coca-cola.com* is also registered to Coca-Cola.

The last three letters in each of these domain names is an abbreviation. The ending *.com* refers to commercial organizations or businesses. The ending *.edu* represents institutions of higher education. And *.gov* refers to United States government organizations. These three-letter abbreviations are top-level domain names. Other common top-level domains include *.net* (network providers) and *.org* (other organizations, including nonprofit organizations).

> **Did You Know?**
>
> New TLDs include *.biz* (businesses), *.pro* (for professionals such as lawyers and accountants), *.name* (for individuals), *.coop* (for cooperatives of more than one organization), and *.museum*.

S TEP-BY-STEP 12.3

1. It is easy to search for a particular domain name to see if it has been previously registered. Go to the **www.domain.com** Web site shown in Figure 12-15 and type your last name in the search box and check **.com**. Click **Go** to see if your domain name is already taken. If it is taken, click the **Whois** link to see who it is registered to. For example, one of the authors of this text asked Whois to search for *mclaren.com*. It found a company in the United Kingdom had registered *mclaren.com* in 2000.

   a. Who has already registered "your" site? _____

   b. What is the purpose of that Web site?

   _____

   _____

   c. Try searching for your first and last name together, as in *catherinesmith.com*. Is your full name available as a domain? _____

STEP-BY-STEP 12.3 Continued

FIGURE 12-15
Domain name registration site

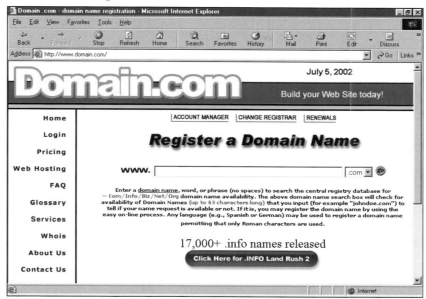

2. Click the **Pricing** link at **www.domaincom**.

   a. How much does it cost to register a new *.com* domain name with Domain.com? _____
   This fee covers the initial registration and updates for a two-year period. You must pay this fee online with a credit card in their secure payment system. Sixty days before the end of the two-year registration period you will be billed for the next two years.

   b. How much is the renewal fee? _____

   c. What happens if you neglect to pay the renewal fee?

   _____

   _____

> **Net Tip**
>
> With most Web site hosting ser- vices, it is possible to use your own domain name or the name of the Web server site followed by your name. For example, the imaginary law firm of McLaren and McLaren could register *mclarenlaw.com* as its domain name. *www.xyzhost.com/mclaren* could refer to the McLaren com- pany's site hosted at *xyzhost.com*.

STEP-BY-STEP 12.3 Continued

3. You can use this Web site to promote your new domain name by submitting it to major search engines and online directories. As shown in Figure 12-16, click the **Services** link and choose the **Search Engine Positioning** link.

   a. What is the cost of the top 50 search engine service? _____

   b. How many of the top 50 sites do you recognize? _____

   c. What does it cost to have domain.com resubmit your site monthly for three months?

   _____

   d. How do you enter the information at this site?

   _____

   _____

Extra Challenge

Why do you think that most organizations want to have their own registered domain name? Should a company be able to sell a domain name to another organization?

FIGURE 12-16
Submit your Web site

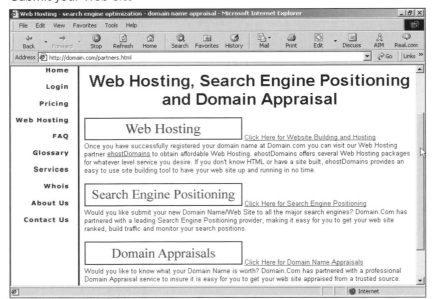

 Net Ethics

Registrars register domain names on a first-come, first-served basis. Do you think it is appropriate for a company to take another company's unregistered name and register it as its own domain name? Should a company whose trademark is properly registered be able to protect that trademark from being used in other domain names?

SUMMARY

In this lesson, you learned:

■ A Web site is made up of some basic components, including optional features of many e-commerce sites.

■ There are several methods for developing a Web site.

■ You can promote your Web site to search engines.

VOCABULARY *Review*

Define the following terms:

24/7	GIF	Top-level domain name (TLD)
Clip art	HTML (hypertext markup	Web editor
Domain name	language)	Web server
Domain registrar	HTML tags	Webmaster
File transfer protocol (FTP)	JPEG	

REVIEW *Questions*

TRUE/FALSE

Circle T if the statement is true or F if the statement is False.

T   F   1. HTML files contain text characters that describe how a Web page should appear in your browser.

T   F   2. After you pay for registering a domain name initially, you have that name forever.

T   F   3. The most common file format for clip art graphic images is MPEG.

T   F   4. To publish your HTML file means to save it on your own computer's hard drive.

T   F   5. You can right-click an image on a Web site and save that image to your own hard drive.

WRITTEN QUESTIONS

Write a brief answer to the following questions.

1. What language is used to prepare Web pages?

2. Why would you want to use a Web editor instead of manually preparing a Web page?

3. What are the disadvantages of using a Web editor?

4. List the mandatory components of a Web site.

5. How do you transfer files to a Web server?

6. What is a Webmaster and why is this person important to a Web site?

7. How do you register a .com domain name?

8. Why does your Web page need a domain name?

9. How much does it cost to register a personal domain name for the Internet?

PROJECTS

 PROJECT 12-1

You want to personalize the Web site shown earlier in Figure 12-4. Open this page at **misnt.indstate.edu/mfbjm/firstpage.htm**. From your browser, view the source for this page in your text editor on your computer, and then fill in the blanks for your own information such as your name, e-mail address, and so forth. Feel free to add more information. Save the file on your own computer, and then open that file in your browser.

 PROJECT 12-2

You want to develop an e-commerce Web site for your online sporting goods store, using Yahoo!Store. Go to Yahoo!Store at **www.store.yahoo.com**. Use the same site you started in Step-by-Step 12-2. Make sure you choose the 30-day free trial link and don't submit your credit card number for a permanent site! Follow the directions in the Yahoo Web site to build your store.

Pick a unique account name for your store. Use your own name and e-mail address as contact information. Add fitness products for your store from the table below. The part number is shown first, along with its description and retail price. Shipping costs are $34 for the first three items and $8 for the next two.

PART NUMBER	DESCRIPTION	RETAIL PRICE
EX123-4	Exercise bike	$199.95
EX127-2	21-speed mountain bike	$349.00
EX390-0	Kid's bicycle	$112.59
EX234-1	Bike pants	$22.95
EX234-6	Bike helmet	$34.95

Write a brief description of your e-commerce site, including its URL. Include a printout of the main catalog showing these fitness items.

SCANS PROJECT 12-3

Continue development of your Yahoo bike store. Add at least five more products to your store, including more bicycles and accessories. Visit another Yahoo!Shopping bicycle store such as **www.gearlink.com** to find similar products. For this project, print a copy of the updated main catalog. Write a brief description of changes that you would like to make to your Yahoo!Store.

SCANS TEAMWORK PROJECT

Each member of your team should search the Internet for suitable photographs or clip art for each of your Yahoo!Store products. You can save the picture/image file on your own disk by right-clicking the image and choosing the appropriate command from the menu. Add the images to your online store to make your pages as appealing as possible. Remember that copyright laws apply to many Web sites and only use images that do not violate these laws.

CRITICAL*Thinking*

SCANS ACTIVITY 12-1

Prepare a brief description of the management reports available for a Yahoo online store. How could a business owner make use of the reports about the e-commerce site?

DEVELOPING A WEB SITE WITH MICROSOFT® FRONTPAGE

OBJECTIVES

Upon completion of this lesson, you should be able to:

■ Evaluate examples of good Web sites and identify principles of good Web design.

■ Create a personal FrontPage Web using the Personal Web template.

■ Use FrontPage to customize a FrontPage Web.

Estimated Time: 4 hours

VOCABULARY

Download

Frame

FrontPage

FrontPage web

Plug-in

Publish

Tasks list

Theme

Thumbnail

Wizard

Design Webs Like a Pro

Lesson 13 will guide you through creating basic Web pages using Microsoft's *FrontPage* 2002, the most popular Web development and Web editor software on the market. You will learn the principles of good Web design and evaluate the design of some award-winning Web sites. Then you will actually create Web pages, edit them, and explore different design choices, including graphics.

Even if you don't have FrontPage, the discussion and illustrations in Lesson 13 will show you how Web development software works. When you are ready to create your own Web site, no matter which development software you buy, you will have a basic understanding that will make learning your new software easy… and fun!

In the last lesson, you learned about the components of a Web site. This lesson will show you how to actually create a Web site using Microsoft FrontPage. To complete the activities in this lesson, you will need to have the FrontPage software installed on your computer. If this is not possible, you can still learn about Web page development by following the activities in this lesson and looking closely at the illustrations.

The lesson begins with some examples of good Web site design, including several award-winning sites. Good Web sites share several common design principles. Most award-winning sites provide attractive graphics that load quickly, organize information for easy access, and don't require any special plug-ins for your browser. Good sites remain fresh, with new information added regularly to capture viewers' interest.

You've visited many sites in your Web tours throughout this book. You are probably starting to form opinions about what makes an effective, vibrant site that will draw visitors again and again. In this lesson, you'll look at some sites that have been honored for their quality, learn why they work so well, and begin to learn how sites are created.

Figure 13-1 shows the home page for Toyota. This site even reminds you that it is a good site! The home page is easy to read, fits on one screen, has pleasing use of color and space, and provides the most important information for the user. The search tool makes finding facts easy for users that don't immediately see what they want in the categories listed across the top. It provides links to specific product lines. Links to consumer information, such as careers at Toyota and corporate information, are found in the About Toyota link. Privacy information is found at the bottom of the home page.

FIGURE 13-1
Toyota home page

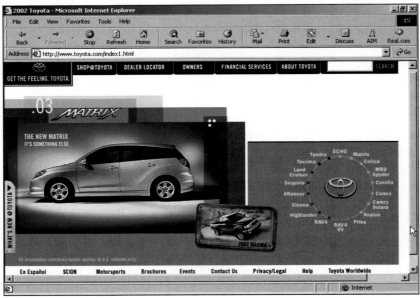

Expertly designed corporate sites and small sites designed by individuals not only share design principles but also are created with the same kinds of Web authoring tools. Many companies sell Web authoring software. Some general-purpose packages such as Microsoft's FrontPage and Netscape Composer are good for beginners and experts alike. Other packages are developed for special audiences. CourseInfo, by Blackboard, Inc., is a package aimed at teachers that want to make a Web site for a class. It even lets teachers post tests online. IBM's ecBuilder Pro is a software package for developing an e-commerce site from your own personal computer.

This lesson will show you how to use FrontPage to create a Web site. If you have FrontPage, you'll be able to experiment with your own site as you follow the activities. If not, follow the steps to see how straightforward creating a site can be. If you have another Web editor, you should be able to complete similar steps, working with hyperlinks, graphics, background colors, and different fonts. Whether or not you will be able to publish your site depends on your facilities.

Will what you learn in this lesson make you an expert Web designer? No, not quite! What it will do is get you started thinking about ways you can incorporate good design ideas into the pages you develop. As you experiment with Web authoring tools, you'll have fun creating attractive and useful pages. And when you are ready to create your own site, you'll be able to learn your software's more advanced features.

Good Web Design

While it is relatively easy to make a home page, it's much more difficult to make a great Web site. Much depends on the purpose of the site. A home page for an individual can be prepared in a matter of hours, while a Web site for a small business could take weeks. Building a Web site for a large organization could take months or years. In fact, to reduce the time, most large organizations assign several people to the task.

Good Web sites share some common design principles:

1. Organize your site into sections, with a separate page for each section. An outline is useful for planning this design.

2. Make your home page functional and attractive.

3. Display current information, and update frequently to keep the site fresh.

4. Design so that your pages will transfer or ***download*** quickly from the server to the user's computer for display.

   ■ Use small images (less than 50 KB).

   ■ Instead of displaying a full-size image, use a smaller version called a ***thumbnail*** that users can click to call up the larger image if they want. FrontPage can automatically create a thumbnail image with a link to the full-size image.

   ■ Instead of one large page, break up the site into several smaller pages.

5. Use colors (for background, text, hyperlinks, etc.) that will display and print well. Remember: Light text colors on a dark background may "disappear" when printed.

6. Write in standard HTML (older browser versions may not be able to handle your page). Caution: Although FrontPage produces standard HTML, it also contains features not supported by all Web servers and browsers.

7. Avoid elements that require browser plug-ins (or offer an alternate version that doesn't require the plug-ins). A ***plug-in*** is a specialty program that works with a major software program to enhance its capabilities.

8. Avoid frames. A ***frame*** is a rectangular section of the screen that scrolls separately from other sections. A frame is commonly used for a table of contents. When users click a link in that frame, the related contents appear in the larger frame. Not all browsers can handle frames, and they take up a lot of space on the screen.

9. Although many users have 800×600 screen resolution, develop your site for 640×480 resolution to avoid horizontal scrolling.

10. Include interactivity with users by providing hyperlinks and an e-mail link.

11. Provide an internal search tool for large sites. Some Web servers have software that can build a site index automatically.

Award-winning Web sites offer good design ideas, even for small sites. When you find a site that looks good, add it to your bookmark list, so you can revisit the site and learn from its design.

STEP-BY-STEP 13.1

1. Each year, the Webby Awards recognize outstanding Web sites. Figure 13-2 shows the **www.webbyawards.com** site. Go to the **Winners** section to learn more about the awards.

FIGURE 13-2
Webby Awards Web site

a. Slide your mouse down the categories on the left side. What happens, and how does this catch your eye?

_____

_____

b. Visit the **Commerce** category and list two good design characteristics for the winning site there.

_____

_____

STEP-BY-STEP 13.1 Continued

2. The Dell Computer Company has frequently been cited as a successful e-commerce Web site. Visit the Dell site, shown in Figure 13-3.

FIGURE 13-3
Dell Computers Web site

a. How many distinct sections or regions do you see on the Dell opening page? _____

b. What happens when you move the mouse to a line with blue text?

_____

_____

c. What is the purpose of the gray banner running across the top of this page (and all Dell pages)? *(Hint: Scroll the mouse across this area and observe the status line of your browser.)*

_____

_____

d. Select the **Home & Home Office** link. What is the purpose of the blue background section at the left side of the Web site?

_____

_____

e. This opening page fits on one screen yet contains a great deal of information. Do you think it is too crowded or compressed? Why or why not?

_____

_____

STEP-BY-STEP 13.1 Continued

3. Open the Web Marketing Association site at **www.webaward.org** and find its most recent winning sites page. Click the **winners** link and choose **all levels** in the **Award Level** box. List one site from each of the following categories and briefly describe one of the site's design elements that you find particularly effective.

a. Best Legal Web Site

_____

_____

b. Best Travel Web Site

_____

_____

c. Best Automobile Web Site

_____

_____

d. Standard of Excellence

_____

_____

e. Best Investment Web Site

_____

_____

> ### Extra Challenge
>
> Evaluate the design of a Web site that you visit frequently. Describe its good features and any design mistakes. Overall, do you think this site is well designed? Why or why not?

 Net Business

Zack Johnson graduated from engineering school and immediately opened his own Internet design and development company. He employs mostly local college students to design, develop, and host Web sites for clients. His market niche falls between the big design houses and the one-person operations. He markets his services by charging a lower hourly rate than most, and including two site revisions in the initial price. He does some Web development by hand using HTML commands as well as using Web development software such as FrontPage. For some applications, Zack builds the Web page "on the fly" by plugging in data from a database such as Microsoft Access. Why do you think this small firm can charge a smaller hourly rate than larger Web developers? Do you think that $750 for preparing a small business Web site is a fair price? For a small Web development firm, how do you think Zack should promote his company to solicit new business?

Accessibility Guidelines

In addition to the Web design tips, Web designers are advised to follow accessibility guidelines that enable physically challenged users to access the Web site. Most of the guidelines represent good Web design principles, as the following list shows:

1. Supply alternate text for all images used on a page. When a blind person uses assistive technology such as special software to read aloud a site, they will hear the alternate text.

2. Design Web pages so that information conveyed with color (e.g., blue for hyperlinks) is also available without color. For instance, make sure hyperlinks are underlined as well. This allows for color-blindness as well as if the page is viewed in black-and-white.

3. Test your page with scripting, style sheets, and multimedia turned off. This represents the browser configuration of some users.

4. Provide redundant text links for each active region of an image map.

5. Include row and column headers for data tables, making it easier for a user to understand when the data are read aloud.

6. Include a link to the appropriate plug-in (a small application called an applet) when your Web page includes use of content that requires the plug-in or applet. For example, this might include Adobe Acrobat Reader for PDF files, Macromedia Flash for Flash animations, or Real Player for audio and video clips.

7. When a timed response is required, alert the user and provide more time if necessary.

8. When you cannot create an accessible page, provide a link to an accessible version. This version will probably be in plain text.

For more information, see the U.S. government section 508 guidelines on accessibility at *www.access-board.gov/sec508/508standards.htm*.

> **Net Fun** ☼
>
> For some practical development advice and online workshops offered in a very upbeat and low-key style, visit WebMonkey *(webmonkey.com)*, a how-to guide for Web developers. You'll find tips from the pros for beginners as well as experienced developers.

Creating a Personal Web with FrontPage 2002

FrontPage is an easy-to-use Web site development and management tool. With it you can create and maintain a FrontPage web or an individual home page. A *FrontPage web* is Microsoft's name for the set of HTML and image files that comprise a particular Web site, including common navigation bars that let users navigate between the pages. We'll use "Web" to refer to the World Wide Web, and "web" to refer to a FrontPage web.

FrontPage consists of the web editor and some optional components, such as Image Composer for working with pictures and Personal Web Server, which converts your personal computer into a Web server. FrontPage has tools for creating, viewing, and managing your web of pages. You can import objects into the web and establish themes for the web. A *theme* is a design template that is used on all pages of a web. It controls the colors, background image, and basic layout of the page. By choosing a theme in FrontPage, you will create a consistent look across all pages in your web. You will learn more about themes later.

FrontPage also lets you create and make changes to individual pages in your web. You can start with a new blank page or you can edit an existing page with the Open command from the File menu. You can double-click any page in your web to open it in FrontPage for changes. The FrontPage menu bar and toolbar resemble those of Microsoft Word and other word processing software. You can highlight text and then format that text by clicking a button, just as with word processing software.

Hot Tip

Based on previous work on your computer, FrontPage may list different existing webs in the top of your New Page or Web task pane.

S TEP-BY-STEP 13.2

1. Click the **Start** button in the taskbar, point to **All Programs**, or **Programs**, and click **Microsoft FrontPage**. *Note*: By default, FrontPage will open to the last web built and in the last view used. You will see a New Page or Web task pane similar to Figure 13-4. The top portion of the task pane lets you select an existing web and the middle portion lets you create a new web. Click the **Web Site Templates** link in the New from template section.

FIGURE 13-4
FrontPage startup screen

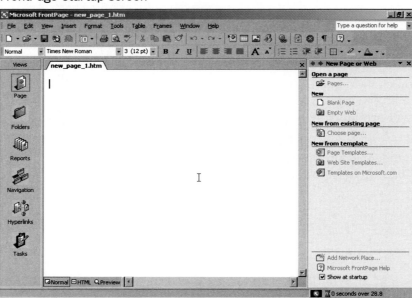

STEP-BY-STEP 13.2 Continued

2. FrontPage will display the Web Site Templates dialog box shown in Figure 13-5. Although FrontPage defaults to the One Page Web in the left pane, click the **Personal Web** template instead. Choose a different name for your web in the text box at the right side. The name of your web will appear whenever someone opens your site on the Internet, so pick something appropriate such as your first name. In this case the web will be called "bruce" and will be stored at C:\My Documents\ My Webs\bruce. Then click **OK** and FrontPage will create all the files associated with your web.

FIGURE 13-5
Web Site Templates dialog box

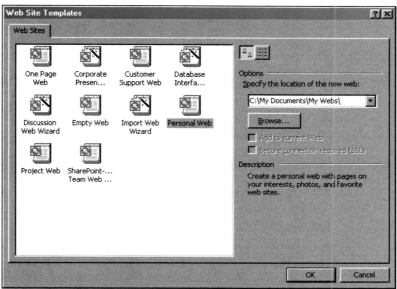

3. To see the files associated with your web, click the **Navigation** button in the Views pane at the left side of the FrontPage window. Your new web now appears in navigation view, as shown in Figure 13-6. The FrontPage template built six HTML page files for your personal web, as shown in the main window. Details and location of the files are shown in the Folder List. Click the **Toggle Pane** button to display the folder list, if necessary. These files contain the outline for a personal web, but you will need to fill in your own information. The main home page file is called *index.htm*.

STEP-BY-STEP 13.2 Continued

FIGURE 13-6
FrontPage web in Navigation view

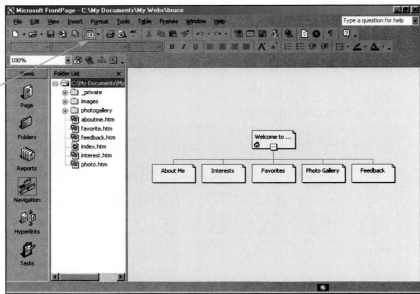

Toggle Pane button

4. To view the contents of your home page in the FrontPage editing window, double-click the **Welcome to** box in Navigation View. The *index.htm* file will open in page view and look like Figure 13-7. The elements on this page came from the Personal Web template. The design formatting is the default theme, Network. This page is an HTML document, even though you don't see any HTML tags in this view. By clicking the **HTML** tab at the bottom of your screen, you can see what the document's HTML code looks like. To see what the page will look like when published, click the **Preview** tab. Print each of the three views of your home page and compare what you see.

FIGURE 13-7
Home page in FrontPage Normal window

Font Color button

STEP-BY-STEP 13.2 Continued

    a. What pages in your web were created by the Personal Web template?

    _____

    _____

    _____

    b. How can you access the other pages in the web?

    _____

5. Now you will make some changes in your home page. Be sure the **Normal** tab is highlighted at the bottom of the FrontPage window—Normal is the window in which you can make changes to the page.

    a. In the top line, _Welcome to my Web site_, replace the word _my_ with your own name, as in _Welcome to Bruce's Web site_. Double-click the Welcome banner and make your correction in the Page Banner Properties box. Click **OK** to save your changes.

    b. Highlight the date just below the page banner, click the list arrow next to the **Font Color** button on the toolbar, as shown in Figure 13-7, and then click **Red** for the text color. (Or open the **Format** menu, click **Font**, click the arrow on the **Color** box, select the color **Red**, and click **OK**.)

    c. Delete the first paragraph in this page. Replace it with a paragraph or two about yourself.

    d. Replace the weather report text with words appropriate for your location and the current weather. _(Hint: use **www.weather.com** to look up information about your current weather.)_

    e. Leave the last paragraph—it contains a special date field that is automatically updated whenever you make changes to the page. Switch to the **Preview** window. Click the **Toggle Pane** button in the Toolbar to remove the Folder List and make more room in Preview. Your home page should now look like Figure 13-8. Print and save your page.

    f. What else do you think should appear on your opening home page? Remember that there are three other pages in this Web site.

    _____

    _____

STEP-BY-STEP 13.2 Continued

FIGURE 13-8
Modified home page in Preview window

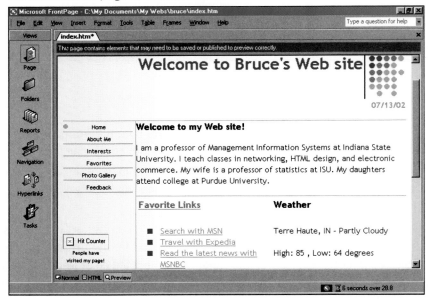

6. Notice that the hit counter at the lower left contains a red *x*, indicating that it does not work. When you publish your web to a Web server that is running special software called FrontPage Server Extensions, active components such as this hit counter will be enabled.

7. If you have made changes since Step 5, click the **Save** button on the toolbar to save your changes in the *index.htm* file. Where are the changes actually saved?

Extra Challenge

FrontPage templates, such as this one that lets you place your words into a standard format, have made it much easier for software users to do complicated tasks. Take a look at the Corporate Presence template in FrontPage to learn what features it can build for a company site.

Customizing Your FrontPage Web

Hot Tip

To enter a hyperlink in the FrontPage Normal window, just type in the URL, beginning with *http://*. FrontPage will recognize the URL and convert it to a hyperlink. If you would like descriptive words other than the URL to appear in the page, first type and highlight the descriptive words. Then click the Insert Hyperlink button in the toolbar and enter the URL that you want to link to your description.

The FrontPage Personal Web template produced a home page and five other related pages. As you saw in the previous Step-by-Step, these pages are connected to the home page through the navigation menu at the left side. When you work with these pages, you can not only enter your own words, but also change the background or theme, bring in a picture or clip art, and add links to other pages on the Internet. If the web you created in Step-by-Step 13.2 is not open, open it now and view your home page in the Normal window.

STEP-BY-STEP 13.3

1. In the FrontPage Normal window for the personal web you created in Step-by-Step 13.2, take a look at the five menu hyperlinks that the template placed on your home page. Place the mouse pointer on the **Interests** link. What is the URL for this link? *(Hint: Look in the status bar at the bottom of the page.)* Hold down the **Crtl** key and click the link to open to the Interests web page for editing.

_____

2. Delete the line that begins, "Here is a good place. . . ." Replace the words in each of the bulleted interests with descriptions of your interests. Include a related URL for one of your interests. Figure 13-9 shows an example. Experiment with fonts and colors for these sentences.

   a. For the Interest 1 bullet, write a few sentences about your hometown.

   b. Write about one of your hobbies in the Interest 2 bullet.

   c. In the Interest 3 bullet, write about your favorite college or pro sports team.

   d. Click the **Save** button in the toolbar to save changes to the *interest.htm* file on your hard drive.

STEP-BY-STEP 13.3 Continued

FIGURE 13-9
Updated Interests page

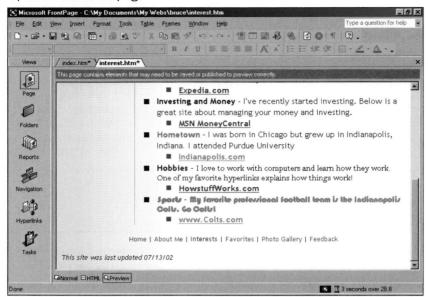

3. Would you like to give your web a new look? Choose **Theme** from the **Format** menu. The Themes dialog box is shown in Figure 13-10. Click several theme choices and preview their designs on the right.

FIGURE 13-10
FrontPage Themes dialog box

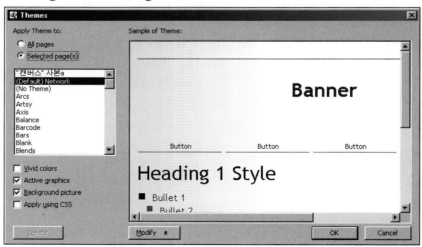

STEP-BY-STEP 13.3 Continued

When you have found a theme you like, click the **OK** button. To check out your web's new look, click the **Preview** tab. Print your Interests page. Figure 13-11 shows the Interests page with the Banner theme. Do you think the colors in this theme are a good choice? Click the **Save** button to make your changes permanent. Remember that you can always re-apply the original theme.

FIGURE 13-11
Interests page with Banner theme

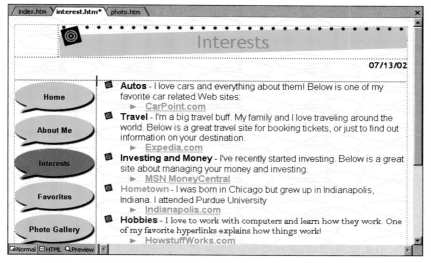

4. Now let's add an image to your home page. Press the **Ctrl** key and click the **Photo Gallery** button at the left of the Interests page to open the Photo Gallery page. As you can see, FrontPage supplies several pictures for this page as part of the template. You can replace these with your own. Double-click a picture to open the Photo Gallery Properties dialog box. Select the **mycat** picture and click the **Remove** button. Then select the **parrot** picture and click in the **Caption** text box. Key the phrase, "Genuine parrot!," and click **OK**. Notice how FrontPage adds the caption next to the bird.

   a. Double-click the photo gallery to open the dialog box. For this Step-by-Step, we'll insert clip art, but you can insert any image you have captured as an electronic file. Click the **Add** button shown in Figure 13-12, and select **Pictures from Files**. Navigate to your clip art selections. Scroll through the clip art and picture selections that FrontPage supplies. Find one you like and click **Open**. Click **OK** and your image is added to this photo gallery.

STEP-BY-STEP 13.3 Continued

FIGURE 13-12
Photo Gallery Properties dialog box

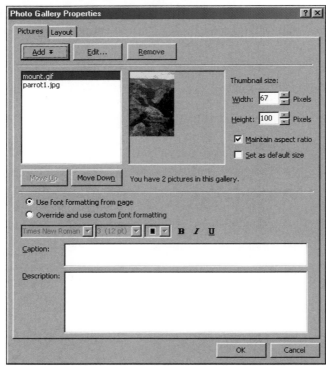

b. You can also add a clip art image anywhere on the page. Highlight the text right above the photo gallery and delete it. Point to **Picture** on the **Insert** menu bar and then select **From File**. Then find an image you want and double-click it to place the image on the page. *(Hint: If you cannot find another image, open **misnt.indstate.edu/mk199/sample.jpg** in your browser. Right-click that picture, click the **Save Picture As**, or **Save Image**, option, and save the image to your disk.)*

c. Click the art you just inserted to select it. You will see little box-like handles appear around it. Move your mouse over a handle until the cursor turns into a double-headed arrow. Then click and drag to resize the art. You can resize it in any direction by dragging the handle on the side you want to change.

d. Now click the art to select it, and click the **Center** button on the Formatting toolbar to center it horizontally on the page. You can also click and drag to move the art around. Figure 13-13 shows the Photo Gallery page after the images were inserted and the text was changed. When you are finished making your changes, save and print your Photo Gallery page.

STEP-BY-STEP 13.3 Continued

FIGURE 13-13
Photo Album page with new text and image

5. Now let's add some hyperlinks to other Web pages from your FrontPage web. Press the **Ctrl** key and click to go to your **Favorites** page. Replace the text for the three existing links with "CNN," "Travelocity," and "ESPN.com."

Highlight each of the hyperlink phrases, one at a time, and click the **Insert Hyperlink** button on the toolbar (or select the **Hyperlink** command on the **Insert** menu). In the Address box, enter the URL for that link as listed below, and click **OK**:

a. CNN: "www.cnn.com"

b. Travelocity: "www.travelocity.com"

c. ESPN.com: "www.msn.espn.go.com/main.html"

Net Fun

If you're looking for more graphic images to put on your page, visit the WebShots Graphics gallery (*webshots.com*). There you'll find a reusable image library, which contains thousands of images that you may use free of charge.

STEP-BY-STEP 13.3 Continued

Figure 13-14 shows the page and hyperlinks. Notice that the mouse pointer is touching the CNN link, and that the URL associated with that hyperlink appears in the status bar. Print and save your Favorites page.

FIGURE 13-14
Favorites page

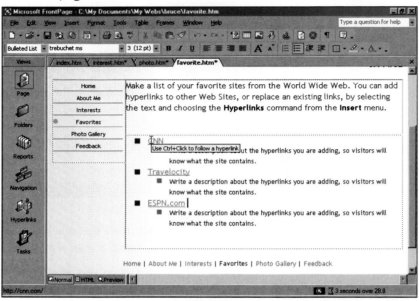

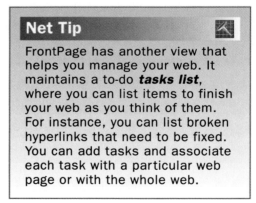

Net Tip

FrontPage has another view that helps you manage your web. It maintains a to-do *tasks list*, where you can list items to finish your web as you think of them. For instance, you can list broken hyperlinks that need to be fixed. You can add tasks and associate each task with a particular web page or with the whole web.

STEP-BY-STEP 13.3 Continued

6. Click the **Hyperlinks** button in the Views bar to display your home page in Hyperlinks view. This view displays all the links in your web. Your screen should look similar to Figure 13-15.

When you are connected to the Internet, FrontPage can check all of your external hyperlinks to see that they still work. If you can connect to the Net, do so now. Then in the View menu of your FrontPage web, point to **Reports**, point to **Problems**, and then click **Broken Hyperlinks**. Click **No** in the **Reports View** window. To begin the check, click the **Recalculate Hyperlinks** command from the **Tools** menu and click **Yes** to verify hyperlinks. You will see green check marks next to the hyperlinks that still work and question marks next to those that failed. In the hyperlink check shown in Figure 13-16, the green check marks indicate that all hyperlinks checked out OK.

FIGURE 13-15
Hyperlinks view

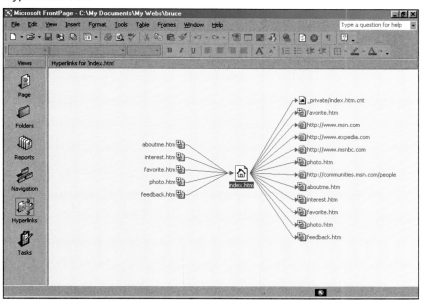

Net Tip

For now, each page in your web is saved on your hard drive. The URL begins with file://. When you *publish* your web, its pages are copied to the Web server and its URL will refer to your Web server. Use the Publish Web button to publish your web.

STEP-BY-STEP 13.3 Continued

FIGURE 13-16
Hyperlinks view with verified links

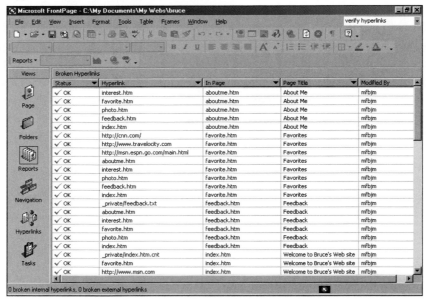

7. Now you'll change the name of one of the pages in your web. In Navigation view, single-click the **Favorites** page to select it. Press **F2** or right-click and choose **Rename** from the shortcut menu. Key **Links**, and press **Enter**. To verify that the name has been changed in all pages, click the index.htm page in Page view to display it. Notice that FrontPage has changed the name of the Favorites page to Links in the navigation buttons at the left of each page. Figure 13-17 shows the final home page, previewed in Internet Explorer.

> **Extra Challenge**
>
> Why would it be helpful to use a FrontPage theme when designing a Web site for an organization? How could the common elements in the theme aid your Web design? Have you noticed common elements in other Web sites?

STEP-BY-STEP 13.3 Continued

FIGURE 13-17
Final home page in browser

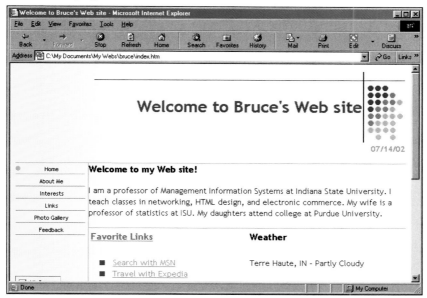

In this introductory book, you are learning about just a small sample of the many features FrontPage has to offer. It has many other templates, or you can create your own pages without the help of a template. When you gain experience with FrontPage, you can create a sophisticated site with extensive links, art and animation, and links to a database. You can create a guest book, a form for user registration, and a search page. If you are interested in learning more about FrontPage, check out the FrontPage Web site at *microsoft.com/frontpage*. When you are ready to create your own site on the World Wide Web using FrontPage, you can buy an easy-to-follow tutorial to guide you through the program's many features. Just go to Course Technology's Computer Education page at *course.com*, and order *Webmastering BASICS Using Microsoft FrontPage*.

Electronic Commerce with FrontPage

Although FrontPage 2002 does not have all the features necessary to develop a fully functional e-commerce Web site, the bCentral Commerce Manager add-in adds that capability. bCentral allows you to build a product database and then use FrontPage 2002 to create a fully-functional e-commerce Web site. It also offers order processing and credit card merchant services (at an extra fee). You can download the Commerce Manager add-in from Microsoft's Web site but must purchase a subscription to bCentral Commerce Manager. The Commerce Manager Standard subscription is currently $24.95 per month (first month is free) or $249 per year. A special version for up to 25 products is available at $12.95 per month or $99.95 per year. The Commerce Manager Canadian edition is specially designed for Canadian e-commerce companies.

Commerce Manager's catalog builder creates an illustrated catalog called a product gallery. It is able to import data from other sources, including Excel workbooks. You can use FrontPage to convert the product gallery into an electronic catalog in your FrontPage web. The Commerce

Manager add-in also enables FrontPage to add a shopping cart to your web. It adds order processing features to your FrontPage web, sending you (and your customer) an e-mail message when an order has been placed and providing management reports for e-commerce activities on your site. Commerce Manager facilitates payments via PayPal and other credit card agencies. The Commerce Manager Product Gallery can also be used to place products on the MSN Marketplace and auction sites such as eBay and uBid. You don't need to have FrontPage or develop your own Web site.

E-commerce add-in products for FrontPage are also available from other publishers. StoreFront at *storefront.net* provides wizards for FrontPage that let you build the various e-commerce features in a FrontPage web. A *wizard* is an automated tool that asks the user a series of simple questions about a feature, and then creates the necessary code to make the feature work. StoreFront comes in standard and advanced editions. The Ponte Vedra Soap Shoppe *(pvsoap.com)* e-commerce site was built with FrontPage and the StoreFront add-in. SalesCart shopping cart add-in software can be viewed in a live demo at *demo.salescart.com*.

SUMMARY

In this lesson, you learned:

- It's important to evaluate examples of good Web sites and identify principles of good Web design.

- You can create a personal FrontPage web using the Personal Web template.

- You can use FrontPage to customize a FrontPage Web.

VOCABULARY *Review*

Define the following terms:

Download	Plug-in	Theme
Frame	Publish	Thumbnail
FrontPage	Tasks list	Wizard
FrontPage web		

REVIEW *Questions*

TRUE/FALSE

Circle T if the statement is true or F if the statement is false.

T   F   1. It is a good idea to organize your Web site into sections with a separate page for each section.

T   F   2. Because most users have large monitors, it is good to design Web sites for 1024 × 768 screen resolution.

T   F   3. Most of the Web site accessibility guidelines are useful tips for all Web sites.

T   F   4. A FrontPage web is composed of a set of HTML files and image files.

T   F   5. A FrontPage theme determines the colors and styles used in every page of a web.

WRITTEN QUESTIONS

Write a brief answer to the following questions.

1. How can you make a Web page download more quickly?

2. What views do you have in FrontPage?

3. What do templates do in FrontPage?

4. How can you view the actual HTML code that FrontPage generates?

5. From the FrontPage editor, how can you open another page in the same web?

6. How can you create a hyperlink in FrontPage?

7. How can you publish the pages in your FrontPage web?

PROJECTS

 PROJECT 13-1

Find three Web sites that you visit frequently, and analyze their content according to the good design principles and the accessibility guidelines. Write a paragraph evaluation of each site. Discuss the good points and the bad points of each site. Be sure to include the URL for each site.

 PROJECT 13-2

Use FrontPage to build a one-page personal web. Include your full name, and your school or place of employment. Describe your hobbies and personal interests. Include a bullet list of ten favorite Web sites that you frequently visit. Insert a picture of yourself or of something that you care about. Include a hyperlink that will send you e-mail. (*Hint: An e-mail hyperlink follows the form **mailto:username@server.com** where you substitute your own username and server address.*) Save your web and print a copy of your site.

PROJECT 13-3

Imagine you are the owner of a lawn maintenance business called Ace Lawn Care in a small college town. You offer year-round maintenance services for lawns as well as snow removal. One reason for preparing your Web page is to offer lawn care services to rental property owners or residents who are away for the summer.

First list the goals for your Web page. What kinds of services will you advertise there? What information do you need to include on your site? You can make up the address, telephone number, fax number, and e-mail address. What pages will you use for your Web site? Write the design in outline form.

Use FrontPage to create a prototype Web site for Ace Lawn Care. You might find the Corporate Presence Template helpful in building your site. That template will ask you detailed questions about the components you want it to put into the Web site, such as:

- Which main pages to include (Home, What's New, Products/Services, Table of Contents, Feedback Form, Search Form)

- The topic for each type of page

- The number of products and services

- What information is needed on the feedback form

- What information should appear at the top and bottom of each page

- What theme to use

After answering these questions, the template will build the web pages and place sample text into each file, just like the Personal Web Template did with your personal web. Then you can go into FrontPage and customize the text to fit your business. Print a copy of all the pages of your site.

  TEAMWORK PROJECT

Together, your team should prepare a site for your company, Ace Lawn Care, as described in Project 13-3. Then each team member should go to the Internet and search for Web sites of lawn maintenance companies. Each person should select a different Web site that can contribute good design ideas to your team's site and print out the pages. Together, your team should decide how to improve your site, based on the sample Web pages each of you found. Then make your site the best, most appealing business site you can.

Prepare to present your finished Web site to the class. Discuss its features and why you decided to include them. Explain how your site will help your company attract business.

CRITICAL *Thinking*

 ACTIVITY 13-1

Now that you have had a chance to work with FrontPage, write a paper for the owner of a small business like Ace Lawn Care, explaining why FrontPage would be a good tool for creating an e-commerce Web site. Do you think the average non-technical Internet user could create an attractive Web site using FrontPage?

DEVELOPING AN ELECTRONIC COMMERCE WEB SITE

REVIEW *Questions*

TRUE/FALSE

Circle T if the statement is true or F if the statement is false.

T F **1.** Most e-commerce sites use a database to hold the product catalog and customer orders.

T F **2.** The HTML code *<B>This is italic</B>* would produce *This is italic* in your browser.

T F **3.** Use JPEG files for photographs and GIF files for animated images.

T F **4.** An e-commerce Web site requires 24/7 access to the Web server.

T F **5.** You can use FTP to modify HTML files.

T F **6.** You contact a domain registrar to register a particular domain name.

T F **7.** To use FrontPage to prepare Web pages you must have a good working knowledge of HTML.

T F **8.** To save Web site download time, use thumbnail images.

T F **9.** Your e-commerce Web site should follow the accessibility guidelines.

T F **10.** FrontPage is able to check your Web site's hyperlinks to make sure that they all lead to a working Web site.

MATCHING

Match the description in Column 2 to its correct term in Column 1.

Column 1

___ 1. Thumbnail

___ 2. HTML

___ 3. Plug-in

___ 4. HTML tag

___ 5. FTP

___ 6. Domain registrar

___ 7. Template

___ 8. JPEG

___ 9. TLD

___ 10. Publish

Column 2

A. Hypertext markup language

B. Organization that registers your domain name

C. Method in FrontPage for applying colors and formatting to a web

D. Process of saving your Web site files to a Web server

E. Compressed graphic image format for photographs

F. Small image with hyperlink to larger image

G. Examples include .com, .org, .edu, and .net

H. Hypertext formatting code

I. Method to transfer files to a Web server

J. Mini application program that displays certain information in a browser

PROJECTS

SCANS PROJECT 5-1

Visit the Lands End Web site at **www.landsend.com** and answer the following Web design questions.

1. Do you believe the home page is functional and attractive? Explain your answer.

_____

_____

2. The opening page does not fill the screen at 1024 × 768 resolution. Explain why this is important.

_____

_____

3. What two features first grab your eye at this e-commerce site and why?

_____

_____

4. Right-click a photograph and choose **Properties**. What types of image files are used there and how large are they? How important are product images for a company such as Lands End?

_____

_____

5. Do you believe that Lands End follows the accessibility guidelines presented in Lesson 13? Explain your answer based on the Web site.

_____

_____

 PROJECT 5-2

Using Microsoft FrontPage, create a one-page web that describes the important components of an e-commerce Web site. Save the web on your hard drive and print a copy.

 PROJECT 5-3

Use the Microsoft FrontPage Corporate Presence template to create a web for a not-for-profit organization in your community. Consider such organizations as the humane shelter, a youth organization, a religious organization, or a shelter. Before you create the web, look through the template to see the information that it needs. Then talk to a representative of the organization to learn more about that organization. Save your web on your hard drive and print a copy of each page.

SIMULATION

 JOB 5-1

Evan Peters would like to build a demonstration Web site for his trading business. What kinds of features would he be able to use with the Microsoft FrontPage Corporate Presence template? What important e-commerce features would *not* be available using this FrontPage template?

 JOB 5-2

Florida real estate agent Gloria Fernandez is interested in creating an e-commerce site for her business. She is not sure how to start but knows that a number of other real estate agents have Web sites. What options does she have for creating a real estate site? Would you recommend that she create a Yahoo!Store? Should she work with a Web developer? Write a recommendation for her.

APPENDIX A

BROWSER BASICS

This appendix will give you a quick tutorial on how to use the most popular Web browser, Microsoft Internet Explorer. You will learn how to get around the Web using links and URLs. You will also learn how to use the features of your browser to find information within a site, to access Help files, to print, and to bookmark your favorite sites.

The Hypertext Concept

VOCABULARY

Browser

Cache

Favorite

Hyperlinks

Hypertext links

HyperText Transport
Protocol

Uniform Resource
Locator (URL)

Hypertext links, or *hyperlinks,* are links from one Web page to another or from one location to another within the same page. Hypertext linking capabilities are the foundation of the World Wide Web. The Web is organized as pages that users can display one at a time. Hypertext links within the pages allow you to jump from one page to another or to other locations in the same page with the click of the mouse.

Hypertext links can appear as words on the Web page, usually underlined and in a different color, such as blue or red. Embedded in this link is the address of another Web location. When clicked, the link takes you to the embedded address.

Hypertext links can also appear as icons or images. You can tell that you have encountered a link when you move your mouse over something on the page and your cursor changes to a hand. When you see the hand, you know that you can click that spot to go to the Web location described by the words or image you see. For example, at *Amazon.com*'s Web site, pictures of books contain hypertext links. When you click the picture of a book, the embedded link will take you to a page containing detailed information about that particular book. Clicking the underscored author's name will take you to a list of other books by that same author.

Parts of an image can contain links as well. For example, a campus map on a university Web site might contain links to more detailed information. The information you get depends on where you click on the map. If you click the computer lab building, for example, the link might take you to a description of how to get there, lab hours, and the resources you will find there.

Well-organized hypertext links can help you easily navigate to the information you want. The top of a Web page might have an index with linked section headings. You can click on a section heading to go directly to that page or part of the document. Well-designed Web pages will also provide hyperlinks that help you go back to the index or home page or to another page when you get to the end of the one you are reading.

Hypertext links can also be organized in layers of detail. Home pages often provide broad overview links. Clicking on one of these takes you to a list of more specific options. For example, at *Yahoo.com*, you can click the Shopping link from among the categories offered on the home page. At the shopping page, you can choose links to different types of products. If you click Sports & Outdoors, you can then choose links to different types of sports. This organization of links helps you to progressively narrow your search until you find just what you want.

Web Browsers

A Web ***browser*** is a program that enables you to view Web pages. When you enter an address in the browser or click a hyperlink, the browser displays the linked page on your screen. The two most common browsers are Netscape Navigator and Microsoft Internet Explorer.

Some of the developers of Mosaic, the first major Web browser, formed the Netscape Company, and produced the next big leap in Web browsers, Netscape Navigator. Navigator, now part of the larger package of Web tools called Communicator, became the leading Web browser in a very short time. Communicator is available at no cost on the Netscape home page.

Microsoft's Internet Explorer is the predominant Web browser today. It is now part of Windows. The latest upgrade for Internet Explorer is available at no cost from Microsoft's Web site. Figure A-1 shows the Microsoft home page displayed in the Internet Explorer browser. The Internet Explorer commands are *very* similar to Netscape Navigator commands. If you are familiar with one browser, you will have little trouble switching to the other. The America Online (AOL) browser is also based on Netscape.

FIGURE A-1
Microsoft Web site

Using a Browser to Explore the Web

This section explains Web browsing using Internet Explorer for most of the examples. If you have Netscape or a different browser, the process will be very similar.

Starting Your Browser

During the installation process, your browser will install itself in the Start menu and should leave a shortcut icon on your desktop. To start Internet Explorer, click the Start button, click All Programs or Programs, and then select Internet Explorer. You can also double-click the Internet Explorer icon on your desktop. To start Netscape Navigator from the Start button, click All Programs or Programs and then select Netscape Navigator in the Netscape Communicator program group. You can also double-click the Netscape Navigator icon on your desktop. If you right-drag the Web browser shortcut from your desktop to the Start button, a new shortcut to the browser will appear above Programs when you click the Start button.

Because your browser requires an Internet connection, it will check for a current connection. If it doesn't find one and you are using dial-up networking, your browser will bring up the Connect To dialog box and wait for you to initiate the connection. It is possible to bring up your browser *without* the Internet connection if you want to display a Web page contained in a file on your disk.

When you first connect to the Internet, your browser will display the default home page. If you have just installed or upgraded Internet Explorer, it will open to the MSN home page at *www.msn.com,* shown in Figure A-2. Netscape Navigator initially opens to the Netscape home page. Later in this appendix you will learn how to change to a different starting page if you like.

FIGURE A-2
MSN home page

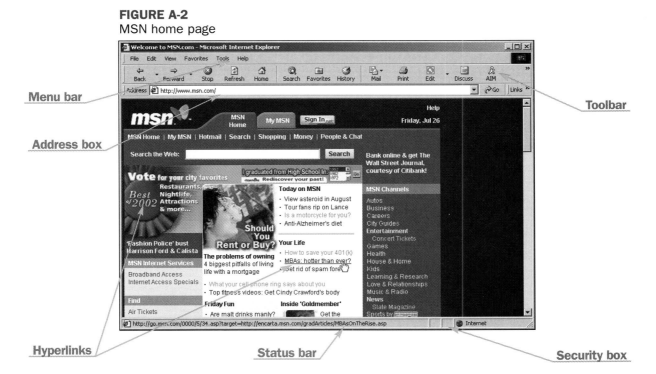

The Main Browser Window

Figure A-2 shows the standard menus, buttons, and tools in Internet Explorer. Like other Windows programs, Internet Explorer features a standard menu bar, with toolbar buttons just beneath it for frequently used commands. The location box just beneath the toolbar shows the Internet address of the particular document being displayed at the moment. You can go to a new location by entering another address in the location box. The Microsoft symbol in the upper right corner of the window is animated. When the browser is retrieving a page, you'll see the symbol rotating like a globe.

The large window in the middle of the screen displays the Web document—in this case, the MSN home page. A Web site's home page is a good starting point for exploring the site. Like a book's table of contents, a site's home page gives an overview of what the site contains. Hyperlinks on the home page help you start "turning the pages" to find the information you want.

At the bottom of the browser window is the status bar. The browser uses the status bar to give you messages about its progress as it retrieves the page you selected. To the right of the status bar is a progress bar. As the browser is retrieving a page, this bar fills with moving color to indicate that the browser is actively locating and retrieving the page.

The padlock in the status bar indicates that the page you are viewing is secure. An empty security box means that transactions you send from this page transmit across the Internet as plain text. A closed lock indicates that transmissions are encoded for privacy. You'll learn more about security in Appendix C.

Figure A-2 also shows examples of two types of hyperlinks. The underlined words are hyperlinks. So is the graphic "Best of 2002." When you move the mouse pointer over a hyperlink, the cursor will turn to a hand and the embedded address will appear in the status bar. The Web developer of this site has purposely coded some hyperlinks with red text to highlight them.

Uniform Resource Locator (URL)

The *Uniform Resource Locator* (*URL*, pronounced "Earl") is the address of a Web page. It defines for your browser the route to take to find the page. The URL for MSN shown in the location box of Figure A-2 is *http://www.msn.com/*.

Every page on the Web has a URL that tells the browser where to find it on the Internet. A URL has several parts:

> **Hot Tip**
>
> Both Internet Explorer and Netscape Navigator (version 4.0 and later) remember previously visited site URLs and will automatically fill in the Address or Location box as you enter a URL. Not only does this feature save time, but it also prevents keying errors.

- *http://* stands for *HyperText Transport Protocol*, the communication rules used to connect to servers on the Web and transmit pages to a browser. You don't have to key the *http://* portion with today's browsers. Because every Web URL begins this way, the browser will insert it automatically in front of whatever you type in the location box.

- *www.msn.com* is the domain address for the Web server on the Internet that holds this Microsoft site. Many URLs on the Web begin with *www*, but this is not mandatory.

- Following the top-level domain extension (*.com* in this case) may be a path to a particular page on the site. For example, if you pass your mouse over different hyperlinks on the MSN page and watch the status bar, you will see letters, numbers, and symbols added to the end of *http://www.msn.com*, each locating the specific page for the browser.

Retrieving a Web Page

You can retrieve a Web page by either clicking a hyperlink or keying the URL into the Location box. The browser knows from the address which server contains the page. It then requests the page from that server and displays it on your screen.

After you click a text hyperlink, you may see it turn to a different color. In Internet Explorer, links usually change from blue to purple. This change in color tells you that you have recently followed that link. By default, this link will stay purple for 20 days before returning to blue. You can change this option in the Internet Options dialog box.

To key in a URL, use Internet Explorer's Open Page command on the File menu or click the Location box in the toolbar. Then type the exact URL into the box and click OK or press the Enter key. You must have the complete URL for the site and type it accurately. If you don't know the URL of a particular site, you can often guess by keying *www.* followed by the organization's name and the appropriate extension (*.edu* for schools, *.com* for businesses, *.org* for organizations, or *.gov* for government sites). Then press Enter. If you guessed right, the browser will go there.

Using the Search Option

Internet Explorer comes with a search button on the toolbar. Clicking this button opens a search pane at the left side of the browser window. You can type in a keyword and instruct Internet Explorer to search for Web pages that contain that keyword. The search is conducted using the MSN Search catalog. You can also use this search tool to look for addresses of persons or to search for businesses.

Many Web users search the Google catalog found at *www.google.com.* Google returns potential Web sites sorted by highest likelihood first. For fun, open the Google home page and search for pages that contain your first and last name.

Viewing Previous Pages

Your browser has two buttons in the toolbar for viewing pages previously viewed during your current session. The Back button will take you backward to the page you viewed immediately before the page currently displayed on your screen. The Forward button will reverse that command. It will take you forward to the page you viewed immediately after the one currently displayed on your screen. You can also right-click the browser window and select Back or Forward from that menu.

Remember, both buttons navigate to pages you have viewed already in this session. If you haven't viewed a page after the one currently displayed, the Forward button will be dim. This means it is inactive. To get back to your browser's home page, click Home in the Go menu or click the Home button.

When you visit Web pages, your browser keeps data from these pages in a temporary storage area called a *cache.* This temporary storage on your machine allows your browser to redisplay these sites more quickly than would be possible if it requested the pages again from the server. A cache is particularly helpful when you redisplay images. Because images take much longer to load than text, the cache will significantly reduce the loading time for pages containing large image files.

Changing Your Default Home Page

You don't have to use the browser's default home page as your starting point when you connect to the Internet. You can change it to any page you want. To change the default home page in

Internet Explorer, use the Internet Options command from the Tools menu and enter the URL in the Address box. Figure A-3 shows the process for changing the default to the Yahoo home page. If you are currently displaying the page you want for your default home page, simply click the Use Current button. Click OK to save your changes. The next time you start Internet Explorer or click the Home button, your new selection will take effect.

FIGURE A-3
Internet Options dialog box

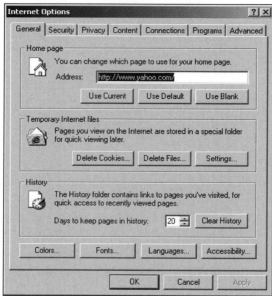

Interrupting a Web Page

If you entered the wrong URL or the current page is taking longer to load than you want to wait, you can interrupt the transfer of a Web page by clicking the Stop button in the toolbar or by pressing the Esc (Escape) key. Your browser will display whatever was transferred before you stopped it.

Your browser transfers the text portions of the Web page first and then the graphic images. Some images are large and take a long time to load. Pressing the Stop button will display the received portion of the page and might allow you to select the next link. If you interrupt a graphic image in the middle, it will be partially saved in the cache. The next time you visit that site, your browser will retrieve the cached portion and download the remaining unsaved portion of the image from the site.

Refreshing a Web Page

If something goes wrong with the display of a page, you can click the Refresh button, or use the Refresh command from the View menu, or its shortcut, F5. Your browser will request that the Web page be retransmitted. The underlying HTML file could change after you open the page. For example, you might be viewing a sports competition for which live statistics are being shown on the Web site. Refresh will cause the latest version of the current Web page to be loaded.

Changing the Text Size

To increase font size, point to Text Size on the View menu, and then select from five sizes ranging from Smallest to Largest. Your browser will modify most text in proportion, and you can change it back at any time. The changes made apply only to that browser window. Note that some HTML programming techniques can prevent your browser from changing the text size with this command.

Getting Help

When you open a menu from the menu bar and highlight a command by moving your cursor over it, the status bar will give you a one-sentence description of what that command will do. You can learn about various commands by selecting a menu item and then moving the cursor over each command to read the description in the status bar.

The most common operations are available with the browser's toolbar buttons. If your browser screen doesn't show the toolbar buttons, point to the Toolbars command on the View menu. Select the Standard Toolbar to turn it on. If you would like to display the button icons along with their names in the toolbar, point to the Toolbars command on the View menu. Select Customize and configure the toolbar buttons and text as desired. Click Close to save your changes.

Many dialog boxes have a Help button for assistance with choices in that box. Choosing the Help button brings up a hyperlinked Help window. From there, you can scroll the contents window on the left, or use the Index button and search for help by keyword. The Find button will search through the actual help display on the right.

For general help, press the F1 function key or use the Contents and Index command from the Help menu in Internet Explorer. Figure A-4 shows the Internet Explorer Help window. As with other Windows Help boxes, you can navigate to the desired topic in the left pane and see the Help document in the right pane. The Index and Search tabs let you search for specific topics by keywords. The Options menu lets you print the current Help document.

FIGURE A-4
Internet Explorer Help window

Printing a Web Page

To print a Web page, click the Print button in the toolbar or use the Print command from the File menu. In the Print dialog box, you can choose to print all of the displayed Web page or specify a range to print. You can also select the number of copies and the print resolution. Click OK to begin printing.

If you click the Print button in Internet Explorer, the entire document is printed without displaying the Print dialog box. This is similar to the Print button's function in Microsoft Office.

Keep in mind that many Web pages are essentially graphic images and may not look as good on a low-resolution printer as they do on your monitor. If you have a color printer such as an inkjet, printed images should look very good but might consume a large amount of ink if there is a background on the Web page. For this reason, you can disable background printing in the Advanced tab of the Internet Options dialog box in Internet Explorer.

Using the Find Command for the Current Page

Although most Web pages are relatively short and are subdivided into sections, some are very long, making it difficult to search manually for a particular keyword. You can scroll up and down in the currently displayed page with the vertical scroll bar, just as you can with any other Windows document. Most Web browsers allow the use of the PageUp and PageDown keys, provided that your cursor is set in the browser window, not the Location box.

You can use the Find button, the Find (on This Page) on the Edit menu, or Ctrl+F to locate keywords in the currently displayed Web page. The Find (on This Page)

> **Hot Tip**
>
> If the Web page you have displayed is very long, use your browser's Print Preview command from the File menu and scroll through the preview. Then print only those pages that are of interest to you by specifying their page numbers in the Print dialog box.

can help with large or complex Web pages. You'll be asked to enter the keyword string in the Find what text box and select the search direction, as shown in Figure A-5. Click the Find Next button, and your browser will search from that point in the desired direction. If a match is found, it will move the pointer to the next point at which the keywords are found and highlight the keyword on the screen. The two option boxes let you specify whether the whole word must match or if you must match the case exactly.

FIGURE A-5
Internet Explorer Find dialog box

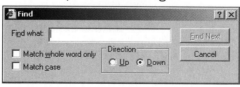

Using Favorites

A *Favorite* is a Web address stored for easy retrieval later. You can use the browser's Favorites feature to store the URLs of your favorite Web sites. Then you can return to the sites easily, without having to memorize their URLs. You can simply click the Favorite and that page will be retrieved. You can organize your Favorites in folders and edit their names and sequence in the Favorites list. In Netscape, Favorites are called Bookmarks.

Adding a Favorite. To add a location to your Favorites list, go to that Web page. In Internet Explorer, click Favorites and then Add to Favorites to add the current page to the Favorites list. In Netscape, click the Bookmarks button and select the Add Bookmark command. The location and description of that location will be placed at the bottom of your Bookmark list.

Jumping to a Favorite Location. To jump to a page in your Bookmark list, click the Bookmarks button in the Navigator toolbar (or the Favorites button in Internet Explorer). Then click the Bookmark of the site you want to visit. Your browser will retrieve that page.

Figure A-6 shows some Favorites in Internet Explorer. Notice that some of the Favorites are folders, indicated by the folder icon at the left side. You can create folders to organize your Bookmarks, just as you can organize your files in Windows Explorer. In Internet Explorer, you can add a new folder from the Organize Favorites command from the Favorites menu. To display the Favorites within a folder, click the folder to open it. Folders can contain other folders, too.

FIGURE A-6
Internet Explorer Favorites list

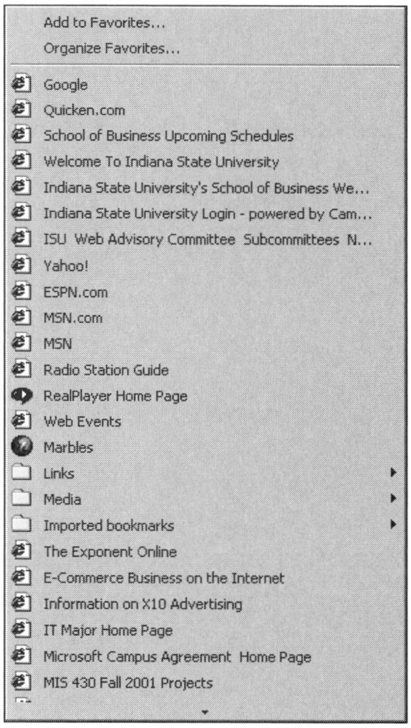

Rearranging Favorites. To change the sequence of your Favorites list, display the Favorites list by clicking the Favorites button, right-drag the particular Favorite to its new location and release the right mouse button. As you drag the Favorite, Internet Explorer displays a black line to show where it will be placed. Favorites can also be rearranged by selecting Organize Favorites from the Favorites menu.

Saving an Image

You can save an image from a Web page on your own computer. First open the Web site so that the image you want appears in your browser window. Then right-click the image to display the Quick Menu, shown in Figure A-7. Choose Save Picture As from the Quick Menu, specifying the name and location for the image. Click the Save button to complete the operation. Remember that most materials on Web sites are copyrighted—be sure to only save materials that you are authorized to copy or reproduce.

FIGURE A-7
Internet Explorer Quick Menu

APPENDIX B

E-MAIL BASICS

This appendix introduces you to electronic mail—the basic tool for sending messages to other users over the Internet. The major e-mail programs operate similarly. If you have a different program from the one illustrated here, you will still be able to apply the concepts to that program you have.

VOCABULARY

Address Book

Clipboard

Electronic mail (e-mail)

Emoticon

Filter

HTML mail

Netiquette

Spamming

How E-Mail Works

Electronic mail, or *e-mail*, is a message transmitted electronically over the Internet or over a local area network to one or more receivers. If you are connected to the Internet through an Internet service provider (ISP), messages sent to you will be stored on a computer at your ISP until you request them. If you are part of a local area network (LAN), a business's internal network, messages sent to you will be stored in your mailbox on the network's server computer.

E-mail shares some similarities with regular or "snail" mail. With e-mail, you must have the receiver's address. You write the message and then mail it by using the Send command. The message is routed from your computer to the receiver's mailbox. But unlike regular mail, e-mail is usually delivered in minutes or even seconds. When you request mail from your mailbox, your ISP (or network server) transmits the mail to your computer and removes it from its computer. After reading your mail, you can delete it or store it on your computer for future reference.

An e-mail message is a lot like a regular letter or memo. It contains a header with the receiver's address, the sender's address, the subject of the message, and the date and time when the message was sent. After the header is the greeting and then the body or text of the message itself. You can also choose to add a signature block to the end of the message.

When you receive an e-mail message, you will see additional text in the header area, reflecting the handling of your message by the outgoing and incoming mail systems. Figure B-1 shows a typical e-mail message next to the mailboxes window. As new messages arrive from your ISP or network server, they are stored in your In mailbox, or Inbox. We will describe parts of this e-mail window later in this appendix.

FIGURE B-1
E-mail message

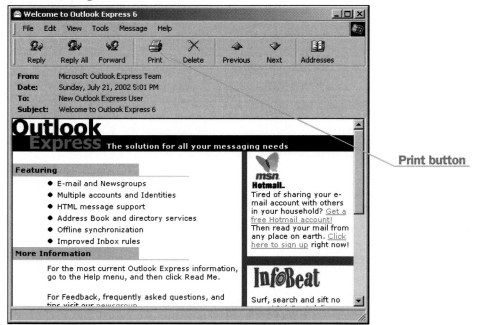

Advantages of E-Mail

E-mail is very fast—your mail is usually delivered immediately if the receiver's mailbox is in the same local area network. It will be delivered in a few minutes when it is sent over the Internet. E-mail is entirely electronic and doesn't require paper unless you want a printed copy. Because the message is electronic, you can use other computer tools, such as a SpellChecker, in creating your message. Most ISPs include electronic mail services as part of their Internet connection fee. Some may charge a nominal fee for low-volume usage.

E-mail is convenient. When you are working on the computer and want to communicate with someone else, it is easy to send an e-mail message. It is particularly convenient for brief messages that don't require the face-to-face or voice-to-voice interaction that some discussions might require. You can arrange meetings, keep up with your friends, or send pictures to family across the country by e-mail.

With Windows or Macintosh, it is easy to copy material from other documents and insert it into an e-mail message. The converse is also true: You can copy material from an incoming e-mail message into other messages or documents.

Disadvantages of E-Mail

E-mail works only if both parties agree to use it to communicate. If either party does not (or cannot) check the mailbox, communication does not take place. Although most e-mail systems are compatible, some advanced e-mail programs add formatting codes that may confuse the receiver's e-mail program.

E-mail is not as personal as meeting with a person face-to-face or talking by telephone. Using e-mail, you miss the nonverbal cues transmitted by body language and the inflection or tone of voice. You also don't get the immediate response that you get from talking with someone directly. Even though e-mail transmits quickly, the receiver must read it before communication is complete.

One of the biggest disadvantages is that e-mail is *not* the same as U.S. mail with respect to privacy. Although the law forbids reading other people's postal mail, electronic mail is not protected. In fact, an employee's e-mail is considered the property of the organization. Company officials can—and often do—read employees' e-mail.

E-Mail Address

Your e-mail address is based on your user name and the domain name of your ISP or organization. For example, one of the author's e-mail addresses is *mfbjm@isugw.indstate.edu*. The letters *mfbjm* are the user name, *isugw* is the name of the network server that contains the mailbox, *indstate* is the designation for Indiana State University, and *edu* represents an educational institution. *indstate.edu* is the domain name that uniquely identifies the server computer at Indiana State.

If you connect to the Internet through an ISP, the domain name in your e-mail address will be that of your ISP. For example, an address with the ISP America Online would take the form: *username@aol.com*.

If you don't know your receiver's e-mail address, there are several ways to find it. Many people now advertise their e-mail address in phone directories and on business cards. If you received an e-mail message from that person, that message will contain the person's e-mail address. Many ISPs and organizations let you search their electronic directories for addresses of people that belong to the same ISP or organization that you do. You can also look up an e-mail address on the Internet. Popular search sites such as Yahoo and *WhoWhere.com* have a people search feature for finding e-mail addresses and telephone numbers.

Using E-Mail

Before you can send or receive messages, you must have an Internet connection and an e-mail account. If your company or school has an e-mail system, your account will be established automatically when you become part of the organization. If you connect through an ISP, your e-mail account will be set up when you establish your Internet account with the ISP.

Outlook Express

Outlook Express is the free version of the popular Outlook e-mail software. You can install a free copy of this Microsoft software when you download and install Internet Explorer. The remainder of this appendix will demonstrate how to perform essential e-mail tasks using Outlook Express for illustrations. Other e-mail programs such as Eudora and Netscape Messenger will operate similarly.

Creating a New Message

The general procedure for sending an e-mail message is:

1. Start the e-mail software from an icon on your desktop or from the Start button.

2. Specify that you want to create a new message by clicking the Create Mail button on the toolbar (or point to New on the File menu and select Mail Message).

3. Supply the receiver's e-mail address and create an appropriate subject header for your message.

4. Key your message into the message window. Be sure to proofread your message before sending it.

5. Click the Send button (or choose Send Message from the File menu) to transmit it to its destination.

Parts of the New Message Window

The Outlook Express message header consists of up to five parts, as shown in Figure B-2. You can send messages or copies to any number of receivers. Simply include all addresses in the appropriate address box. Most e-mail programs will remember your address and will automatically enter it for you in the From box.

You may write a message directly to someone and want others to receive a copy. If you want everyone to know who received copies, enter the addresses of the people to be copied in the Cc (carbon copy) box. If you don't want others to know who received copies, use the Bcc (blind carbon copy) box. By default, the Bcc header does not display. *Hint*: To display all headers, use the All Headers command on the View menu.

In the Subject box, key in a brief description of the topic of your message. Your receivers will see this subject in their mailbox listing, so choose a subject wording that tells them at a glance what your message is about.

You can attach electronic files of any kind to an e-mail message. When you attach a file, the file name will appear in the Attach box of Outlook Express. In other e-mail programs, the file name and an icon appear in the message box. You will learn more about attaching files later in this appendix.

FIGURE B-2
Parts of a New Message window

Send button

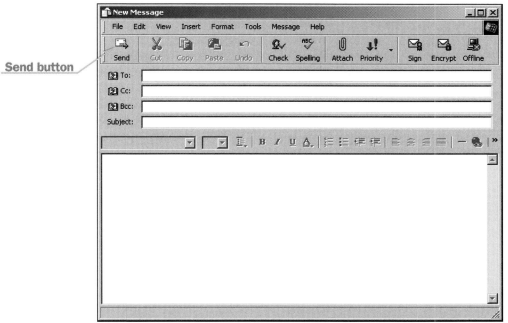

Creating the Message

Most e-mail systems contain a limited-feature word processor for creating and editing your messages. Simply begin keying on the first line of the message box and continue keying until you reach the end of the paragraph. The editor will wrap your message at the end of the line, so press the Enter key only at the end of a paragraph. Use the arrow keys or the mouse to move the cursor to different places in the message. The e-mail program's word processor will have commands for such things as deleting a word, deleting a line, and so forth. Outlook Express uses many of the same text editing shortcut commands as Microsoft Word. Delete and Backspace have the usual effects. Ctrl+Delete deletes the word to the right of the cursor location. Ctrl+Backspace deletes the word to the left of the cursor location. Ctrl+Home moves to the top of the message. Ctrl+End moves to the end of the message.

Some e-mail programs will automatically reformat lines for you as you insert or delete text, while others require that you issue the reformat command yourself. If you are using a Windows-based e-mail program, most of the usual Windows commands will work. For example, you can use the Windows *clipboard* to copy or cut text from one message and paste it elsewhere in the same message or into a different message. You can even bring text into an e-mail message from another Windows document via the clipboard.

Sending the Message

Once you have finished your message, proofread it before sending it on its way. If your mail system has a SpellChecker, use it now. In Outlook Express, click the Spelling button or use the Spelling command on the Tools menu. When you are ready to send the message, click the Send button illustrated in Figure B-2. Most mail programs automatically keep a copy of all outgoing messages. Outlook Express stores these copies in the Sent Items mailbox. Other e-mail programs store the copies in a mailbox labeled Out, or similar. Your mailbox can rapidly fill with these copies. You should periodically empty your Out or Sent Items mailbox of unneeded messages (printing any you wish to save).

Reading a Message

Depending on how your e-mail program is configured, it may prompt you when you have unread mail in your mailbox, or you may not know if you have new mail until you request it. To request your mail from the mail server, click the Send/Recv button in the toolbar, pictured in Figure B-3. Other programs may label this button Check Mail, or similar. You can also check for mail using a menu command. In Outlook Express, point to Send and Receive on the Tools menu, and select Receive All.

FIGURE B-3
Outlook Express main window

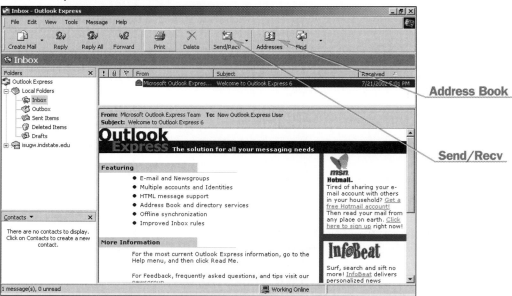

Some mail systems (including Outlook Express) require you to enter a password before you can retrieve messages. You can configure most e-mail programs to remember your password so you don't have to enter it each time. Be cautious with this setting, however. In an environment where other people have access to your computer, unscrupulous users can gain access to your e-mail account and read your e-mail or send objectionable messages under your name.

Select the message you want to read in your incoming mailbox and double-click to open it. The message will be displayed in the message window, as shown in Figure B-1. After reading the message, you have several options: Delete it, save it in a mailbox, forward or redirect it to another user's mailbox, or prepare a reply to the original sender. Most e-mail programs will let you leave the read mail in the Inbox. This is helpful if you want the message to appear as a reminder to answer it or do something else with it later.

Replying to a Message

Often, you will want to reply to the message you just read. To do so, highlight the message and use the one of the reply commands on the Message menu or click the Reply button in the toolbar. The Outlook Express Reply button is pictured in Figure B-1. The e-mail program will open a new message window and place the address of the original sender in the To box and your e-mail address in the From box. You can use the same subject, modify it, or replace it with your own subject. Then move to the New Message window and create your reply.

Most e-mail programs will include a copy of the original message with your reply. To distinguish the original from the reply, the program may put a > or other character before each line of the original message. You can key your responses next to relevant portions of the original message, or key your entire reply in one place. You can also delete parts of the original message that aren't relevant to your reply.

One caution in replying to a message originally sent to a group of people. Do you want your reply to go to just the original sender or to the entire group? As with Outlook Express, most e-mail programs let you choose Reply All or Reply, which goes only to the sender. You could be embarrassed if you accidentally send to all receivers a reply you intended for the original sender only.

Printing a Message

To print a message with Outlook Express and other e-mail programs, select the message and click the Print button, similar to the one pictured in Figure B-1. If you use the Print command on the File menu, a dialog box will appear that will let you choose the pages you want to print (default is all pages) and other printer options.

Outlook Express will print a special header and footer in bold for each page of the message. The sender's name, date, time, and subject appear in the header, while the receiver's address and page number appear in the footer. As with Outlook Express, other e-mail programs let you choose options such as font, page margins, and print quality. Use the Options command on the Tools menu. Switch to the Read tab and click the Fonts button to select the fonts for your incoming mail messages.

Forwarding a Message

To forward a message to another user, highlight the message in the mailbox and choose the Forward command in the Message menu or click the Forward button in the toolbar, pictured in Figure B-1. Outlook Express will open a message window with a blank line followed by the contents of the original message. Enter the address of the person to whom you are sending the message. You can make changes or comments as needed to the body of the message. Click the Send button to forward the message.

Deleting a Message

To delete a message in Outlook Express, select the message and click the Delete button, or press the Delete button on the keyboard. Other programs may use a trashcan or some other icon for deleting a message.

When you delete a message, it will be copied to the Deleted Items mailbox folder (or Trash folder in other programs). To get rid of your deleted messages completely, you must empty the contents of the deleted folder. To do this in Outlook Express, use the Empty Deleted Items command from the Special menu. In other programs, you will find a similar command, such as Empty Trash Mail. Like the Windows Recycling Bin and the Macintosh Trash Can, this two-step process allows you to retrieve a deleted message from the deleted folder before it is gone completely. Most users appreciate the value of this extra step. However, it is also possible to configure Outlook Express to automatically empty the deleted items folder when you exit from Outlook Express.

Using E-Mail Features

Many e-mail programs offer features such as group mailings, attaching document files to the message, and multiple mailboxes. Some also allow you to request notification when a message you sent has been delivered and read by the receiver.

Address Book

You can use your e-mail program's *Address Book* to store names and e-mail addresses of the people with whom you communicate. Some address books can also store other information about your correspondents, such as street addresses, phone numbers, and even notes about them that you want to record on their address cards. To add a new contact in Outlook Express, open the Address Book by clicking the Addresses button in the toolbar. Click the New button and then click New Contact. (Other programs call this button New Card or New Contact.) A dialog box will appear, similar to the one pictured in Figure B-4. Fill in the person's name, e-mail address, and other contact information, and then save the card.

FIGURE B-4
Outlook Express Address Book Properties dialog box

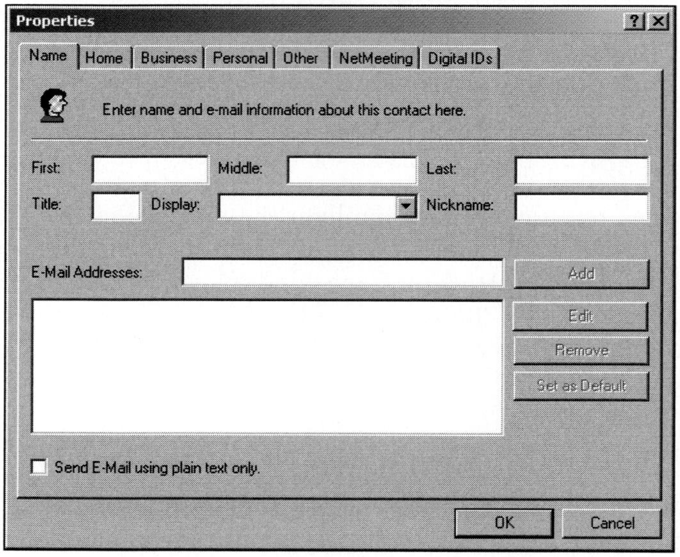

Once someone's e-mail address is stored, you can retrieve it from the Address Book whenever you want to send a message to that person. To use the Address Book for addressing a new message, create a new message and key in the name that you used in the Address Book. Your e-mail program will fill in the full e-mail address when your message is sent. Or in some programs, you can click To in your new message header to bring up the Address Book. Then click the person's name from the list in your Address Book, and the e-mail address will be inserted into the To box.

You can also create a group mailing list and store it under one group name in your Address Book. To create a group list, open the address book by clicking its icon on the toolbar or using the Address Book command from the Tools menu. In the Address Book dialog box, click the New button and then choose New Group. Select a name for the group. Then add the e-mail address of each user you want in the group, clicking the Add button after you have entered the e-mail address. In some programs, you can add user addresses to the group by selecting them from the Address Book.

Give your group a name. Then click OK to complete the group and close the address book. When you want to send a message to everyone in the group, just enter the group name in the message's To box or select the group name from the address book.

Attaching a Document File

Most e-mail programs allow you to transmit other files as attachments to your e-mail message. You may want to send someone a report you wrote in Word, a graphic image stored as an electronic file, or even a program file. Also, any file stored on disk can be transmitted as an e-mail attachment.

To attach a file, create a new e-mail message as usual. Before you send the message, click the Attach button in Outlook Express to open the Insert Attachment dialog box, shown in Figure B-5. In other programs, this button might be called Insert File, or similar. You can also use the File Attachment command in the Insert menu, or a similar one in other programs. Navigate to the file you want to attach. Select the name and click Attach to append it to your e-mail message. The file name will appear in the Attachment header in your message.

FIGURE B-5
Outlook Express Insert Attachment dialog box

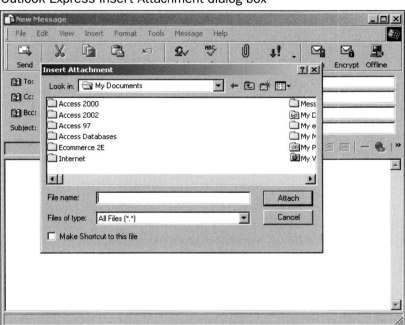

When you send the message, the attached document will be carried along. At the destination, the receiver will be told that the message has an attachment. For example, Outlook Express displays a paperclip icon to the left of a message that has an attachment. When you receive an attachment, you can open it by double-clicking its icon or filename in the message. You can also save the file to your hard disk or to a disk by using the Save Attachments command in the File menu, and specifying where you want to save the attachment.

Priority Level

Some e-mail programs allow you to assign a high priority to an important message, so that it will stand out from other unread messages. The high-priority message usually appears in a different color or with an exclamation point in the receiver's mailbox. In Outlook Express, click the Priority drop-down button in the message toolbar to select a priority level. Outlook Express maintains three priority levels: Low, Normal, and High. The priority level will show with your message's listing in the receiver's mailbox. Take care not to abuse the high or highest priority— remember the boy who cried "Wolf!"

Cancel Message

Few systems let you cancel a message that has already been sent. This feature, although rare, can be particularly useful when you have sent a message in error, or when you sent a hasty response that you later regret. The Cancel feature is not available with Outlook Express.

Mailbox System

Most systems let you set up a mailbox or folder system, in which you can store messages according to their content. It is a convenient way to organize messages. Standard Outlook Express mailboxes include:

- An Inbox folder, where incoming messages are placed.

- An Outbox folder, where copies of messages to be sent are stored.

- A Sent Items folder, where copies of sent messages are stored.

- A Deleted Items folder, for messages you no longer want to keep.

- A Drafts folder, where copies of messages that you are working on are stored.

When you have many messages stored, it's hard to find a particular message. To get organized, you can create a filing system of mailbox folders, similar to the folder system on your hard drive. Designing a useful structure early on will save you grief later as your messages multiply. Suppose you are working on a couple of projects and have exchanged e-mail messages with several colleagues. You might want to file their replies in a mailbox associated with each project. That way, in the future you can more easily refer to messages about that project.

Creating a Mailbox

To create a mailbox in Outlook Express, point to New on the File menu, and select Folder. Key the name of the folder, and select the folder in which the new folder is to be placed. Click OK to create the folder. The current mailbox names are displayed in the mailbox window at the left side of the Outlook Express window.

Transferring a Message to a Mailbox

You can transfer a message to a folder in Outlook Express by selecting that message, and then dragging it from one folder to another folder with the left mouse button.

Message Signatures

Most e-mail systems let you create a personal e-mail signature that is automatically added to the end of outgoing messages, saving you time. Rather than resembling your written signature for checks or correspondence, the mail signature contains your name and address and any other information you would like to accompany your messages to all receivers. Many people include their telephone number and Web site address.

To create or edit a signature in Outlook Express, use the Options command on the Tools menu. Click the Signatures tab to display the signature settings. Enter the information you would like in your signature, similar to Figure B-6, and then close the Options dialog box. Outlook Express will add this signature text to the end of all outgoing messages unless you delete the signature from the message. You can turn off the signature in the Options dialog box by unchecking the Add signature to all outgoing messages line.

FIGURE B-6
Author's e-mail signature

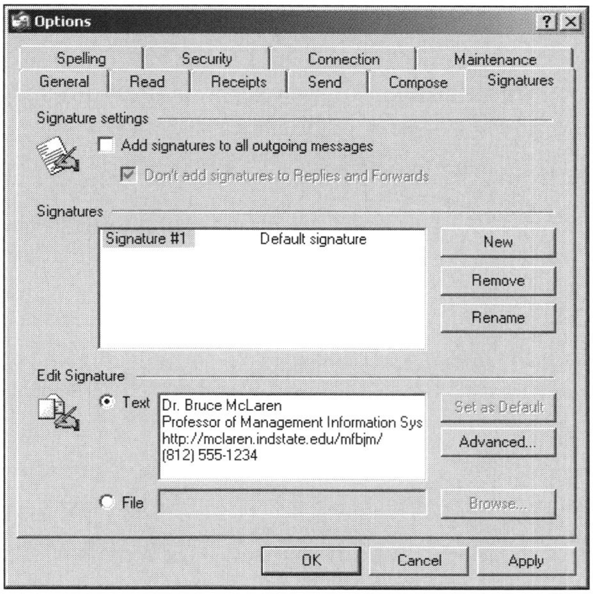

Emoticons

The whimsical images known as **_emoticons_** are a set of keyboard characters that, when viewed sideways, indicate the writer's emotion. Because they can be created with any keyboard, they are popular for expressing feelings in e-mail messages. It is much more difficult to communicate subtle meanings with an e-mail message than with a phone call or face-to-face meeting. This is a good reason to use emoticons. But when you want to project professionalism, use emoticons sparingly or not at all.

Here are some typical emoticons:

:-)   smile

:-D   wide smile or grin

;-)   wink or light sarcasm

:-1   indifference

:-(frown or anger

:-0   shock or surprise

:-/   perplexed

- Identify yourself in the message. Fill in your personal name in the mail configuration, so that your name appears with your e-mail address in the From message header box.

- Avoid inflammatory or intimidating statements. Consider your response carefully before snapping off something you'll be sorry about later.

- Use ordinary capitalization. ALL CAPS is equivalent to shouting in e-mail.

- Read your mail promptly. Most senders expect their messages to be read as soon as they are received.

- Use emoticons when appropriate.

- Keep message length to a minimum, particularly when sending to a group or attaching a file. Most people don't want to wade through lengthy dissertations to get to the meaning in your message.

- Repeat portions of your sender's message when replying. That way, the receiver will have a context for your reply.

- Minimize the number of people to whom you send copies of messages. Most users are busy and don't want to spend time reading messages that are not relevant to them. Sending copies of one message to many people is called *spamming*.

An infamous spamming incident occurred in 1994 when an Arizona law firm sent thousands of messages offering their immigration services to discussion and news groups. Some people estimate that up to 20% of the e-mail at AOL is junk e-mail.

Message Filters

Some mail systems provide *filters* that let you specify criteria for allowing some messages to pass through to your Inbox folder while rejecting others, or for directing incoming messages to different mailboxes. A filter can help you keep unwanted e-mail from cluttering your Inbox folder. You can specify e-mail addresses or subjects to be filtered. You can use filters to direct incoming e-mail into particular folders by subject or sender. That way, you can read new mail according to its subject or by priority. If someone is using e-mail to bother you, you can filter mail from these individuals into the Deleted Items folder.

Outlook Express supports use of e-mail filters through message filters. Point to Message Rules on the Tools menu, and then select Mail. In the Message Rules dialog box you can specify the content of any of the header blocks (To, From, Subject, and so forth) and give the filter condition (contains certain text, is more than a certain size, is marked as priority, and so forth). The action section lets you specify what to do when a message matches that condition: Delete it, copy to, or transfer to another folder. E-mail filters are especially useful when dealing with spam messages or making sure you see high-priority messages.

Spelling Check

You can configure Outlook Express to automatically check spelling of outgoing messages in the Spelling tab of the Options dialog box. If you don't have a SpellChecker in your e-mail program, then proofread carefully before you send the message.

Plain Text or HTML Mail

Older mail programs send plain text in e-mail messages. Newer programs are able to display formatting such as bold, italic, and different fonts through the use of *HTML mail*. Outlook Express can embed HTML tags in outgoing messages and is able to display incoming e-mail messages that contain HTML tags. To use the formatting features of Outlook Express, simply click the appropriate formatting buttons on the toolbar when creating a new message.

Because some e-mail systems cannot handle HTML mail, Outlook Express also provides the capability to strip the HTML tags from the outgoing message. You can select Plain Text, or HTML, in the Send tab of the Options dialog box, or simply refrain from using formatting options when you send mail to someone that requires plain mail.

WEB SECURITY

In this appendix, you will learn how e-merchants secure information sent over the Internet and how electronic payment systems work.

Providing Privacy for E-commerce Visitors

You have seen many examples of electronic commerce in this book, from *Amazon.com* to *ZDNet.com*. Virtually every e-commerce site has an online catalog, a shopping cart to keep track of your purchases, and a method for gathering information about payment, which is usually made via credit card. To protect sensitive customer information, your browser encrypts the data before it is sent back to the e-commerce Web site. *Encrypted data* is data that is scrambled or coded to prevent unauthorized individuals from understanding it if they intercept it as it travels across the Internet to its destination.

VOCABULARY
Authentication
Cookie
Digital cash
Digital certificate
Encrypted data
Encryption key
Firewall
HyperText Transport Protocol Secure (https)
PayPal
Pretty Good Privacy (PGP)
Secure sockets layer (SSL)
Smart cards
Spoofing

Secure Sockets Layer

Secure sockets layer (SSL) is the most common method for encrypting data on the Web. Browsers that support SSL are able to communicate with a Web server that encrypts data. Both Internet Explorer and Netscape Navigator (v. 2.0 and later) support SSL. The symbol for a secure session is a closed lock in the status bar. Figure C-1 shows the Internet Explorer browser with a secure connection to Lands' End, as indicated by the closed lock in the status bar. Notice that the URL in the Location box begins with *https* for **HyperText Transport Protocol Secure (https)**. The *https://* designation in the URL directs the transmission to a secure Web server. Normal unencrypted sessions begin with *http://*.

Not all of a merchant's Web site needs to be encrypted. Public areas for displaying product information don't involve sensitive information. Most e-commerce Web sites only encrypt the checkout area. Encrypting the Web page slows down the process of sending information between the Web server and your browser. Online merchants often offer three options for placing an order: Order online using the secure session; phone in the order with a toll-free number; fax the order.

FIGURE C-1
Secure browser session

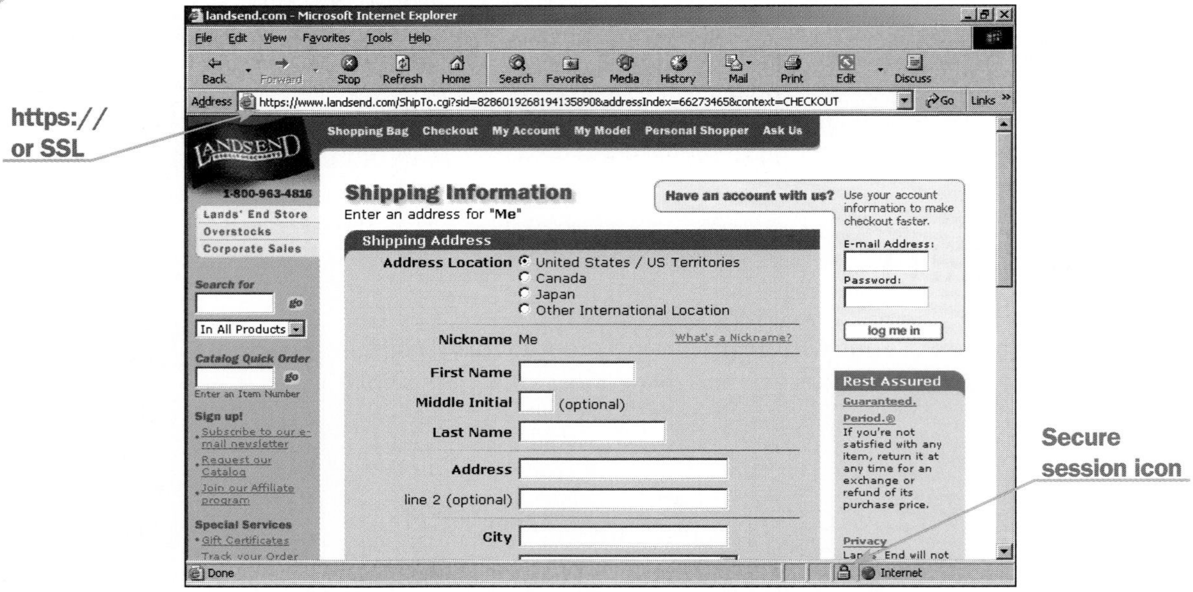

https://
or SSL

Secure
session icon

Although details about encryption methods are beyond the scope of this book, the procedure is fairly straightforward. The ***encryption key*** is a series of digits that are added to the original text using a formula. At the other end, the message must be decoded by applying another key.

The Caesar cipher is a simple version of encryption. Suppose you replaced each letter of the original text with a letter 11 places later in the alphabet. When you got to Z, you would start over again at A. For example, INTERNET would appear as TYEPCYPE, as shown in Table C-1. If you want to do one yourself, prepare a sheet of paper with the letters A-Z and their place position from 1 to 26. When you add the key (11 in this case), be sure to start over again at A when you go past 26.

TABLE C-1
Caesar Cipher Example

TEXT	PLACE POSITION	PLACE POSITION +11	CIPHER TEXT
I	9	20	T
N	14	25	Y
T	20	31 -> 5	E
E	5	16	P
R	18	29 -> 3	C
N	14	25	Y
E	5	16	P
T	20	31 -> 5	E

The longer the key, the more secure the encrypted information. Hackers try to break the code by repeatedly trying all possible combinations for the key. Older versions of Internet Explorer used a 40-bit key but the current version has a 128-bit key. Some online banking Web sites require the 128-bit version, but most secure sites will work properly with the 40-bit version. It is estimated that a high-speed computer could crack a 40-bit key in several hours but would take much longer to break a 128-bit key, even working around the clock. Note that Microsoft will not export 128-bit encryption products to some foreign countries.

Public Key Encryption

Most encryption systems on the Web use two keys—a public key and a private key. The browser uses the public key to encrypt information at the customer's computer. The private key is held only at the Web server. The private key can unlock the message, and having two keys means that the Web server does not have to transmit its key to customers' browsers, avoiding the possibility of an unauthorized person gaining access to the private key during transmission.

Digital Certificates

A *digital certificate* is a digital ID that verifies the identity of the owner of the Web site. When you initiate a secure connection with a Web site, your browser requests a copy of the digital certificate from the Web server. That certificate contains the public key to encrypt further transmissions to that site. It also assures you that you are dealing with the real owner of the Web site.

Digital certificates are issued by commercial organizations such as VeriSign that research the business and verify that the Web address does indeed belong to the authorized owner. This is one way to prevent *spoofing,* an illegal practice in which a third party "steals" the Web site and sets up a storefront to steal information about the site's customers.

Pretty Good Privacy (PGP)

Pretty Good Privacy (PGP) is low-cost encryption software developed by Pretty Good Privacy, Inc. In fact, it is free for non-commercial use. Using some of the same encryption technology as commercial organizations, PGP is available in many forms. While it is used primarily for encrypting e-mail messages between individuals, it can also be used to encrypt FTP and Web traffic. PGP uses the public key method of encryption. For more information, see the FAQ list at *www.dk.pgp.net/pgpnet/pgp-faq/.*

Authentication

Another way of securing information is to provide for an authenticated session. *Authentication* is a process for establishing the user's identity, usually requiring a username and password. When a Web site uses authentication, the login screen, such as that shown in Figure C-2, asks for an account ID (username) and password. Only users whose account ID and password match the data on file at the Web server will be granted permission to access the next Web page. It is possible to both authenticate *and* encrypt the same Web page.

FIGURE C-2
Authentication login screen

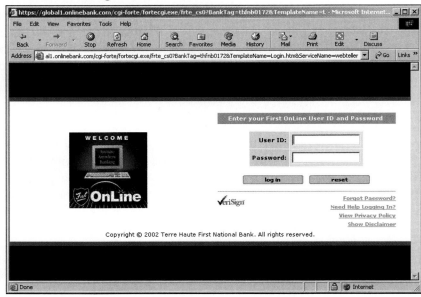

Of course, no authentication security measure is truly foolproof. If you leave your account ID and password out in the open, someone could copy the information and use it to access the server. Make sure your password is hard for someone else to guess. Make sure you log out from the session when you leave the computer, even if only for a few minutes.

Lands' End offers another layer of security in addition to SSL. You can create a personal shopping account at Lands' End and create a password. When you arrive at the site, you'll be asked to sign in and verify your identity through the password. Of course, this can backfire if customers have trouble remembering all their passwords at different Web sites!

When choosing a password, don't use names of friends or relatives. Your password ought to be at least five or six characters long with a mixture of upper- and lowercase letters and digits. For example, use something like frY8bee. You should change your password every few months.

Cookies

A *cookie* is a small text file stored on your computer that contains some identifying information and is associated with a Web site. Rarely is any sensitive information (such as a credit card number) stored in the cookie file. For example, when you buy something at *Amazon.com*, a cookie file containing your account ID is created and stored on your hard drive. When you revisit *Amazon.com*, the Web server directs your browser to open the cookie file and send its contents to the server. The server can look up information in its own database about your previous purchases and display information in the Web site that matches your reading interests. Notice in Figure C-3 that *Amazon.com* identified one of the authors by name—evidently picking up this information from a cookie file.

FIGURE C-3
Web site personalized for the user

The Web server should have permission before it can direct your browser to save information in the cookie file. Customers who do not want cookies stored on their computer can turn off this feature with a browser command. In Internet Explorer, use the Internet Options command on the Tools menu and select the Privacy tab, shown in Figure C-4. The security slider can be used to select from six privacy levels for the Internet zone, from Block All Cookies to Accept All Cookies, with several intermediate levels. The default value is Medium security in which some cookies are permitted. Move the slider all the way to the top to block all cookies.

FIGURE C-4
Internet Options Privacy dialog box

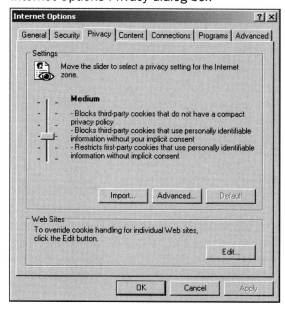

In Netscape, choose the Preferences command on the Edit menu and double-click Privacy & Security to expand the menu and then select Cookies on the submenu. There you can disable cookies altogether, accept certain cookies, or ask to be warned each time a cookie is accessed. In general, you will benefit from cookies, because you don't have to key as much to identify yourself.

Firewalls

Customers expect e-merchants to protect information about them from outside users. This can be accomplished with physical security at the data center as well as implementing a firewall.

A *firewall* is hardware and/or software that isolates an organization's computers from the outside world. A firewall prevents outside users from accessing information inside the firewall. It also may selectively prevent individuals in the organization from accessing information outside the firewall. Visualize the firewall as a checkpoint that all information must pass through.

Another role of a firewall is to restrict internal users from accessing certain sites on the Internet. In other words, as your browser requests a certain URL, the firewall software must decide whether you are eligible to access that site. Some organizations restrict certain users from accessing anything outside the firewall. Other employees might have partial access.

Yet another role of the firewall software is to log the sites that users visit. For example, your employer would know if you regularly visit *espn.com* while on the job!

Paying for Merchandise Online

Most users pay for goods ordered online with a credit card. With proper encryption, there is little reason to think that credit card information is any less secure than when you call a toll-free number and give your credit information over the phone. In fact, if you order merchandise with a portable telephone, someone could intercept the telephone call from the street in front of your house!

Credit Card Processing

To be able to accept credit card payments, a merchant opens a credit card agreement with a financial institution, such as a bank. The merchant pays a small fee for this service. The same is true for online credit card sales. Some ISPs offer credit card processing bundled along with other merchant services when you host your site with that ISP.

Most e-commerce sites process credit cards immediately, verifying the customer's credit worthiness online and making a decision about the credit sale at the same time. Of course, if you are using an ISP to host your site, the ISP will probably already have links to the credit card verifying sites and the necessary links for your site. In fact, you will probably use a standard Web site to verify and process payment. If you are hosting your own e-commerce Web site, then you must create the credit card validation pages yourself. Some packages, such as IBM's Startup for e-business, offer instant credit card processing.

Visa and Master Card have been working on an SET (Secure Electronic Transaction) standard for credit card payments. This standard will improve the ability for e-merchants to make sales online. In this system, your credit card number is sent over the Internet in pieces, making it more difficult for thieves to steal your information.

PayPal is the best known method to pay for items bought at electronic auctions such as eBay with over five million transactions made via PayPal. With PayPal a buyer must first register a credit card (or a debit card) over a secure link. Sellers who anticipate being paid via PayPal must also register their e-mail addresses and credit card or bank accounts so that credit can be given. When a buyer makes a purchase, the buyer can pay the seller by completing a PayPal transaction, providing the seller's e-mail address and the transaction amount. The credit card of the buyer is charged for the amount and the seller's credit card account is credited with the transaction amount. There is no charge for individuals to use this service—PayPal earns its revenue by taking advantage of the float on payments made. Business members pay a fee for premier services, similar to a merchant account for credit card processing. There is a small fee for international accounts—PayPal is now in 38 countries.

Digital Cash and Electronic Wallets

Some customers do not want to give their credit card information online. Customers can instead use *digital cash,* an online account into which customers deposit funds and then use to pay for purchases. Think of this as an electronic debit card—you provide authentication information, and the merchant receives payment from your digital cash account. It is somewhat safer than a credit card because only you can give the authentication information and the account information remains offline, at the digital cash company, not the merchant. The downside is that you can only shop at merchants that are compatible with your digital cash institution.

CyberCash was one of the earliest digital cash providers and was recently acquired by VeriSign. As e-commerce grows, emphasis on making payments more efficient and more secure will also grow. In fact, VeriSign offers an array of Internet payment services to e-commerce merchants, including online credit card processing.

Some electronic payment methods keep your credit card information off the Internet altogether. When you make a purchase, you authorize the payment provider to make a direct charge against your credit card on behalf of the merchant. Your credit card information never appears on the Internet, safeguarding the information. This is similar to having a personal payment account with a merchant, established offline via telephone. When you are ready to pay, you give the personal account information but not the credit card information. Of course, you must still safeguard the personal account information through secure sessions, but should the information get out, it can only be used for purchases made at that merchant.

In most cases there is no cost to the consumer for using these digital cash solutions. Rather, the merchant pays a fee, similar to the credit card arrangement. InternetCash has worked to make it easy to transfer funds from your own bank to a prepaid InternetCash account. Some digital money providers refer to the account as an electronic wallet.

Microsoft's .NET Passport program is designed to help the buyer make a purchase more easily by providing a single sign-in. After the buyer registers to obtain a .NET passport, the passport can provide stored information to the seller automatically. The buyer can register for a .NET wallet that stores credit card information in encrypted form along with billing and shipping information. The user can make express purchases and the passport program helps the merchant authenticate that buyer. Hundreds of e-commerce sites are compatible with the .NET Passport. The .NET Passport home page shown in Figure C-5 is found at *www.passport.com*.

FIGURE C-5
.NET Passport home page

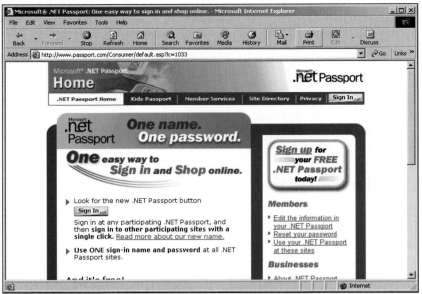

Smart Cards

Smart cards are credit cards with a built-in microprocessor and memory used for identification, or for financial transactions. These cards might contain a cash balance, or could have a non-reproducible serial number or PIN. When customers are ready to make a purchase, they insert the card into a reader attached to their computer. Thus, only the person in possession of the card can conduct a transaction.

The downside is that customers must have a card reader attached to their computer. For now, that is not practical for most users. But in the future, smart cards could become commonplace, particularly if there are serious security breaches in e-commerce.

The Old-Fashioned Way

Of course, it is still possible to shop electronically and pay with check, money order, or other offline payment method. This adds a few days to the purchase cycle and introduces new security risks through the mail. But for consumers who aren't satisfied with any amount of online security, they can still shop online and pay using one of these other methods.

The Final Guarantee

Several e-merchants have announced guarantees against any customer losses due to fraudulent use of credit card information. OfficeMax and Lands' End both have elaborate security and privacy discussions in their Web sites. In fact, Lands' End states that since going online in 1995, there have been no confirmed cases of fraud reported by customers as a result of credit card purchases there. Both firms say that they will pick up all liability owed by the customer in such cases, including the first $50.

GLOSSARY

A

Acronym A group of letters, usually the first letters of the words of a phrase, that form an abbreviation for the phrase. Sometimes acronyms can be pronounced as words and become a recognized term. "FBI" and "scuba" are both acronyms.

Address Book E-mail program feature that stores names and e-mail addresses that can be retrieved easily for addressing e-mail messages.

Alt-text lines Short text phrases that appear in an image's location while the image is loading.

Animated GIF ad Web advertisement containing a graphic image that moves.

Assessment tool A questionnaire or other means for gathering information. When tallied, your answers to the questions will indicate your interests or other characteristics about you.

Asynchronous Activities not synchronized in time or place.

Auction service Online site that allows anyone to offer an item for sale to the highest bidder.

Authentication The process of establishing the user's identity, usually requiring a username and password.

Automatic withdrawal Regular, pre-authorized payments taken from a bank account. Customers often use these for loan payments or savings plans.

B

Banner ad A large, splashy advertisement that appears on a Web page and often has a hyperlink to the advertiser's own Web site.

Bricks and clicks Retailers with both physical and online stores.

Browser Program, such as Netscape Navigator or Microsoft Internet Explorer, that enables users to view Web pages.

Business-to-business sales (B2B) Sales made by one business to another.

Business-to-consumer sales (B2C) Sales made by a business to a consumer.

C

Cache Temporary storage area in a computer that helps a browser display previously visited Web pages more quickly than it could by requesting the page from the server again.

Career A profession for which you receive training and may hold several jobs during your lifetime. A career is usually a long-term pursuit.

Clearinghouse An agency that gathers, stores, and exchanges information. Online job clearinghouses are large databases that store information about jobs and job seekers, and match jobs with people.

Clip art A collection of electronic drawings, pictures, and icons, created for use in Web pages and other documents.

Clipboard Feature that allows information to be cut or copied from one document and pasted into another document or into another location in the same document.

Consumer The ultimate owner or user of a product.

Cookie A file of information about you that some Web sites create and store on your hard drive when you visit the site.

Cooperative ads Pairs of ads placed in complementary sites. Viewers at one site would likely be interested in products at the other site.

CPM Cost per thousand impressions, the basis used for determining advertising rates.

D

Database A large collection of information arranged in linked tables for easy search and retrieval.

Data port An RJ-11 analog telephone jack that lets a user connect a computer's modem through a telephone when a direct wall connection is unavailable.

Demographics Characteristics of human populations, such as age, gender, income, and ethnic background.

Digital cash Online accounts that customers deposit funds into and then use to pay for purchases.

Digital certificate A digital ID that verifies the identity of the owner of the Web site.

Direct deposit Paperless transfer of funds from an employer or other agency to the account of an employee or beneficiary.

Discount broker An investment agent who buys and sells securities at the client's request, but does not provide extensive advice or other services.

Domain name The last part of a URL that includes the organization's unique name followed by a top-level domain name designating the type of organization, such as *.com* for "commercial" or *.edu* for "educational."

Domain registrar A company like VeriSign that enables an organization to register its domain name such as *course.com*.

Download Transfer of electronic files from one computer to another.

Drill down To refine a search by examining successively more specific categories.

Dynamic ads Ads that appear when certain keywords are entered in a search engine.

E

E-commerce (electronic commerce) Any electronic business transaction or exchange of information to conduct business.

Electronic data interchange (EDI) Electronic exchange of business information.

Electronic mail (e-mail) A message transmitted electronically over the Internet or local area network to one or more receivers.

Electronic shopping cart A small program at a retail Web site that keeps track of your selections as you shop.

E-mail ads Personalized e-mail advertising messages sent to a particular customer, usually with a link to the advertiser's Web site.

Embedded hyperlink A link between one object and another that, when clicked, opens your browser and loads the linked document or Web site. Hyperlinks can be embedded within an e-mail message as well as in any other kind of text or graphics.

Emoticon Icon created with keyboard characters that, when viewed sideways, indicates the writer's emotion.

Encryption Coding data for security.

Encryption key A series of digits added to the original text using a formula, for secure transmission over the Web.

Entrepreneur Someone who starts and operates a new business.

E-procurement Internet based automation of obtaining or accessing goods.

Extranet An intranet that uses the Internet to transmit private information beyond the company's own premises, but keeps its pages private by requiring user authentication.

F

FAQ (frequently asked questions) A list of answers to common questions that customers ask.

Favorite Web address stored for easy retrieval later.

File transfer protocol (FTP) Method for transferring files over the Internet from one computer to another.

Filter In e-mail, criteria you specify for allowing some messages to pass through to your In mailbox while rejecting others, or for directing messages to different mailboxes.

Firewall Hardware and/or software that isolates an organization's computers from the outside world.

Frame A rectangular section of a Web page that scrolls separately from the main section.

FrontPage Web site development and management software from Microsoft Corporation.

FrontPage web The collection of HTML and image files that comprise a particular Web site, including the hyperlinks that let users navigate between the pages.

G

GIF (graphics interchange format)   The universal standard format for storing images for display in Web browsers. It is used for most lettering, small pictures, and animations.

H

Hit counter   An electronic counting device that keeps track of the number of visits to a Web page during a particular time period and provides limited identity information about viewers.

HTML-enhanced e-mail   E-mail programs capable of displaying messages with embedded HTML commands that link to Web pages.

HTML tags   Computer codes that tell your Web browser how to display information on your screen. HTML tags are surrounded by < > symbols. For example, <B> means to turn on bold and </B> means to turn off bold. HTML tags are used to indicate such features as bold, character size, font color, hyperlinks, and images.

Hypertext links (hyperlinks)   Links from one Web page to another or from one location to another within the same page.

Hypertext markup language (HTML)   Language used to create Web pages by adding formatting tags to text.

Hypertext Transport Protocol (HTTP)   The communication rules used to connect to servers on the Web and transmit pages to a browser.

Hypertext Transport Protocol Secure (HTTPS)   Method for accessing a secure Web server.

I

Image map   A picture that is separated into sections, each of which contains a link that will take users to different Web locations.

Interest (loan)   A fee for the use of borrowed funds.

Interest rate (loan)   The percentage of a loan amount charged to the borrower.

Internet   A network of public networks, generally available everywhere.

Intranet   A private information network for company employees that is available only within the company's premises.

J

Job   A specific position you hold with a specific employer.

JPEG (Joint Photographic Experts Group)   Standard graphics format for compressing still images, such as large photographs and art for use in Web browsers. JPEG files do not render lettering well.

L

Lemon   Car with so many problems that the manufacturer repurchases it.

M

Mailing list service (LISTSERV)   Automated e-mail system on the Internet to which users may subscribe to receive regular news on a specified topic.

Meta-site   The prefix "meta," from the Greek for "between, with, or after," has come to mean "going a level above or beyond." So a meta-site would be a super site with many links, larger and more extensive than a customary Web site.

Mirror site   A twin Web site placed in another country or continent to reduce the download time by eliminating the need to connect to the distant master site.

Mortgage   A loan for the purchase of real estate.

MP3   A compression format that has revolutionized the way high-quality digital music can be delivered over the Internet.

Multinational corporation   Companies that have manufacturing, supplier, and distribution sites in multiple countries.

N

Netiquette   Etiquette on the Internet.

O

Online mall   Internet site that offers links to a large number of stores in one convenient place.

P

Packets   Blocks of data used to transmit Web pages and messages through the Internet.

PayPal Electronic payment system that lets the buyer pay with a credit card or debit card by providing the e-mail address of the seller.

PDF (portable document format) A file format generated by the Adobe Acrobat program that makes it possible to download and read files on different computers, using the free Acrobat Reader program.

Pixel (PIX [picture] ELement) One or more dots that operate as the smallest element on a video display screen.

Plug-in A specialty program that works with a major software to enhance its capabilities.

Pop-under ads Ads that appear in a separate browser window beneath the base Web page.

Pop-up ads Ads that appear in a separate browser window on top of the base Web page, which remains open in the background.

Portal sites Web sites, such as search engines, that offer users a good starting point for entering the Web.

Portfolio A collection of stocks, bonds, and other investments.

Powered by Run by a search engine or database that provides the background resources for a site.

Pretty Good Privacy (PGP) A low-cost encryption software developed by Pretty Good Privacy, Inc.

Private trading network (PTN) An online site to bring together buyers and sellers with similar interests.

Publish To transfer an HTML file from your computer to a Web server.

Pull technology Internet information retrieval system in which users actively seek information by visiting sites.

Push technology Internet information retrieval system in which users specify the information they want, and the system finds and downloads it automatically to the users' computer.

R

Reach The number of potential customers who view an ad.

Recall A manufacturer's request to return a product because of severe risks to health or safety.

Request for quotation (RFQ) A detailed description of a product or service needed, published so that providers can offer a bid.

Resume A list of personal information, educational background, and professional experience.

Retailing Selling goods and services to the ultimate consumer.

Richness (in advertising) Degree to which ad content can be designed for a specific market segment.

Rotation ad Banner ad that rotates between advertisers. Each time the page comes up, the advertiser changes.

S

Secure sockets layer (SSL) Most common method for encrypting data on the Web.

Security Protection from unauthorized access to data.

Shopping cart A detailed list of items and their features compiled prior to completing an electronic sale.

Smart cards Credit cards with a built-in microprocessor and memory used for identification or financial transactions.

Socially responsible investing A policy of promoting environmentally and socially responsible operating practices by investing in corporations with good records in these areas.

Spam Copies of an e-mail message sent to many people.

Spoofing "Stealing" a Web site to set up a storefront to steal information about the site's customers.

Static ad Advertisement that always appears in a given location on the Web page, regardless of the keywords used to get to the page.

Supply chain Integrated activities that enable businesses to get what they need at the right place and time.

T

Tasks list In FrontPage, a helpful utility in Explorer to keep track of "to-do" items associated with a project.

Term (loan) The duration of a loan.

Theme   In FrontPage, a collection of design elements, such as colors, fonts, bullets, background images, and navigation bars, that are applied to all pages in a web, giving the site a consistent "look."

Thumbnail   A smaller version of the full image used to reduce download time. The viewer can click the thumbnail image to display the full image in the browser.

Ticker symbol   Company abbreviation made up of several letters, used for reference in stock quotes.

Top-level domain name   Three-letter abbreviation at the end of a domain name, designating the type of organization that owns the site.

24/7   24 hours a day, 7 days a week.

U

Uniform resource locator (URL)   The address of a Web page that defines for the browser the route to take to find the page.

V

VeriSign   One organization that registers domain names.

Virtual marketplace   Links purchasers and suppliers online.

Vortal   A site that provides industry- or interest-specific information and encourages collaboration.

W

Web editor   An easy-to-use program for creating Web pages. The Web editor resembles a word processor and automatically inserts the proper HTML tags into the file when you have selected a certain format or feature.

Web server   Computer that holds the pages and images that form a Web site and accepts requests from Web browsers to download them. The Web server is the host for the Web site. The Web server must be connected to the Internet all of the time, so that users can view the Web site.

Web spider   Robotic search tool that is constantly examining sites around the Web and adding them to a search engine's catalog or index.

Webmaster   Web developer who is responsible for creating and maintaining the HTML files that comprise a Web site. The Webmaster knows HTML and usually has programming skills.

Wizard   An automated tool for Web building that asks the user a series of simple questions about a feature, and then creates the necessary code to make the feature work.

INDEX